The 1980 Presidential Election

Ronald Reagan's victory in the 1980 presidential election marked a watershed moment in the history of the United States, heralding the triumph of the American conservative movement. Once a supporter of the New Deal, Reagan had come to symbolize the union of three diverse forms of conservatism—anti-communism, social traditionalism, and libertarianism—that were increasingly intertwined under the banner of the Republican Party. The unlikely development of this new conservative coalition was based upon the larger impacts of the civil rights movement in reshaping the dynamics of the Democratic and Republican parties, the social "backlash" of the Nixon era, the emergence of the religious right, and the economic and political crises that directly set the stage for Reagan's stunning victory.

In five original, engaging chapters, *The 1980 Presidential Election* shows how Reagan's journey to the White House was connected to the wider transformations of post-1945 American history. Supplemented by a fresh collection of primary documents—including previously unpublished transcripts of Reagan's radio addresses of the late-1970s—this book is an ideal introduction to the origins and impact of the American conservative movement.

Jeffrey D. Howison is Assistant Professor of Sociology at Yeditepe University in Istanbul.

Critical Moments in American History
Edited by William Thomas Allison, Georgia Southern University

The Assassination of John F. Kennedy
Political Trauma and American Memory
Alice L. George

The Battle of the Greasy Grass/Little Bighorn
Custer's Last Stand in Memory, History, and Popular Culture
Debra Buchholtz

Freedom to Serve
Truman, Civil Rights, and Executive Order 9981
Jon E. Taylor

The Battles of Kings Mountain and Cowpens
The American Revolution in the Southern Backcountry
Melissa Walker

The Cuban Missile Crisis
The Threshold of Nuclear War
Alice L. George

The Nativist Movement in America
Religious Conflict in the 19th Century
Katie Oxx

The 1980 Presidential Election
Ronald Reagan and the Shaping of the American Conservative Movement
Jeffrey D. Howison

The 1980 Presidential Election

Ronald Reagan and the Shaping of the American Conservative Movement

Jeffrey D. Howison

Taylor & Francis Group
NEW YORK AND LONDON

First published 2014
by Routledge
711 Third Avenue, New York, NY 10017

and by Routledge
2 Park Square, Milton Park, Abingdon, Oxon OX14 4RN

Routledge is an imprint of the Taylor & Francis Group, an informa business

© 2014 Taylor & Francis

The right of Jeffrey D. Howison to be identified as author of this work has been asserted by him in accordance with sections 77 and 78 of the Copyright, Designs and Patents Act 1988.

All rights reserved. No part of this book may be reprinted or reproduced or utilized in any form or by any electronic, mechanical, or other means, now known or hereafter invented, including photocopying and recording, or in any information storage or retrieval system, without permission in writing from the publishers.

Trademark notice: Product or corporate names may be trademarks or registered trademarks, and are used only for identification and explanation without intent to infringe.

Library of Congress Cataloging in Publication Data
Howison, Jeffrey D.
  The 1980 Presidential Election: Ronald Reagan and the Shaping of the American Conservative Movement/Jeffrey D. Howison.
  pages cm.—(Critical moments in American History)
  Includes bibliographical references and index.
  1. Reagan, Ronald—Influence. 2. Conservatism—United States—History—20th century. 3. United States—Politics and government—1981–1989. 4. Presidents—United States—Biography. I. Title.
  E877.H69 2013
  324.973′0927—dc23
  2013012397

ISBN: 978-0-415-52192-5 (hbk)
ISBN: 978-0-415-52193-2 (pbk)
ISBN: 978-0-203-08150-1 (ebk)

Typeset in Bembo and Helvetica Neue
by Florence Production Ltd, Stoodleigh, Devon, UK

Irmak için, aşkım

Contents

Series Introduction		ix
List of Figures		x
Acknowledgments		xi
Timeline		xiv
Preface		xvii
1	Introducing American Conservatism	1
2	The South, Civil Rights, and the Transformation of the Republican Party	27
3	The Social Backlash: Riots, Religion, and Realignment	54
4	Crises, Carter, and the Triumph of Ronald Reagan	87
5	The Image and Reality of Ronald Reagan and American Conservatism	113
	Documents	145
	Notes	199
	Bibliography	209
	Index	217

Series Introduction

Welcome to the Routledge *Critical Moments in American History* series. The purpose of this new series is to give students a window into the historian's craft through concise, readable books by leading scholars, who bring together the best scholarship and engaging primary sources to explore a critical moment in the American past. In discovering the principal points of the story in these books, gaining a sense of historiography, following a fresh trail of primary documents, and exploring suggested readings, students can then set out on their own journey, to debate the ideas presented, interpret primary sources, and reach their own conclusions—just like the historian.

A critical moment in history can be a range of things—a pivotal year, the pinnacle of a movement or trend, or an important event such as the passage of a piece of legislation, an election, a court decision, a battle. It can be social, cultural, political, or economic. It can be heroic or tragic. Whatever they are, such moments are by definition "game changers," momentous changes in the pattern of the American fabric, paradigm shifts in the American experience. Many of the critical moments explored in this series are familiar; some less so.

There is no ultimate list of critical moments in American history—any group of students, historians, or other scholars may come up with a different catalog of topics. These differences of view, however, are what make history itself and the study of history so important and so fascinating. Therein can be found the utility of historical inquiry—to explore, to challenge, to understand, and to realize the legacy of the past through its influence on the present. It is the hope of this series to help students realize this intrinsic value of our past and of studying our past.

William Thomas Allison
Georgia Southern University

Figures

1.1 Ronald Reagan delivers "the Speech" at a GE plant in October of 1955 — 8
2.1 The heart of the "Solid South" was flipped inside out during the 1964 presidential election by the conservative candidacy of Barry Goldwater — 52
3.1 Hardhat workers demonstrate in New York City in May of 1970 — 70
4.1 In an address from the Oval Office on July 27, 1981, President Reagan uses a cartoonish prop to explain the rationale and potential benefits of tax reduction — 96
5.1 President Reagan shakes hands with Arkansas Governor Bill Clinton at the signing of the Welfare Reform Act of 1988 — 143

Acknowledgments

I wrote this book in Istanbul, mostly during the 2011–2012 academic year, during which time I taught six courses per semester—a teaching load that is not too unusual for us recent PhDs. Amid the long commutes and the blur of students and daily lectures, I juggled my teaching and faculty responsibilities while trying to preserve enough time and energy to read, to think, and to write about Ronald Reagan and American conservatism, from whose presence I was far removed. It was not easy, although I have been fortunate to have had the support of colleagues, friends, and family, without whom I would have been unable to complete this project. I hope the following people feel pleased, rather than implicated, by their association with me and with this publication of my work.

I would like to thank my colleagues at Yeditepe University. In the Department of Sociology, Aykut Toros, Demet Lüküslü, and Banu Koçer Reisman welcomed me with friendship and intellectual camaraderie while I assimilated to life and to work in new surroundings. Çok teşekkürler hocalar! Thanks to Hilal Özateş, whose warm presence makes coming to work in the morning much more enjoyable than it would otherwise be. In the Department of History, thanks to Şefik Peksevgen for encouraging me to offer a survey course on American history and to Feroz Ahmad for welcoming me in his office for tea, and for talking with me about history. Thanks, too, to Bora Özerinç and to Emre Şakar for showing me the ropes around campus and around town.

While I was writing this book, I attended two academic conferences. I benefited from discussions at the 2012 European Association of American Studies meeting in Izmir, Turkey, and the excellent conference, "Conservatism, Radicalism and Fundamentalism," sponsored by the Department of Political Science at Debrecen University in Hungary.

Alf Tomas Tønnessen and Barış Ünlü generously provided me with very constructive criticism on the manuscript. Their comments saved me from a couple of embarrassing errors and helped me to reconsider the general themes of this book. I probably should have taken their advice more than I actually did, and the mistakes, misjudgments, or just plain bad writing that might follow are my own.

I am privileged to have studied with wonderful professors at Miami University, the University of Toledo, and the State University of New York at Binghamton. My teachers molded my scholarly interests and gave shape to my life: William C. Flint, Peter Linebaugh, Martin J. Murray, William G. Martin, and Michael O. West.

Thanks to Bill Allison, editor of this book series, for giving me the "thumbs up" to contribute to his exciting project and for his encouraging comments, including things I might do to improve the manuscript. At Routledge, Rebecca Novack, Kimberly Guinta, and Genevieve Aoki guided me in a friendly way through the unfamiliar process of writing a book. The three reviewers for Routledge who gave critical comments on my initial proposal were very insightful. They thought of things I didn't, and I benefited from and tried to make use of their knowledge and recommendations.

Thanks to Scott Nesbit, who replied to a query I sent to the H-South discussion list. He and the folks at the Voting America Digital Scholarship Lab of the University of Richmond created the political maps that appear in the second chapter. Thanks to Carin Johnson, who facilitated the permission for my use of the powerful Garry Winogrand photograph, "Hard Hat Rally," that appears in the third chapter.

This book contains a number of primary documents. Many thanks to the following people and institutions for their generosity in granting me their permission, or in helping me track down those who could. *New Left Review* allowed me to publish excerpts of C. Wright Mills' "Letter to the New Left." Much to my pleasant surprise, Tom Hayden responded to an email I sent him, and he gave me permission to reprint excerpts from the "Port Huron Statement." Thanks to Jack Fowler, publisher of *National Review*, for granting permission to reprint the 1960 "Sharon Statement" of the Young Americans for Freedom. Sarah Farber and Brandon Burke from the Hoover Institution were of tremendous help in directing my request to transcribe several of Reagan's radio commentaries through the proper channels. Joanne Drake of the Ronald Reagan Presidential Foundation ultimately granted me permission to make the transcriptions, and I am most grateful to her and to the Reagan Foundation for that. As I completed them myself, I am responsible for any errors that may have been made in the transcription process.

I would also like to thank the managers of the international file sharing servers. For those of us who live in countries without adequate English language research libraries, the services of these websites are invaluable. They function as a global library and facilitate the acquisition of knowledge and the publication of more books, such as this one, that in an earlier age of technological history could not have been written outside of the United States.

I am privileged to be part of an international family. Here in Turkey, Berna "Annecegim" looks after us and treats me as a son; "eline sağlık!" to Mehmet. Back in Ohio, I'm thankful to have the love and support of my brother Ben, my sister Jodi, and my parents, Jim and Jean, who stood firmly behind my decision to become an academic. As a testament to their open-mindedness, my mother and father gave me the independence required to develop my own ideas, even when my thinking diverged from their own. I'm not sure we've ever managed to reach a political consensus (and I suspect we never will), but our differing political views have never come between us or the love we have for one another.

Finally, I would like to thank my wife, Irmak Ertuna-Howison, to whom this book is dedicated, for reading through the manuscript and for giving me advice about my writing and ideas. But much more than that, she tolerated those lost weekends and pampered me while I stared at my laptop and drank coffee. During our trips back from the United States, she allowed me to fill our precious luggage space with books about Ronald Reagan and American conservatives. Her love drives me, and without it, I'd be . . . well, nothing really.

Jeff Howison
Istanbul, November 2012

Timeline

February 11, 1911	Ronald Wilson Reagan is born in Tampico, Illinois
October 29, 1929	The New York Stock Exchange crashes, triggering the Great Depression
November 1932	Democrat Franklin D. Roosevelt elected president and launches New Deal policies
April 1933	Reagan begins work with WHO radio in Davenport, Iowa
March 1937	Reagan arrives in Hollywood and signs a contract with Warner Brothers
January 26, 1940	Reagan marries his first wife, the actress Jane Wyman
December 7, 1941	Japanese attack on Pearl Harbor, United States enters WWII
April 1947	Reagan works for the FBI as an anticommunist informant
1947	Reagan becomes president of the Screen Actors Guild for the first time
August 1948	The States' Rights Democratic Party, or "Dixiecrats", break from national Democratic Party and nominate Strom Thurmond for president
March 4, 1952	Reagan, recently divorced, marries his second wife, the actress Nancy Davis
1954	Reagan begins work as spokesman for the General Electric Company
November 19, 1955	William F. Buckley Jr. publishes the first issue of *National Review*
1962	*General Electric Theatre* cancelled, Reagan leaves General Electric
1964	Reagan appears in his last role as a professional actor, with Lee Marvin and Angie Dickenson in NBC's "The Killers"
October 1964	Reagan enters party politics with "A Time for Choosing" speech in support of Barry Goldwater
August 1965	Watts Riots erupt in Los Angeles, Reagan and conservative leaders call for "law and order"
November 8, 1966	Reagan becomes Governor of California in a landslide victory over the incumbent, Democrat Pat Brown
April 4, 1968	Martin Luther King Jr. assassinated in Memphis, setting off widespread rioting across the country
August 1968	Reagan is defeated by Richard Nixon in the Republican presidential primaries
November 3, 1969	Nixon delivers the "Silent Majority" speech

May 1970	Hardhat rallies take place in New York City as blue collar union members assault antiwar protestors
November 3, 1970	Reagan reelected as Governor of California
October 1973	Arab members of OPEC launch oil embargo, leading to worldwide recession and "stagflation" in the United States
January 6, 1975	Reagan's second term as Governor of California ends, he does not seek reelection
April 23, 1975	President Ford announces end to Vietnam War, one week later Saigon falls to the communist North Vietnamese as the American embassy is evacuated
August 1976	Reagan is defeated by Gerald Ford in the Republican presidential primaries
November 4, 1979	52 Americans taken hostage in Tehran; Iranian hostage crisis begins
December 1979	Soviet forces invade Afghanistan
November 4, 1980	Ronald Reagan elected President of the United States
January 20, 1981	Reagan takes office; American hostages in Iran are released
March 30, 1981	Reagan shot by gunman John Hinckley Jr., barely surviving assassination attempt
August 5, 1981	PATCO strike ends as Reagan fires more than 11,000 air traffic controllers
August 13, 1981	Reagan signs the Economic Recovery Tax Act of 1981, lowering tax rates for individuals and corporations
March 23, 1983	Reagan proposes the Strategic Defense Initiative, dubbed the "Star Wars" program by the press
November 6, 1984	Reagan reelected in landslide victory over Democrat Walter Mondale
October 5, 1986	CIA plane shot down in Nicaragua, triggering the discovery of the Iran-contra affair
December 8, 1987	Reagan signs Intermediate-Range Nuclear Forces (INF) Treaty with the Soviet Union
January 2, 1988	Reagan signs the Canada-United States Free Trade Agreement
January 20, 1989	Reagan leaves office amid high approval ratings; George H.W. Bush succeeds Reagan as president
November 10, 1989	The Berlin Wall falls
December 25, 1991	National independence declared for Soviet satellite states, effectively ending the Cold War in Eastern Europe and marking the fall of the Soviet Union
January 1, 1994	The North American Free Trade Agreement (NAFTA) takes effect
November 5, 1994	Reagan writes letter disclosing he has been diagnosed with Alzheimer's disease
November 8, 1994	"Republican Revolution" in U.S. Congress, the party achieves a majority in the House of Representatives for the first time since 1952
June 5, 2004	Reagan dies at his home in Bel Air, California, at the age of 93

Preface

In the aftermath of the 1980 presidential election, journalists, academics, and ordinary American citizens attempted to make sense of what they had just witnessed: what did the election of Ronald Reagan signify for the past, present, and future of the United States? Reagan had been the icon of the American conservative movement since 1964. He was a former Hollywood actor and Republican Governor of California who had unsuccessfully run for President in 1968 and in 1976, both times failing to win his party's nomination. This time around, not only did he win the nomination, he crushed in an electoral landslide the incumbent Democrat, a trained nuclear engineer, peanut farmer, "born-again" Christian and former Governor of Georgia, Jimmy Carter. Kathleen Frankovich, a leading pollster for CBS News whose quantitative research was the basis of a widely discussed book published shortly after the election, wrote, "There is no evidence that indicates a turn to the right by the nation. Reagan was not elected because of the increasing conservatism in the country . . . In 1980 voters were no more likely to call themselves conservatives than they were in 1976."[1] Frankovich is correct: between the years 1976 and 1980, the number of Americans who self-identified as being "conservative" had not risen in any substantially quantifiable sense. More than any other factor, Frankovich pointed to the widespread dissatisfaction with the Carter administration in handling foreign policy and especially the economy, which was struggling to recover from the bleakness of "stagflation." Thus, the outcome of the presidential election of 1980 was a referendum on the Carter presidency just as much as—if not more so than—it was a mandate for Reagan and for conservatism.

But this characterization is true only in the short-term sense. American people did not suddenly become more conservative during the four years that separated the election of Jimmy Carter from that of Ronald Reagan—

although a number of important conservative organizations *did* emerge during this period. Instead, the victory of Ronald Reagan was a culmination of social changes that had gradually taken place in American society since the end of the Second World War. The most general way to characterize what had happened during this period is that the United States had become increasingly conservative. This is a book about how and why that process occurred, and what Ronald Reagan had to do with it.

In order to avoid misleading readers, I should say that despite the implication of its title, the 1980 presidential election is not the primary focus of this book. Other books, written by people with direct access to Ronald Reagan and to Jimmy Carter, to their staffs and to their advisors, all of whom were personally involved in the day-to-day events of the campaigns, would be of greater use on the specific topic of the election than anything I would be capable of producing. The minute details of the election constitute neither the bulk nor the main purpose of this book. Instead, this book takes as its central premise that the presidential election of 1980 was a critical moment in the larger history of the United States, and that the victory of Ronald Reagan signified the ascendancy of the conservative movement in American society. Furthermore, some of the ideas that Reagan advocated would establish new political and economic trends that would transcend party divisions: they would be embraced not only by conservative Republicans, but by supposedly liberal Democrats as well.

This is a unique book in relation to others that have been written about the conservative movement and the legacy of the Reagan presidency. In order to answer the questions concerning why the Reagan victory in 1980 was important and how it related to the rise of the conservative movement in the United States, it is necessary to use a flexible historical point of view that can blend biographical, intellectual and social histories. This is not a biography of Ronald Reagan, although parts of the book discuss the contours of his life in some detail. This book contains elements of "top-down" history: the stories of powerful politicians and what they did to create and to capitalize upon the feelings of ordinary citizens. In parts, it is also a "bottom-up" history that looks at the ways in which conservatism developed from the grassroots of society. It also focuses upon the role of conservative organizations and how they interacted with public sentiment and government policies.

The chapters of this book are organized chronologically as well as thematically, and each one incorporates Reagan's relationship to the development of the conservative movement. The first chapter is composed of three parts: a biographical portrait of Ronald Reagan, an overview of the different forms of American conservatism, and a summary of how, by the early 1960s, conservatives and their nascent movement were gaining momentum in American society and within the Republican Party. The second chapter offers a longer-term discussion of the role of the American South in the evolution of party politics. One of the key developments that presented new opportunities for conservative Republicanism during the 1960s had to do with the civil rights movement and the reaction of white southerners to the social changes taking place in the region. The chapter concludes with an analysis of the Barry Goldwater campaign of 1964, which marked Reagan's entry into politics.

The third chapter discusses the complex historical backdrop of the period after the 1964 presidential election and through the middle of 1970s, and focuses upon what many authors have referred to as "the backlash." It was during this period that conservatism found receptive new audiences, particularly in the emerging opposition to the social movements and political developments of the era. In a stunning landslide victory over the Democratic incumbent Pat Brown, Reagan was elected Governor of California in 1966 in large part because of his stance against the campus protests at Berkeley and the Watts Riots, both of which shook the foundations of liberal political assumptions and voter coalitions. I argue that what happened in California was essentially a harbinger of what would subsequently occur at the national level. Liberal policy decisions, such as the use of busing to achieve racial balance in schools, as well as the antiwar, feminist and gay rights social movements, spurred conservatives of various stripes—patriotic blue collar workers, suburban parents and the "religious right"—to launch a thermidorian reaction, or backlash. Together, these groups would constitute the foundation of an unprecedented political entity in the United States: a national conservative coalition.

The fourth chapter discusses the political and economic conditions of the late-1970s, which directly set the stage for Ronald Reagan's 1980 victory. It was during this period that the United States faced several overlapping crises that contributed to the appeal of Reagan's unique blend of simplistic optimism and hard-line anticommunism and militarism, which had remained fundamentally unchanged since his entry into politics. The chapter concludes with an analysis of the 1980 election results. The final chapter suggests a new framework for understanding Reagan's relationship to the three branches of American conservatism: social conservatism, anticommunism and libertarianism. Although Reagan can indeed be considered a conservative throughout his political career, his relationship to the movement today remains largely symbolic and is often at odds with the reality of his beliefs and the policies he advocated—or failed to advocate. Nevertheless, Reagan played a leading role in legitimizing conservative ideas in relation to a range of issues, although it is ironic that, because the Republican Party continued to move well to the right after his presidency, if Reagan were alive today he would not be considered a conservative Republican. Reagan's contribution to economic conservatism remains his most lasting legacy, and his economic philosophy would contribute to the shaping of a new era in American—and indeed, *world* history.

The appendix of this book contains 13 primary documents, presented chronologically, which are related to the development of the American conservative movement and to Ronald Reagan. Included in this section are excerpts from a well-known speech entitled "A Time for Choosing," which Reagan made in 1964 in support of Barry Goldwater. With this exception, the documents compiled here have not been widely reprinted and do not appear in other books on the topic of American conservatism. I have included excerpts from the "Letter to the New Left" by C. Wright Mills (1960), as well as the "Port Huron Statement" of the Students for a Democratic Society (1962). The inclusion of two documents of the new left might seem grossly out of place in a book about American conservatism. However, these documents will allow readers to compare the reactions of conservatives *and* radicals to the social conditions with which they were both profoundly unsatisfied during the post-WWII period. The rise of the American conservative movement, or new right, was in many ways the flip-side to the rise of the new left, as both movements developed in part through their mutual antagonism. But by the middle of the 1970s, the new right would continue to play a major role in American society, while the new left had essentially disintegrated.

I have also included the "Sharon Statement," a short founding document of the conservative movement produced by the Young Americans for Freedom (1960), as well as Richard Nixon's "Silent Majority" speech of November 3, 1969. Nixon was not directly connected to the conservative Republican tradition, although he capitalized on the backlash of the 1960s and 70s by exploiting fissures in the Democratic constituency, having realized the potential for a reconfiguration of the historic Republican and Democratic coalitions on a national scale. In language that resonates with the subsequent American wars in Afghanistan and Iraq, Nixon explains his rational for "Vietnamization" and calls upon the "silent majority" of Americans to support his policies and to defend the United States from the "humiliation" of antiwar dissenters.

The remaining eight primary documents, which I personally transcribed, are from Ronald Reagan's radio commentaries of the late-1970s. During this period Reagan did not hold political office but remained active in addressing social, political, and economic issues. These broadcasts, to my knowledge, appear here in print for the first time (other than in

Reagan's handwritten notes). The commentaries I have selected include Reagan's thoughts on serious political subjects such as the Guantanamo Naval Base and sanctions (which he opposed) against the apartheid government in South Africa, as well as more light-hearted musings, including the use of hyphenated surnames and his retelling of a children's fable meant to illustrate the benefits of free market capitalism. The range of documents will allow readers to become familiar with the substance and style of Reagan as a public figure and as a politician. I have offered short introductions to each of these documents that explain their historical context and larger significance.

A brief word is in order about my own political views in relation to the subject about which I have written. I am not a subscriber to the objectivist view of history. To paraphrase the historian E.H. Carr, I do not believe that the piling up of "historical facts" makes for good history any more than the piling up of bricks makes for good architecture. In both cases, what matters is the way we *choose* to construct the piles. The existing scholarly literature on Ronald Reagan and various aspects of the conservative movement can itself be divided into two general piles: one hagiographic and one critical. This book will likely be among those in the latter pile, although I have not set out to cast judgment upon the movement, in either a positive or negative light, without first attempting to understand it. To paraphrase C. Wright Mills, I've tried to be objective, but I don't claim to be detached. My purpose is neither to celebrate nor to condemn Reagan and American conservatism. Instead, I have analyzed the social forces that gave rise to the conservative ideas adopted by large segments of the American people in the decades after the Second World War. Ronald Reagan was a product of those forces, and he became a symbol of those ideas. Without the conservative movement, there would have been no Ronald Reagan. And without Ronald Reagan, the conservative movement may very well have ended up a footnote, rather than a critical part of twentieth-century American history. I hope readers will find this book useful as they continue to form their own judgments.

CHAPTER 1

Introducing American Conservatism

From the first moments of the Reagan presidency, it was clear that change had arrived in Washington. After his narrow 1976 victory, on the day of his own inaugural ceremony, Jimmy Carter opted to walk down Pennsylvania Avenue rather than to ride in the limousines of the presidential motorcade. He did this to symbolize his humility and the reduced stature of the office of the presidency in the aftermath of the Watergate affair. Carter was casual: he often dressed informally and prepared his own meals during the time he spent in the White House. Four years later, as Ronald Reagan was inaugurated, the festivities could hardly have been more different. Reagan's swearing-in ceremony on January 20, 1981, was held on the stately West Front of the Capitol Building, a site that his advisors and the president-elect himself thought better suited to emphasize the grandeur of the American presidency than the traditional location of the inaugural ceremonies, the more banal East Front of the building. The celebrations later that evening featured black-tie galas, Hollywood celebrities, and five-star menus. "The President's thousand-dollar morning suit, the First Lady's $10,000 gown, the sixteen-million-dollar inaugural price tag, the private planes landing at National (soon to be Reagan) Airport, the limousines deployed on the ground . . . all signified Reagan's new direction."[1]

The ritzy atmosphere of Reagan's inauguration prompted many observers—including some of his historic allies—to remark on what they considered to be offensive displays of wealth during difficult economic times. Barry Goldwater, the conservative Republican senator from Arizona whose 1964 presidential campaign changed the direction of the party and launched Reagan's career in politics, seethed, "When you've got to pay $2,000 for a limousine for four days, $7 to park, and $2.50 to check your coat, at a time when most people in this country just can't hack it, that's ostentatious."[2] In addition to the glamour of celebrity, Reagan's formality contrasted with Carter's folksiness even in the most mundane tasks of the presidency. "Reagan, despite his views that he was 'one of the people' and inseparable from them, suspected that . . . calculated displays of ordinariness detracted from the dignity and purpose of the presidency . . . his approach . . . was consciously respectful, reflected in [his] refusal to take off his coat whenever he worked in the Oval Office."[3]

But Reagan's 1980 victory, and what it came to symbolize, was much more than a stylistic departure from earlier protocols of presidential behavior—although, as will be seen, style and the use of imagery is a crucial aspect of Reagan's rise to power, his presidency, and his legacy. It was also much more than the usual celebrations that mark the "change" brought about by the election of a new president. Instead, Reagan's election signified a critical moment in American history for more profound reasons: it represented the ascendance of the American conservative movement as one of the key historical outcomes of the social changes that had taken place in American society during the long post-WWII period. Furthermore, not only was Reagan's election a culmination of these changes, it was also a watershed moment in the "conservative turn" in American politics: it helped to legitimize conservative positions in relation to a wide range of social, political, and economic issues.

In order to understand Ronald Reagan and his relationship to the American conservative movement, we should first define exactly what we mean by these terms. Of course, Ronald Reagan is one of the most recognizable Americans of the twentieth century, so it might seem redundant to "define him." But to appreciate his relation to the American conservative movement, it is necessary to chart the course of his personal biography and the historical forces that shaped his life and his political views. Additionally, it is important to "get to know him" on a somewhat more personal level before examining the significance of his election and presidency, for one of the keys to Reagan's success has to do with the features of his personality, which in turn informed how he understood his role as a politician.

RONALD REAGAN: A BIOGRAPHICAL PORTRAIT

Ronald Wilson Reagan was born on February 6, 1911, in Tampico, Illinois, to a Protestant mother and an Irish Catholic father; he grew up in the nearby town of Dixon. His family was not wealthy, and although they would struggle under the conditions of economic crisis during the

1930s, they were squarely part of that ambiguous American category, the "middle class." Despite graduating from the obscure and socially conservative Eureka College during the height of the Great Depression, Reagan's background in the performing arts, coupled with his persistence and quick wits, helped him soon find work as a radio broadcaster in Davenport, Iowa. By all accounts, Reagan had a natural talent as a sports announcer, not so much because of his interest in sports, which was considerable, but because of his background in the theatre, his easy Midwestern charm, and his vivid imagination, all of which enabled him to absorb the storylines of the players and teams quickly, even in contests with which he had been entirely unfamiliar. Reagan was soon promoted to the larger market of nearby Des Moines, and it was there, through his work in sports radio at the NBC affiliate station WHO, that he began his career as a public figure. By 1934, although not exactly a household name, "Dutch" Reagan (in his early years he was known by the nickname bestowed upon him by his father) had emerged as an affable small-time celebrity as the voice of the Chicago Cubs baseball team in the Midwest:

> [Reagan's] success had not diminished his extreme modesty, the way he had of holding a slightly receding posture so that people often had to lean toward him to hear what he was saying (a manner that created an almost instant sense of intimacy). And then there was his distinctive voice—hospitable and at the same time persuasive, seductive and without sham. An investigative reporter could search long and hard and not find one man, woman or child who disliked Dutch Reagan in the 1930s.[4]

In March of 1937, under the pretext of covering a Cubs spring training game in California, Reagan, through the help of his agent, set out to test the waters of Hollywood and the prospects of a career in film. Reagan seemed personally immune to the effects of the Depression, a feature of his biography that likely contributed

> Although he never achieved the fame of a leading Hollywood star such as Humphrey Bogart or Cary Grant, Ronald Reagan appeared in more than 50 motion pictures during his 20-year film career, including: *Girls on Probation* (1938), *Brother Rat* (1938), *Code of the Secret Service* (1939), *Smashing the Money Ring* (1939), *Murder in the Air* (1940, the last in a series of films in which Reagan portrayed Lieutenant "Brass" Bancroft), *Knute Rockne—All American* (1940), *King's Row* (1942), *This is the Army* (1943), *The Voice of the Turtle* (1947), *Bedtime for Bonzo* (1951), and *Law and Order* (1953).

to the later development of his individualistic worldview. After his first audition he was offered a contract with Warner Brothers (who advised that he should use his given name of Ronald, rather than "Dutch"), and he began to appear in films almost immediately. In his first film role, Reagan aptly portrayed a Midwestern radio announcer, and he would continue to portray throughout his film career characters who reflected his own personality and reputation as a good natured "all American." Reagan's life—his general outlook, the people with whom he associated, and, as some have suggested, his perception of reality—would be tremendously influenced by his Hollywood career. It was in the entertainment industry that Reagan met both of his wives: his marriage to the actress Jane Wyman ended in divorce in 1949; he married his second wife and life partner, the actress Nancy Davis, in 1952.

Although Reagan's poor eyesight kept him out of combat during the Second World War, he served as an officer in the Cavalry Reserve in Fort Mason, California, during which time he appeared in and narrated several U.S. Army propaganda films. It should come as no surprise that the Second World War and its aftermath had a deep impact on Reagan's political views. Prior to the war, Reagan had been, like many Americans during the 1930s, a New Deal Democrat who idolized Franklin D. Roosevelt. And indeed, even after his ideological conversion to conservatism and growing opposition to New Deal social programs, Reagan remained a great admirer of FDR, albeit on a personal rather than ideological level. Over the course of his presidency, Reagan borrowed liberally from several FDR speeches, including the line "rendezvous with destiny," which Roosevelt had used at the 1936 Democratic National Convention.

Despite his eternal admiration for FDR, after the war Reagan morphed into a hard-line anticommunist and increasing opponent of the central premises of New Deal liberalism: namely, he came to oppose state intervention in the economy and a range of "collectivist" federal social programs. The reasons for Reagan's personal transformation from a New Deal Democrat to a conservative Republican have been the subject of much debate. Historians and Reagan biographers have largely failed to come up with a convincing singular explanation as to why this change in his personal political beliefs occurred, although one general factor is beyond dispute: Reagan's views were shaped by the same historical forces that transformed the views of countless other Americans, and these social changes would slowly reconfigure the ideologies and constituencies of both the Democratic and Republican parties and would culminate in Reagan's election as President of the United States in 1980. These forces will be explored at length throughout the pages of this book, but suffice it to say that the Cold War, a general reaction against the "consensus" politics of the 1950s and the social movements of the 1960s and 70s (including radical and conservative mobilizations) all played a part in shaping Reagan's views.

In the immediate postwar years, Reagan increased his role in the labor politics of Hollywood through the Screen Actors Guild (SAG), where he joined the administrative board of directors before going on to serve as president an unprecedented seven times during the late-1940s and 50s. During this period, Reagan was increasingly associated with the rising tide of anticommunism, which, as will be seen, was one of the three ideological pillars of American conservatism in the twentieth century. Through his leadership position inside SAG, Reagan worked as an FBI informant (as did his brother, Neil) and as a friendly witness before the House Select Committee on Un-American Activities (HUAC), during which time he secretly "named names," directly contributing to the larger purges of suspected communists in Hollywood that occurred through the creation of the infamous "blacklists."[5]

During the second half of the 1950s, as Reagan's career in Hollywood was in decline, he began a new position for which he was well suited, one that allowed him to continue his balancing act of keeping one foot in the world of show business and the other in the world of politics. In a position that perhaps foreshadowed twenty-first century attempts at the seamless integration of corporate advertising into "real life" through product placement and "guerilla marketing" campaigns, Reagan accepted the lucrative position he once described as his own "postgraduate education in political science": a multifaceted role as the public face and spokesperson for the General Electric Company. From 1954 to 1962, Reagan was the host of the *General Electric Theatre* television program, while acting as a "symbol and spokesman for the entire GE endeavor, what a publicist called the company's ambassador of goodwill to the public at large."[6] Furthermore, Reagan also advertised and represented the lifestyle of the "modern American consumer." In addition to his hefty salary, he was given a house complete with the latest technological gadgets and appliances, with which he frequently appeared and which he endorsed both on screen and in print. Reagan embarked upon extensive tours of the United States to make personal appearances at each and every one of GE's 135 production facilities across the country. During these tours, he spoke with workers, managers, and their families about a wide range of social issues. Through both the television program and the factory tours, Reagan had a dual platform to deliver the company's and, increasingly, *his own* vision for America.

It was through Reagan's work at GE that he became a student and practitioner of "Boulwarism," a management and public relations method named after Lemuel Boulware, a fellow executive at General Electric.

Boulware's main objective at GE was to break the power of the United Electrical Workers (UE), the labor union whose massive 1946 strike rocked the company and set the tone for the rising power of organized labor in the post-WWII era. In earlier periods of American history, the violent clashes between unions and corporations had taken place in the streets. For Boulware, however, the most important terrain of the conflict was the mind. He embarked upon a wide-reaching campaign to shape the political ideology of GE workers toward antiunion positions. "Boulware made fighting the unions come to seem moral, a righteous cause, forward looking, necessary to make a better America."[7] Although Boulware was vehemently opposed to labor unions, he believed "it was not enough to win over company employees on narrow labor issues . . . but [to] pass on GE's essentially conservative message . . . helping the company to win voters at the grass roots who would elect officials and pass legislation" that would ultimately serve the corporation's political and economic interests.[8] Through Boulwarism, General Electric developed the field of corporate public relations as it went "over the heads of union officials directly to the blue-collar workers, their families, and their neighbors" in an effort to influence the opinions and mold the political ideology "within the company and in other companies, and the public at large."[9] Under the tutelage of Lemuel Boulware, Reagan's views moved increasingly to the right, as he stood in a unique position to appear as a television personality and corporate front man, while simultaneously working to shape the political ideology of his audiences.

Throughout the 1950s, Reagan polished his public speaking and finalized his break with New Deal liberalism while solidifying the principles that would define his political legacy: in addition to his fierce opposition to communism, he developed a growing opposition to labor unions, to the federal regulation of business, and to taxes—principles that were indistinguishable from those advocated by GE and other major American corporations. Reagan sought to convince his audiences of the merit of these positions through a standard stump speech, which he delivered countless times across the country, inside factories, at banquet dinners, and in more informal settings. During the eight years of Reagan's employment at GE, he "was giving the same speech year after year, making it vivid and enjoyable, though its message was apocalyptic: a slow invisible tide of socialism was engulfing America, held back only by a few brave businessmen."[10] These speeches laid the foundations for Reagan's political style. Through his innumerable conversations with GE workers and their families, Reagan mastered the art of reducing complex issues to simplified arguments that appealed to the traditional sensibilities of many ordinary Americans. This way of addressing his audiences became the hallmark of

Reagan's rhetorical style, and he would use it effectively throughout his political career, including during the course of his presidency.

"The Speech," as it is known among Reagan's biographers, was characterized by its abundant and scattershot use of anecdotal rather than well-documented evidence. It invariably centered upon the evils of communism and the ways in which the principles of Soviet totalitarianism were increasingly reflected in the monolithic power of the United States federal government bureaucracy, which, from Reagan's point of view, arbitrarily tormented the lives and productive capacities of the American people through an array of illogical and stifling regulations, all of which were underwritten by excessive taxation. For Reagan, there were always simpler solutions to be found for the problems of modern American society, solutions other than government action. Instead, social problems were best solved through individualistic common sense. For some of Reagan's contemporaries, "the Speech" was political ideology delivered with the silver-tongued confidence of a traveling salesman. Lawrence Williams, an actor who worked with Reagan during the 1930s, remarked:

> Statistical information of all sorts was a commodity Ronnie always had in extraordinary supplies . . . Not only was this information abundant, it was stunning in its catholicity. There seemed to be absolutely no subject, however recondite, without its immediately accessible file. Ron had the dope on just about everything: this quarter's up—or down—figure on GNP growth, V.I. Lenin's grandfather's occupation, all history's baseball pitchers' ERAs, the optimistic outlook for California sugar-beet production in the year 2000, the recent diminution of the rainfall level causing everything to go to hell in summer [in] Kansas and so on.[11]

Reagan's time at GE ended in 1962 after he was dismissed in part because of his increasingly controversial viewpoints and associations with individuals and groups on the far right wing of American politics, including the John Birch Society and various southern politicians whose careers had been defined by their attacks on black civil rights. In what would become a trademark of his position on southern racism and other divisive issues, "Reagan did not embrace the bigoted opinions and platforms . . . but . . . was more than willing to associate himself with racists and conspiracy theorists, demagogues and anti-communists."[12] Thus, in light of his background in the anticommunist politics of Hollywood and through his position at GE, by the early 1960s Reagan was widely recognized as a staunch voice of the nascent conservative movement in the United States,

Figure 1.1 Reagan worked for General Electric and hosted the *General Electric Theatre* from 1954 until 1962, where he learned the art of "Boulwarism." Here, at a GE plant in October of 1955, he delivers "the Speech." Courtesy of Ronald Reagan Library.

although he was still a television personality who regularly took up political issues, rather than a politician who appeared regularly on television.

This would change in 1964, as Reagan made his formal entry into American party politics in a format with which he was intimately familiar: a made-for-television speech. "A Time for Choosing" was the latest version of "The Speech," but instead of delivering it on behalf of GE, it was tailored to support the presidential candidacy of Barry Goldwater, who was facing an insurmountable battle against the incumbent Democrat, Lyndon Johnson. Reagan derived the title of his address from the 1964 pro-Goldwater book by the conservative activist Phyllis Schlafly, *A Choice, Not an Echo* (Schlafly would be a key figure in the rise of social conservatism during the 1970s, and she will be discussed in greater detail in Chapter 3). Although Goldwater's advisors initially hesitated to use Reagan in light of what were perceived to be his increasingly extremist political views, the address was a smashing success both for Reagan personally and for the emergent conservative movement within the Republican Party, and it is estimated to have generated more than $8 million for the Goldwater campaign.[13] Despite the apparent setback for American conservatism after Goldwater's trouncing by Johnson in the 1964 presidential election, two years later Reagan rode the unyielding conservative wave in California to a stunning landslide victory over the incumbent governor, the Democrat Pat Brown. With his victory in 1966, Reagan had successfully transformed himself from an actor and corporate spokesperson into the most visible conservative politician in the United States.

One of the first celebrities to be elected to a major political office (the actor George Murphy, himself a former SAG president, was elected as a Republican Senator from California in 1964), Reagan appeared well suited to politics. Many of Reagan's contemporaries, who observed how easily his screen presence as an actor translated into a political persona, quickly realized his apparently unlimited potential in party politics—some of them even predicted that Reagan would become President of the United States long before he became directly involved in party politics, and despite his lack of any experience working in government. Indeed, to many, Reagan simply *seemed* presidential. During the filming of *King's Row* in 1941, Reagan's friend Sam Wood, the anticommunist film director who served as president of the Motion Picture Alliance for the Preservation of American Ideals, asked, "Ronnie, have you ever considered becoming President some day?" To which Reagan is said to have replied, "President of what?" Wood clarified his question, "President of th̄e ̄ ̄ ̄ ̄States."[14] Hunter S. Thompson, the pioneer of "Gonzo" journalis̄ ̄ ̄ ̄ ̄nal thorn in the side of countless politicians and authority fiḡ ̄ ̄ ̄te in a merciless February 1965 letter, "Ronald Reagan is the ̄ ̄ ̄ ̄e of the new mythological American, a grinning whore who will ̄ ̄ ̄ ̄meday be President."[15] Reagan himself also presumably realized h̄ ̄ ̄ ̄tential, although he was perhaps getting ahead of himself when, ̄ ̄ ̄ ̄idst of the 1966 gubernatorial campaign, before he had ev̄ ̄ ̄ ̄d in government, he "suddenly put down his reading material ā ̄ ̄ ̄nced, 'Damn. Wouldn't it be fun to be running now for tḡ ̄ ̄ ̄ncy? Wouldn't that be great?'"[16]

Reagan's potential as a professional politician was, of course, realized. He served as a two-term governor of California, from 1966 through January of 1975, an era marked by social conflict throughout the United States: student protests related to the war in Vietnam, racial uprisings and the emergence of the black power movement, feminism, and the ongoing conflicts over divisive cultural issues such as gay rights and abortion. Reagan constantly pursued the presidency: he made unsuccessful runs in 1968 and again in 1976, both times losing in the primaries. Reagan remained somewhat out of the public eye during the second half of the

1970s, although he continued to broadcast his views regularly through a series of radio programs, *Viewpoint with Ronald Reagan* and *Ronald Reagan Radio Commentary*.

In 1980 the stage was set for Reagan to make another run for the Republican presidential nomination. This time, he found success. Although they were in a virtual dead heat in the weeks leading up to the election, Reagan won the presidency in 1980 by a margin that was far larger than any observer could have credibly predicted at the time: he won more than 90 percent of the Electoral College and received seven million more popular votes than the incumbent Jimmy Carter. And although there have certainly been other presidents in American history who can be considered "conservative," Reagan was the first president directly associated with the American conservative movement. The oldest president-elect in American history, he served two terms and left office in January of 1989 at the age of 77. In 1994, Reagan disclosed what many observers had suspected: he suffered from the devastating effects of Alzheimer's disease. Reagan died on June 5, 2004, having lived out of the public eye during the last decade of his life.

Although Reagan is today unequivocally lauded by conservative Republicans—and by many Democrats—as one of the most iconic presidents of the twentieth century, there is no such consensus among historians and political commentators. Like the conservative movement more generally, the issues and events that are inextricably linked to Reagan and his presidency—"supply-side" economics, the deregulation of financial markets, defense spending, tax cuts, the federal budget and deficit, the politics of labor unions and religious groups, the Iran-contra affair, and the collapse of the Soviet Union (all of which will be discussed in greater detail in the following pages)—are not merely subjects of historical disagreement, their implications are often at the heart of debates taking place in contemporary American society.

WHAT IS THE AMERICAN CONSERVATIVE MOVEMENT?

In order to understand the significance of Ronald Reagan's 1980 victory as a critical moment in American history, it is necessary to understand and define the key features of the American conservative movement. As the subtitle of this book implies, something called the American conservative movement surely exists—but what is it? The answer to this question is not a simple one; there are several definitional and conceptual issues that must be addressed in order to formulate an understanding of what the conservative movement is, where it came from, and its changing historical relationship to American politics and society. Indeed, scholars, journalists, politicians, and ordinary citizens have struggled to define conservatism and its principles not only in the abstract, but also in a more concrete sense as they argue over who and what can properly be labeled as being a conservative in the context of today's United States. As we construct a historical description of American conservatism and of the conservative movement, it is necessary both to limit the discussion in two important ways as well as to provide a definition that is broad enough to include the range of individuals and groups that consider themselves (or who are considered by others) to be conservative.

Among the most immediate conceptual problems that arise in discussions of conservatism is that, as a general form of ideology, conservatism, of course, is not exclusive to the United States. Different ideologies and belief systems that can be considered "conservative" in one way or another have existed throughout history, all over the world. But in the following pages, the analysis of conservatism is restricted to the United States. Although American conservatism has ideological connections to older European traditions, those traditions are not considered at any great length in this book, the purpose of which is not to provide a definition or analysis of conservatism as it may or may not have appeared in all times and in all places, but rather to understand its development within the relatively recent history of the United States. Only in the concluding chapter is any attempt made to link American conservatism and Ronald Reagan to larger global processes and trends. As a second limiting premise, although portions of this book discuss American social and political history using a longer-term perspective (particularly in portions of the second chapter), here the discussion of conservatism in the United States is limited to the era after the Second World War. This is another necessary step that will help to avoid the inherent pitfalls that would arise in an attempt to provide a more universal understanding of conservatism that is geographically or temporally unspecific. Furthermore, this way of limiting the discussion allows us to see that although today's conservatives in the United States are not a homogeneous group, they have emerged in the context of a common set of historically specific conditions against which they have engaged in an ideological battle.

But even if we limit our own discussion of conservatism to a post-WWII American context, there are several additional issues that remain. Namely, what do we mean when we identify something or someone as conservative? In fact, there are ongoing debates about this thorny issue not only among outside observers but among self-professed conservatives as well. For example, during the 2012 Republican presidential primaries,

Mona Charen, a columnist for *National Review* (a leading conservative publication that will be discussed throughout this book) attempted to uncover who among the prospective candidates was the "true conservative." She came to the conclusion that while all of the candidates had the appearance of conservative credentials, the "true" conservative was, in fact, Mitt Romney, not Newt Gingrich, Rick Santorum, or any of the other contenders.[17] The implication of her effort is that although a particular individual might profess or appear to be a conservative, all conservatives are not created equal. In other words, there are authentic conservatives and there are imposters.

The approach used throughout this book is quite different from Charen's effort to locate a singular "true" conservatism. Instead, one of the key points established by historians of conservatism in the United States is that it has always lacked a singular ideological or organizational fountainhead. Rather, American conservatism has developed from multiple—and occasionally conflicting—sources. This is one of the basic premises conveyed by George Nash, whose work, *The Conservative Intellectual Tradition in America Since 1945*, was first published in 1976 and remains unsurpassed in its depth and influence. For Nash, there is no such thing as "true conservatism," and Charen's attempt to locate it would seem to be a futile and purely ideological exercise.

Instead, in Nash's formulation, there are three broad currents of twentieth-century conservatism, all of which have contributed to the development of the movement as we know it today: libertarianism (or economic conservatism), anticommunism, and traditionalism (or social conservatism). Nash writes, "No rigid barriers separated the three groups. Traditionalists and libertarians were usually anti-Communists ... Nevertheless, the impulses that comprised the developing conservative movement were clearly diverse."[18] Although these three traditions were historically distinct, during the long post-1945 period they became increasingly intertwined. The merger of these three varieties of conservatism was not always a smooth or even intuitive process, although the three groups did move closer together during the post-1945 era. Their fusion was the basis of the American conservative movement, which gradually consolidated its power within the Republican Party and in American society more generally. There is reason to speculate that the merger of these three ideological traditions may be a historically temporary phenomenon, as today there is compelling evidence that points to signs of increasing animosity between them—particularly between the traditionalist and libertarian factions. For example, within the tea party movement, as Theda Skocpol and Vanessa Williamson have noted in their recent study, libertarians have clashed with the social conservatives, who have attempted to promote their anti-abortion concerns in meetings designed to focus on economic issues such as taxation. In interviews conducted with the conservative activists, many voiced concerns that the movement had become "too churchy."[19] In fact, there has always been tension—if not outright conflict—that has existed within the varieties of American conservatism. For this reason, it might be more accurate to speak of American *conservatisms* rather than a singular or "true" conservatism.

The first form of American conservatism is economic, and it is often referred to as libertarianism. This ideology is derived from older traditions of what is known in a European context as "classical liberalism." The central premise of this ideology is straightforward: the market economy should not be regulated or otherwise influenced by institutions of government. In the United States, this belief was heavily influenced by the earlier writings of "liberal" European economists such as Friedrich Hayek and Ludwig von Mises, although it was also present in earlier periods of American history as well, most notably during the "Gilded Age" of the late nineteenth century. These early libertarians attempted to present free market capitalism as a moral imperative rather than as a strictly economic question. "For Hayek and Mises, the market meant something more than private property, dispersed ownership, or free competition . . . The market created a space of freedom, a world in which individual actions could revolutionize society."[20] Libertarianism would become a significant ideological force in the United States only in later decades, because during the 1930s and 1940s, as the world economy had collapsed during the Great Depression, the ideology had little public support and was associated with wealthy elites whose beliefs had no connection to the economic interests of ordinary American citizens. As will be seen, the historical conditions of the postwar decades would change this, and the appeal of libertarianism would greatly expand among the white middle class as free market ideology became increasingly intertwined with larger social and cultural issues.

The second historical component of American conservatism during the post-1945 era is

> Although in a contemporary American context, the term "liberal" is widely understood to denote essentially the opposite of "conservative," the term "liberalism" has European roots and was historically used to refer to the "conservative" ideology that advocated *laissez-faire* capitalism and the belief in the infallibility of the free market. In the United States it is common to refer to this ideology as "libertarian" rather than "liberal," and the misuse of the latter term continues to cloud the judgment and analyses of many students and even some leading scholars, a point to which we will return in the concluding chapter.

anticommunism. Although there was relatively constant opposition to communism in most mainstream political circles following the October 1917 Russian Revolution that gave rise to the "Red Scare" in the United States, in light of the American–Soviet alliance during the Second World War it was not until after 1945 that anticommunist ideology fully took hold as a principal aspect of American foreign and domestic policy. In terms of foreign policy, immediately following the war there emerged a widespread consensus within the federal government that sought to limit the influence of communism around the world, with the leading role given to the United States military in pursuit of that goal. The apparent urgency of this task was especially amplified after the "fall of China" in 1949, which bolstered the regional power of the Soviets and undermined what had been a primary objective of American foreign policy: to maintain an "open door" for American political and economic interests in China, with the country acting as a bulwark against the expansion of communism in Asia. Although there was a three-way split between the isolationists on one hand, versus those concerned with containing the western front of communism (the "Europe First" school) and those who were more concerned with its eastern expansion in Asia (the "Asia First" school), there was a general consensus within the federal government that the forces of international communism posed a direct threat to American geopolitical interests. Indeed this "specter of communism" gave rise to the Cold War and was the basis of overt and covert American military operations around the world for nearly 50 years, including throughout the Reagan presidency. But opposition to international communism was not a trait that was exclusive to American conservatives. Indeed, it was arguably the most important unifying aspect of mainstream party politics in the postwar United States.

Far from being limited to the employment of the American military in conflicts around the world, beginning in the 1950s, anticommunism became the primary ideological backbone for emerging conservative positions relating to a wide range of political, economic, and social issues *inside* the United States. In other words, anticommunism as a key aspect of American conservative ideology is related to its function in domestic rather than foreign policy. The strength of anticommunism as a powerful component of conservative ideology is largely derived from its malleability. Although it began as simply the prevailing logic of an American foreign policy that attempted to curtail the influence of the Soviet Union (particularly over the former European colonies, the so-called "third world"), the scope of its application was gradually broadened to encompass criticisms of an incredible array of issues: New Deal social and economic policies, the civil rights movement and school desegregation/integration, the student free speech and antiwar movements, the feminist movement, and even sex education in public schools. In one way or another, all of these movements and issues have been depicted by conservatives as being either inspired or led by agents of international communism who actively sought to subvert "traditional" American values and institutions.

There were several key developments in the rise of conservative (or "domestic") anticommunism, the most well known of which was undertaken by the Republican senator from Wisconsin, Joseph McCarthy. Although McCarthy hardly pioneered the issue, he used it to his own political advantage and greatly extended the scope of individuals and organizations accused of acting as agents of communism. McCarthy (once dubbed by his fellow congressmen the "Pepsi Cola Kid" because of his close relation to the sugar industry) became the most infamous figure of the anticommunist crusade. His role in those efforts began with a speech he delivered in Wheeling, West Virginia, on February 9, 1950, during which he produced a piece of paper that he claimed listed the names of more than 200 communists who had infiltrated the State Department and who were active Soviet agents. This set off a series of new efforts (as well as intensifying old ones) at the highest levels of American government that sought to identify, arrest, and/or purge suspected communists from their positions within government and from within the private sector.

> The John Birch Society, which still operates today, was founded in 1958 by Robert Welch Jr. and several leading American businessmen, including Fred Koch, the industrialist whose family fortune would play a key role in funding other conservative organizations, such as the Cato Institute (founded in 1974). The charges of communism leveled by members of the John Birch Society against high-profile Americans knew no limits. During the height of the organization in the late-1950s and early 1960s, "Birchers" claimed that among the agents of the international communist conspiracy were President Dwight D. Eisenhower and Chief Justice of the Supreme Court Earl Warren.

The cause of anticommunism was championed by government officials and citizens' groups as well. One such group on the extreme end of the anticommunist spectrum was the John Birch Society. The historical consensus concerning the Birch Society and McCarthyism is one of near-universal condemnation and ridicule. And although the majority of mainstream conservatives—including, after much prodding during the 1966 California gubernatorial election, Ronald Reagan—would ultimately break from or publically denounce the efforts of the Birch Society leadership and the more extremist forms of anticommunism, this aspect of conservative ideology proved the most effective way to discredit a variety of social movements and programs, as well as to unify large segments of the American public. In light of the fall of the Soviet Union at the end of 1991 and the apparent American "victory" in the Cold War, anticommunism may appear no longer to be the force it once was in American politics. Indeed, during the 1990s anticommunism all but vanished from the rhetorical landscape of American conservatism. But with the election of Barack Obama in 2008, conservative rhetoric against communism (or now more frequently, "socialism"), has returned with a vengeance, particularly in criticisms of federal initiatives such as health care reform.

Although the role of anticommunism in the larger formation of the conservative movement is most directly related to the Cold War battle against the Soviets, it can also be conceptualized in a more general sense to refer to the ways in which mainstream political ideology in the United States has remained committed to individualism rather than to collectivism. Countless authors have referred to "American exceptionalism" in their explanations of why, for example, there has never been a viable labor party in the United States. This question cannot simply be reduced to an opposition to Soviet communism, but must consider a more general spirit of individualism that has frequently defined life in the United States. Among the various historical factors that have contributed to this, scholars have pointed to the absence of feudal relations or a state church, along with the existence of the frontier. This aspect remains useful in explaining why anticommunism has continued to persist even after the fall of the Soviet Union.

The third form of postwar American conservatism is the somewhat more ambiguous category of "traditionalism," or social conservatism. Here we can include the diverse efforts that have been made to preserve or restore beliefs, customs, and social relations that may once have existed—or were thought to have existed—in earlier periods of American history. Just as Bob Dylan once sang in his observation of the emerging social movements of the 1960s, "the times they are a-changin'," so too would the fictional folksinger-turned-conservative politician Bob Roberts (played by Tim Robbins) sing in a 1992 parody film, "the times they are a-changin' *back*." Several variants of traditionalism have influenced the development of the American conservative movement. During the 1960s and 70s, social conservatives coalesced around a dizzying array of causes, including efforts to stop the passage of the Equal Rights Amendment, a proposed change to the United States Constitution outlawing gender discrimination. Conservative leaders and grassroots organizations also organized against other social movements concerned with issues of gender and sexuality, such as the gay rights movement, which they assailed as an assault not only on longstanding sexual mores and gender identities but upon traditional "family values."

Another important component of social traditionalism concerned white southerners who attempted to preserve racial segregation during the era of the civil rights movement. Despite the work of leading American historians who have shown that racial segregation in the southern states was a relatively recent historical invention that emerged during the 1890s, southern politicians and citizens' groups assailed efforts of both the federal government and civil rights activists during the 1950s and 60s as infringing upon the "traditional southern way of life." The efforts of these white southerners would be a key development for the political organization of the conservative movement, as they broke ranks with the Democrats and realigned with the new conservative faction within the Republican Party (this process is discussed in detail in the following chapter).

Another indispensable faction of social conservatism has been the religious (or evangelical) right, which has steadily increased its level of political and organizational strength as well as its ability to define the terms of debate that have surrounded various social issues. Although there is indeed a much longer history of politicized religion in the United States, the evangelical right emerged only during the 1970s and quickly became a highly organized, well-funded part of the conservative political scene. Notwithstanding initial reservations that it was "unchristian" to politicize religion, the evangelical movement has since occupied the leading edge of the traditionalist segment of American conservatism. The movement has evolved in a number of ways, including in the issues with which it is concerned as well as in its general political orientation. As will be seen, Jimmy Carter had high levels of support among those who identified themselves as being evangelical, but during the late-1970s the movement's ironic rejection of Carter—the first American president to profess his "born again" faith—was a crucial development for Reagan's 1980 victory.

Thus, the American conservative movement has been historically composed of the diverse and occasionally contradictory ideological elements of libertarianism, anticommunism, and traditionalism. In addition to the diverse origins of American conservatism, it is also somewhat problematic to speak of a unified conservative *movement* as a coherent historical entity in light of the nature of the movement's ideology. This is because one of the hallmarks of conservative philosophy is a celebration of individualism rather than collectivism. Indeed, conservative ideology is often hostile toward any sort of collective identity, including social movements. Ayn Rand, the Russian-American author whose writings have influenced many American conservatives (although her staunch atheism severely limited her wider appeal to traditionalists), wrote famously in her novel *Atlas Shrugged*, "I will never live for the sake of another man, nor ask another man to live for mine." This individualistic rather than cooperative mindset tends to deter collective action, including the already difficult tasks involved in the organization and maintenance of a mass social movement. Margaret Thatcher, the Conservative British Prime Minister and one of Reagan's closest confidants during his presidency, quipped in reference to the issue of homelessness and the responsibility of governments to provide shelter and food for the poor, "[The homeless] are casting their problems on society. And, you know, there is no such thing as society. There are [only] individual men and women." Thatcher's response to the question of governmental—or even individuals'—responsibilities toward their fellow citizens, underscores the Randian approach to the question of social responsibility: namely, that individual people need only worry about themselves, and not seek assistance from one another—and certainly not assistance from government.

If individualism is indeed a hallmark of its ideology, it would seem that, by definition, conservatism would tend to function as an independent rather than a cooperative endeavor. This contradiction has crept into analyses and explanations of the tea party movement, and was noted by Anthony DiMaggio in his dismissal of the group as a social movement: "A primary reason the Tea Party is not a social movement is its contempt for collective identity and action . . . the entire idea of collectivity is rejected on an ideological level by tea partiers . . . This group is quite different in their contempt for collective action than the public as a whole, which opinion polls demonstrate remain sympathetic to collective action and social movements."[21] Thus, because of the nature of its ideology, it is somewhat wrongheaded to describe American conservatism as a "social movement" analogous to the civil rights movement for example, which not only championed specific social and political issues, but embraced the philosophies and tactics based upon collective identity. However, although a conservative "movement" tends to be antithetical to the very philosophy of conservatism itself and an apparent contradiction to the inner logic of its ideology, conservative individuals and organizations have indeed worked together quite frequently in attempting to influence political leaders, the policies of the United States, and, by extension, their fellow citizens. In this sense the conservative movement has been quite real in its impact on American society.

CONSERVATIVES AND THE REPUBLICAN PARTY

One of the primary factors that helps to explain the growth of the movement during the postwar era is the confluence of its three ideological tributaries—libertarianism, anticommunism, and traditionalism—whose complex merger produced a mighty river of conservatism. This process of convergence has occurred in ideological as well as organizational terms. Ideologically, there have been countless examples (many of which will be discussed in the following chapters) of social issues that functioned to bring together groups of conservatives who previously shared little in terms of tangible common interests. For example, one of the major controversies that persisted as a key issue in the 1970s involved the tax exempt status of religious schools, particularly in the southern states. The national controversy climaxed in 1978 around the case of Bob Jones University, a "Christian" university that had denied admittance to unmarried black students until 1971 and which forbade interracial dating among its students. As will be seen, the issue appealed to economic conservatives in light of the tax dimension of the conflict, but it also galvanized social traditionalists, including religious and racial conservatives who were more concerned with what they perceived to be federal encroachment and judgment upon their cultural preferences.

In addition to processes of ideological convergence, conservatives came together organizationally by uniting under the banner of the Republican Party while simultaneously gaining an increasing and ultimately *dominant* voice within the party apparatus. In light of today's partisan reality, it is necessary to remind ourselves that the direct association of conservatism with Republicanism is a very recent development in American political history. In the past, both the Democratic and Republican parties contained a stunning array of ideological variety among their respective politicians and the constituencies that supported them. To be sure, there have always been conservative Republicans and liberal Democrats, and there is some continuity between earlier political configurations and the parties as they appear today. But historically, conservative Republicans were but one faction within the party; they were hardly the driving force they would become in later decades.

Prior to the "Republicanization" of the American conservative movement, the party was defined by its diverse ideological admixture, various factions that attempted to exert influence over the party platform and nominate candidates whose beliefs were closest to their own. Historians have recognized at least three distinct Republican groups that coexisted within the party in the past and that correspond also to a loose geographical regionalism. First, the "modern Republicans" (who are also commonly referred to as "moderate Republicans") were a reformist wing of the party based in the northeastern states. As Geoffrey Kabaservice notes:

> Like the fiery New England abolitionists who had helped found the Republican Party, [modern Republicans] rallied to the standard of civil rights and civil liberties; like the Bull Moose progressives [Theodore Roosevelt's third party of 1912], they were willing to use government power to promote economic growth and social development.[22]

The modern Republicans were internationalist in terms of the foreign policies they advocated, including their strong support for U.S. military intervention in World War Two. Although they were not a leading force in the black freedom struggle, they would come to support the goals of the civil rights movement during the 1950s and 60s, including the Civil Rights Act of 1964.

There were also conservatives within the Republican Party. These party "stalwarts" were historically based in the Midwest and were led by a powerful figure from a dynastic family in American politics: the Tafts of Ohio. In terms of the early formation of postwar conservatism, it was Robert Alphonso Taft (not to be confused with his son Robert Taft Jr., or grandson Robert "Bob" Taft III, Governor of Ohio from 1999–2007) who played the leading role. Taft and the stalwarts opposed military cooperation with international forces such as the North Atlantic Treaty Organization (NATO) and the United Nations (UN), as well as international legislative bodies such as the World Court. Consistent with this isolationism, they also strongly opposed American involvement in the Second World War. Taft, unlike the moderate Republicans, was a supporter of *laissez-faire* capitalism. The stalwart Republicans are often referred to as the "old right" of the party. As one of the economists of the old right, Murray N. Rothbard, has written, "The Old, original, Right realized the horrors of the New Deal and

> Moderate Republicans held positions of power at all levels of American government throughout the twentieth century, although they would largely disappear during the 1970s as the conservative faction increased its power within the party. The most prominent moderates were President Dwight Eisenhower, New York Governor Nelson Rockefeller, and Michigan Governor George Romney. Richard Nixon is also generally considered a moderate Republican, despite the fact that during his presidency his socially conservative rhetoric was often indistinguishable from the conservatives'. But Nixon was frequently attacked by party conservatives in light of his positions on civil rights, economic regulation, and international diplomacy.

predicted the collectivist road on which it was setting the nation . . . it was solidly united: all opposed the New Deal and were committed to its total repeal and abolition lock, stock, and barrel."[23]

During the 1950s, the moderate traditions were at the forefront of the Republican Party. It requires a keen political eye to distinguish the ideologies of these moderate Republicans with their "liberal" Democratic counterparts during the era. Most of the disagreements between them were in degree rather than in kind. Indeed, political commentators were so struck by the apparent lack of substantive dispute between the parties and between the contending classes in American society that they developed the idea of the "end of ideology" and of the "liberal consensus": "the productivity

Old Right, New Right

Robert A. Taft led the Republican contingent that was opposed to American involvement in both the First and Second World Wars. Taft and other isolationist Republicans were also outspoken against the economic policies of the New Deal and continued to support the ideology of free market economics during the Great Depression. These party "stalwarts" are also associated with the "old right," and are sometimes referred to as "paleo-conservatives," in reference to the Paleolithic era of human prehistory. The rationale for these somewhat derisive characterizations is two-fold. On one hand, they hint at the generally archaic and unpopular nature of these positions, particularly in light of the fact that millions of Americans—including Ronald Reagan's father, Jack—would not have survived the Depression if not for the intervention of the federal government. Opposition to the New Deal simply did not exist on a widespread level during the Depression era. Second, the influence of the old right was eclipsed by ideological developments that took place in later decades, having to do with social and cultural, rather than strictly economic issues. Thus, the *new* right refers to the more populist aspects of American conservatism that emerged after the Second World War.

The distinction between the old versus new right parallels the distinction between the "old left" and "new left." The former, of course, refers to the industrial working class, who, as envisioned by Karl Marx and Frederick Engels, were thought to constitute the revolutionary force in capitalist societies. But during the 1960s, commentators and social theorists recognized the emergence of a "new left" that was composed of groups other than traditional blue collar workers. In the United States, the term has been used to encompass student radicals of the free speech and antiwar movements, feminists, the black power movement, the gay rights movement, and the American Indian movement, among others. While the new right became a dominant force in American politics, the new left had largely dissolved by the mid-1970s.

of American capitalism and its capacity to spread affluence throughout the social order had made questions of class inequality meaningless and that political conflict would be limited to well-regulated and institutionalized struggles among interest groups over how much affluence would come their way."[24] The moderate wing of the Republican Party achieved a reasonable level of grassroots strength, and there was also a concerted effort to publish moderate newsletters and magazines (such as *Advance*) that sought to build institutional and ideological support across a wider audience. But these efforts would pale in comparison to the rising conservative Republican faction, which was successfully linking their efforts with new constituencies, including anticommunists, southern segregationists, and business interests aligned against the framework of the New Deal.

In terms of presidential politics, the Republicans were on the sidelines during the post-WWII era, with the notable exception of General Dwight D. Eisenhower. But Eisenhower's two-term presidency (1953–1960) was largely the result of his personal popularity rather than that of the party, which tended to remain largely an elitist rather than populist organization. At the conclusion of the Eisenhower presidency, Republicans faced not only the prospect of a vacuum of leadership in the absence of the war hero "Ike," they were also devoid of a clear set of ideological positions that set them apart from the Democrats. "For eight years the party had basked in the national popularity of Dwight Eisenhower, but the general's personal popularity failed to rub off on other Republican candidates . . . There was no automatic conservative vote ready to back Republican candidates. The party had no national power; it was 'recognizably a corpse.'"[25] It was in the context of this larger institutional void that conservative politicians and activists sensed their opportunity to agitate for a stronger position both within the party and on the national stage. Their efforts would be paralleled by a small group of intellectuals who began to call for new forms of populist conservatism that could potentially appeal to a wider audience, while at the same time serving as an alternative to what they derided as the unprincipled "me too" politics of the Eisenhower administration (implying that under the leadership of the moderates, the Republicans merely adopted the ideas and policies of the Democrats). During the second half of the 1950s, several related developments would begin to lay the political and ideological groundwork for the emergence of the American conservative movement, while undermining the claims of those who declared an end to substantive ideological difference between the parties. Indeed, conservative authors and activists began to formulate the ways in which their ideas could reach new audiences and potentially create new and transformative conservative coalitions in American politics.

The most important early effort came from the pen of William F. Buckley Jr. Buckley's father, William Sr., was a land speculator and oil magnate who made a fortune in Mexico before being expelled from the country in 1921. "To the elder Buckley, the Mexican and Bolshevik revolutions seemed one in the same. It was a lesson he imparted to his ten children . . . It was the ideal training for a young conservative: serious, confident, faintly aristocratic, and sharply critical of mere 'materialism.'"[26] Thus, Buckley grew up in an atmosphere that was well suited to the formation of a conservative intellectual. By the time he graduated from Yale in 1950, he was already an outspoken critic of the prevailing trends in American society. His first book, *God and Man at Yale*, was published in 1951 and attacked the "liberal bias" and "godlessness" that pervaded his alma mater. But it was through the pages of *National Review*, the first issue of which was published in 1955, that Buckley quickly became an icon of the nascent conservative movement. Buckley was:

> in the age of Madison Avenue, the cause's most engaging and relentless publicist, the figure who managed to weave the disparate strands of conservatism together and make them respectable again . . . [he] had found in patriotic anticommunism a new focus and new political glue that could bind its disparate parts together.[27]

Although *National Review* had only a modest initial circulation, it would come to act as a lightning rod for the conservative cause in its effort to bridge the anticommunist, libertarian, and traditionalist factions of the movement. As will be seen, Buckley (in the pages of *National Review*) took many controversial positions through the years, none more so than his early stance against the civil rights movement, which was the first major national issue that clearly differentiated the "new right" from earlier forms of Republican conservatism, and which would propel the party in an unprecedented direction. But Buckley was merely an intellectual, not a politician. And although his writing would inspire many conservatives around the country, he was not directly involved in the daily affairs of the Republican Party. Like all social movements, intellectuals require activists who are willing to engage in the day-to-day tasks of putting ideas into action. It was here that the activities of several organizations, as well as movement intellectuals, began to coalesce around a rising figure inside the Republican establishment, the Senator from Arizona, Barry Goldwater.

Goldwater was a lifelong Republican, and he represents an important stream of conservatism that flowed from the American West. Like California, Arizona would be transformed by the massive flows of migrants

> ### It's a Family Affair
>
> With the exception of Ronald Reagan, William F. Buckley Jr. (1925–2008) is arguably the singular embodiment of postwar conservatism in the United States. A devoted Catholic, Buckley worked as a CIA operative in Mexico City in the early 1950s and later became a nationally syndicated columnist who published dozens of books and served as host of the television program *Firing Line* for more than 30 years. His magazine, *National Review*, inspired a new generation of conservative activism on college campuses, including new student publications that paid it homage as a namesake. During his presidency, Ronald Reagan once quipped that *"National Review* is to the West Wing of the [Reagan] White House, what *People* magazine is to your dentist's office."
>
> Buckley and several of the leading figures of the early conservative movement were related not only through the overlap of their ideologies, but through personal and familial relations. Barry Goldwater had been an ardent supporter of Joseph McCarthy—as was Buckley—even through the dark days of the senator's congressional censure in 1954. Goldwater hired one of McCarthy's former speechwriters, Brent Bozell Jr., who was a friend and classmate of Buckley's at Yale, to work on his staff. Bozell was the co-author, with Buckley, of the 1954 book *McCarthy and His Enemies*, and the ghostwriter for Goldwater's 1960 breakthrough book, *The Conscience of a Conservative*. Bozell married Buckley's sister, Patricia, and he later became a militant anti-abortion activist. In June of 1970 Bozell was arrested after breaking into the Student Health Services building at George Washington University, having attempted to beat an intervening police officer with a giant wooden cross. Bozell had ten children, including Brent Bozell III, who would also become a significant conservative voice as founder in 1995 of the Parents Television Council, whose self-described mission is to "restore responsibility and decency to the entertainment industry."

coming from the Midwest (many of whom had backgrounds as Taft-style Midwestern Republicans), who gravitated toward jobs related to the "Pacific Theatre" of American involvement in the Second World War. In 1909, Phoenix had a population of only 30,000, but by 1963, the population had skyrocketed to more than 800,000. "Phoenix developed on the basis of military installations, electronics, climate, water and power projects constructed by the federal government, and a fantastic in-migration. By 1960, two-thirds of its citizens had come from elsewhere."[28] The Midwestern transplants, the hyper-patriotism that resulted from the concentration of defense industries, and the *laissez-faire* economic outlook that was a product of the perception of life on the western frontier, all contributed to the growth of conservatism during the 1950s and 60s in the American West.

Goldwater was born into a political family in Phoenix in 1909, three years before Arizona became a state. He grew up as manager of the family department store and he maintained a strong anti-labor philosophy throughout the course of his life. Although he had been a member of the United States Senate for seven years by the time of its publication, it was his 1960 book, *The Conscience of a Conservative*, that established his leading role in the conservative movement. The book, which is striking for its tone as well as its substance, deals with foreign and domestic policies concerning taxes, agricultural subsidies, labor unions, and, of course, the "Soviet menace."

A mere 117 pages in length, *Conscience* effectively disabused those who were convinced of the supposedly bipartisan, consensus nature of American politics. The book set its sights on what conservatives would refer to in later decades as "big government"—which, for Goldwater, bore an alarming similarity to Soviet-style totalitarianism. Throughout the text, Goldwater juxtaposes powerful Washington bureaucrats with the threat of a Soviet takeover:

> Our tendency to concentrate power in the hands of a few men concerns me. We can be conquered by bombs or by subversion; but we can also be conquered by neglect—by ignoring the Constitution and disregarding the principles of limited government. Our defenses against the accumulation of unlimited power in Washington are in poorer shape, I fear, than our defenses against the aggressive designs of Moscow.[29]

Goldwater remained both a hard-line anticommunist as well as a vehement critic of federal power, and the larger significance of *Conscience* lies in the fact that it began to direct conservative ire "away from the McCarthyite witch-hunts and toward a political rhetoric that sought to exploit fissures in the postwar liberal consensus."[30]

Immediately after the publication of the book, Goldwater was hailed as the figure who would lead the emerging conservative movement into power. Activists inside the Republican Party in Arizona and in California began an effort to "draft Goldwater" to run for president. These conservative activists, under the banner of the Young Americans for Freedom (YAF), were attempting to break the dominance that the northeastern modern Republicans exercised over the party. Not only did they want to nominate one of their own to run for president, they hoped to bring about the creation of a new political coalition based upon a reconstitution of the Republican and Democratic parties. "If the moderates could be thwarted and a true conservative like Goldwater could gain the Republican presidential nomination, the parties at last would divide along ideological lines, and a newly energized conservative majority would sweep the Republicans to victory."[31]

As will be seen, Goldwater was thrust into a battle for the 1964 Republican presidential nomination in a showdown against his bitter political rival and the symbol of modern Republicanism, New York Governor Nelson Rockefeller. But the struggle between these two regionalized Republican factions, which would come to a head at the 1964 Republican National Convention in San Francisco, was only the tip of the iceberg of a much larger social and ideological conflict fomenting in American society. And if conservatives were indeed determined to construct a new national coalition, they would have to come to terms with the political implications surrounding the civil rights movement in the southern states.

CHAPTER 2

The South, Civil Rights, and the Transformation of the Republican Party

> I believe in states' rights ... I believe that we've distorted the balance of our government today by giving powers that were never intended in the constitution to the federal establishment. And if I get the job I'm looking for, I'm going to devote myself to trying to reorder those priorities and to restore to the states and local communities those functions which properly belong there.[1]

This affirmation of the principle of "states' rights" elicited resounding cheers from the audience that had gathered to hear Ronald Reagan give his first campaign speech after he officially received the Republican nomination in 1980. But as news of his remarks spread through the national media, these seemingly mundane words contributed to a controversy that continues to haunt the legacy of the Reagan presidency, as well as the Republican Party and the American conservative movement more generally. In order to understand this controversy, it is necessary to appreciate the historical role of American regions in shaping the Republican and Democratic parties, their constituencies and ideologies, and the key issues that have, in turn, shaped the country's political geography.

Ronald Reagan, the hometown hero of Dixon, Illinois, outgrew the confines of Midwestern sports journalism and set out for Hollywood, eventually entering into California politics. But he did not launch his triumphant 1980 presidential campaign in either California or Illinois—the two states most directly related to his own biography. Instead, at the behest of his campaign advisors, including the South Carolinian Lee Atwater and a young Republican congressman from Mississippi named Trent Lott, Reagan kicked off his official campaign in what appeared to be the most unlikely of locations. On August 3, 1980, Reagan traveled to the heart of the Deep South, where he spoke at the Neshoba County

Fair in Mississippi, within walking distance of the site of the heinous murders of the civil rights activists James Chaney, Andrew Goodman, and Michael Schwerner, which had occurred 16 years earlier in 1964—a year that remains enormously symbolic in American political and racial history. Not only was the summer of 1964 the climactic moment of the civil rights movement, it was also the year in which the Republican Party realigned itself on the side of southern whites who opposed the civil rights movement. As will be seen, it was no coincidence that these two historical developments overlapped.

In his "States' Rights Speech," Reagan drew upon the familiar pro-business and anti-tax themes he had delivered countless times across the country on behalf of General Electric and which he echoed during his "A Time for Choosing" speech in support of Barry Goldwater, the "extremist" Republican presidential candidate of 1964 whose opposition to the Civil Rights Act made him the improbable darling of large segments of the white South. Reagan also drew upon a distinctly southern rhetoric that was deeply intertwined with the region's notorious history of racism. In so doing, Reagan ensured that racial politics would remain central to the conservative discourse of the Republican Party. Furthermore, Reagan symbolically confirmed that the party had, in a stunning culmination of its longer rupture with its regional and ideological history, cemented its new affiliation with the conservative white South.

> The philosophy of states' rights is most often associated with the South, although it is not exclusive to it. The American West has also been home to many conservative anti-federal appeals to the rights of states, such as during the "sagebrush rebellion" of the 1970s, which called for the return of federally owned and protected lands to the individual states for the purpose of privatized economic development. In a move that paralleled his visit to Neshoba, during his presidential campaign Reagan also traveled to Salt Lake City, Utah, where he proclaimed, "I happen to be one who cheers and supports the sagebrush rebellion. Count me in as a rebel!"

From elected public officials to journalists to media celebrities, today's conservative leaders are not only outspoken in their defense of Reagan's speech in Mississippi, but are also quick to point out that it was the Democratic, not the Republican Party that was the political force of southern segregationism. For example, Ann Coulter has attempted to link southern segregationists, who were historically loyal to the Democratic Party, to the Democratic Party of the Obama era, writing that, "It was the Democratic Party that ginned up the racist mob against blacks and it is the Democratic Party ginning every new mob today."[2] Other conservatives have followed suit, emphasizing that the Republican Party was the party of Abraham Lincoln and that it can therefore boast of irrefutable historic connections to abolitionism and in supporting the civil rights of black Americans. According to the former U.S. Representative from Kansas, the conservative Republican Todd Tiahrt, "History tells us [the Republican Party] is the party of Lincoln . . . It was the party that fought for the thirteenth, fourteenth and fifteenth amendments to our Constitution . . . You have to wonder why more African Americans aren't Republicans."[3] In a 2011 broadcast entitled "How Reagan Attracted Independents," the conservative radio host Rush Limbaugh defended the Republican Party against claims that it was culpable in its opposition to the civil rights movement.

> It's like somehow the Republicans stood in the way of the Civil Rights Act [of 1964]. No, no, no, no. It was the Democrats that stood in the way of the Civil Rights Act . . . A greater percentage of Republicans in the Senate voted for the Civil Rights Act than Democrats.[4]

Coulter, Tiahrt, and Limbaugh are factually correct: southern segregationists were Democrats; Lincoln was a Republican; the Republican Party was against slavery and worked to produce the Reconstruction Amendments of the post-Civil War era; the Civil Rights Act of 1964 had more Republican than Democratic support in Congress. But these factual statements obscure larger historical truths about the parties and their relationship to black civil rights in the South. First, Barry Goldwater, the Republican presidential candidate of 1964 whose nomination was the first significant (albeit short-lived) political victory for the American conservative movement, broke from the congressional and gubernatorial moderate Republican tradition and made his fierce opposition to the Civil Rights Act of 1964 the defining issue of his failed campaign. Thus, as Geoffrey Kabaservice has written, "the credit—even the glory—that the Republican Party should have enjoyed for its support for the Civil Rights Act of 1964 was effectively negated when its presumptive presidential nominee voted against the measure."[5] Second, 1964 was a watershed year in the historic transformation of the Republican Party, and the way in which it was changing had everything to do with the issue of race and southern civil rights. Simply put: in a political transformation that was central to the larger changes taking place in American society during the post-WWII era, conservative white southerners abandoned the Democratic Party *en masse* and became Republicans. This was not a change that occurred overnight. It was an uneven process for presidential and congressional politics, and in the ways in which white southerners would come to identify themselves with the Republican Party. But over time, from Goldwater's 1964 candidacy to Reagan's 1980 triumph, the transformation was completed. And not only did the white South "vote with its feet" by leaving the Democratic Party, which had become through several historical coincidences inextricably linked to the pursuit of black civil rights, but Republican politicians and their strategists actively pursued the support of southern segregationists in what would become known as the party's "southern strategy."

The significance of this changing geographical and ideological orientation of the Republican Party can only be seen by taking a step back and examining the shifting landscape of American politics through a larger historical perspective. In order to understand the controversy that still surrounds Reagan's campaign speech in Mississippi, and the connections between American conservatism and southern racism, it is necessary to examine how the Republican Party has changed its relationship to the southern states over a longer period of time. Such a larger historical perspective can not only answer Congressman Tiahrt's question about "why more blacks aren't Republicans," it can also illustrate part of the larger significance of Reagan's 1980 election and how it represented the culmination of longer-term changes that had taken place in American society. The origins of this story are rooted in the sectional conflict that culminated in the American Civil War.

SOUTHERN EXCEPTIONALISM AND THE RISE OF THE SOLID SOUTH

One of the most important historical features of the Republican Party is that from its inception in the mid-nineteenth century and during much of its subsequent existence, it was essentially a regionalized rather than national organization. Although both the Republican and Democratic parties would eventually develop bases of support throughout the country, the Republican Party—until only very recently in its long history—was an organization that simply did not have a presence in the American South. This aspect of its history stems from the fundamental differences that developed between the northern and southern regions of the country during the antebellum (1820–1860) era: while the economy of the northern states was increasingly based on free labor, urbanization, and manufacturing, antebellum southern society was itself increasingly based on the production of cotton for export, and the foundation of this social and economic system was, of course, racially based slavery. This basic regional difference shaped the competing ideologies of northern and southern politicians, their corresponding political parties, and the citizens who supported them.

During the decades preceding the Civil War, as new territories were being incorporated into the United States, the expansion of slavery was inherently tied to the fates of the broader interests of the ruling political and economic classes of the two general regions of the country. The elites of the North and South stood in sharp contrast over various aspects of national policy—most of which were direct corollaries of the slavery issue—and both groups wanted to ensure that their own agendas would prevail. For example, one of the most important disagreements was the issue of the tariff. Because northern politicians represented the general interests of the industrial capitalist class, they supported the protective tariff on European manufactured goods in order to maintain their own monopoly in the American market. On the other hand, politicians and agrarian interests from the South took the opposite position and favored anti-tariff policies that would open the southern market to cheaper imported goods. Southerners also feared a retaliatory English tariff that would potentially hurt their own cotton exports.

The South also faced direct threats to the institution to slavery, and thus to the basis of its regionalized social system. The abolitionist movement was gaining momentum in the northern states as growing numbers of American citizens, black and white, petitioned to abolish the "peculiar institution." Abolitionism reached its peak during the 1830s and 1840s as figures such as William Lloyd Garrison and Frederick Douglass roused audiences in their calls for an immediate end to slavery. David Walker, a black printer living in Boston, also frightened the southern "slaveocracy" when he published his *Appeal to the Colored Citizens of the World* in 1829, which advocated a large-scale violent slave rebellion. John Brown played perhaps the greatest role of all abolitionists in striking fear in the southern slave owners. In 1855 he traveled to Kansas and began, with other "Jayhawkers," an armed campaign against settlers who had brought slaves into the western territories. Four years later, in 1859, he and his followers attempted to raid the federal armory at Harper's Ferry, Virginia, where they hoped to seize and distribute weapons to slaves who would then begin a great revolt. Other challenges to slavery came from the slaves themselves, as Denmark Vesey and Nat Turner illustrated during their respective 1821 and 1831 rebellions.

It was in this historical context of rising sectional conflict and growing southern anxieties over the survival of slavery that southern politicians began to craft a unique political ideology that was overtly hostile to the federal government and toward the notion of "outside interference" with the "southern way of life." These politicians began to advocate the principle of states' rights as a way to resist northern or federal attempts to meddle with the institution of slavery. In 1828, John C. Calhoun, a wealthy politician and slave owner from South Carolina, published "The South Carolina Exposition and Protest," an anti-tariff pamphlet that outlined the ideas of states' rights and nullification—ideas that would remain central to southern politics for more than 150 years and which would later be incorporated into conservative ideology on a national scale. While the various branches of the federal government might claim to act as agents of the general welfare, he argued the source of actual sovereignty can only exist in the states themselves. By extension, when citizens of a particular state became unhappy with a federal law, Calhoun argued, states could individually "nullify" it by opting out of the social contract into which they entered as sovereign entities. Calhoun's arguments went beyond existing ideas about state autonomy as described by Thomas Jefferson and James Madison, because this southern principle of "nullification" was developed in a specific effort to protect slavery as an institution and to promote slaveholding interests in shaping national policies.

The deep sectional and ideological conflict that marked this period of American history was an important factor that shaped the rise of the modern two-party system. The Whig Party, a remnant of what historians refer to as the "first party system" in the United States, split over disagreements concerning the expansion of slavery into the new territories and soon dissolved from the American political landscape. The Democratic Party was created in this context as a national political organization that would downplay the issue of slavery and could thus be supported by both northern and southern citizens. In contrast to the early Democrats, the northern antislavery factions formed the Republican Party, founded just prior to the Civil War in Ripon, Wisconsin. "In the new [Republican] party, belief in the superiority of the 'free labor' system of the North and the incomparability of 'free society' and 'slave society' coalesced into a comprehensive world view or ideology."[6] Thus, from the moment of its inception, the Republican Party was inherently "un-southern": it was perceived (quite correctly) by southern politicians and citizens to stand in opposition to the "southern way of life" and to slavery, the most fundamental of all southern institutions.

When Abraham Lincoln was elected as the first Republican president in 1860, neither his name nor his party appeared on the ballots in the southern states. Historians have since shown that Lincoln was not an abolitionist and that he had no desire upon his election to free the slaves. Nevertheless, southern leaders were so repulsed by Lincoln and the Republicans that they withdrew from the United States and formed the Confederate States of America, complete with its own president, capital, currency, and flag. With the defeat of the Confederacy and emancipation of the slaves during the Civil War, the newly strengthened federal government, under the auspices of the Republican Party, embarked upon a program to rebuild the South—politically, institutionally, socially, and physically—which had been decimated by war. The subsequent period of Reconstruction would further galvanize southern white resentment toward and alienation from the Republicans.

The South faced essentially two competing paths as it attempted to resolve the complex questions related to the end of the Civil War and the rebuilding of its social system in the aftermath of the emancipation of the slaves. In one direction was an interracial democracy that would move beyond the legacies of slavery; in the other direction stood a "Herrenvolk" system of racialized caste relations. For a brief historical moment following the end of the war, the federal government pursued policies of racial progress in the South and the region was prodded down the first path. Through the Republican Party and the Freedmen's Bureau—at the time the largest and most ambitious government agency ever created—federal authorities built schools, homes, and infrastructure projects while overseeing the social and political advancement of black southerners. The spirit of racial progress was most strikingly illustrated by the election of former slaves, now Republican politicians, into various state and federal offices, including as members of the United States Congress—a political development that would be unthinkable in later decades.

The period of Reconstruction created a widespread backlash among white southerners directed at the newly empowered black population and at the Republican federal government, which was perceived as an "occupying power" interfering with southern affairs. Historians sympathetic to this point of view, such as William Dunning and Claude Bowers, referred to Reconstruction as the "tragic era" that was defined by widespread political corruption and incompetence of both "scalawags" (pro-Reconstruction white southerners) and "carpetbaggers" (northerners who came to the South after the war to exploit the region's devastation for their own political and economic interests).[7] It is perhaps not surprising that Reconstruction came crashing down in 1877 under a political compromise in which the white Democratic South agreed to back the Republican presidency of Rutherford B. Hayes in exchange for the withdrawal of the remaining federal troops in the region. The subsequent "redemption" that restored southern "home rule" had disastrous consequences for black southerners who would, in the famous phrase of W.E.B. Du Bois, be pushed "back toward slavery."[8]

The southern civil rights gains associated with Reconstruction were immediately erased. Mississippi led the way in this creative destruction by devising numerous loopholes and legal absurdities that collectively disenfranchised its black citizens (and some poor whites as well) through such mechanisms as the poll tax, the literacy test, the "understanding clause," the "good character clause," and—most infamously—the "grandfather clause," which exempted white voters from disenfranchisement. By the end of the century, southern blacks were, by and large, left without social, political, or legal rights, at the mercy of the ruthless white power structure in the region, which was backed by constant threat of the lynch mob, a distinctly southern form of organized terror that emerged during the era, and which would remain part of the southern caste system in ensuing decades.

The United States Supreme Court also played an important role in this racial "counter-revolution." The Court first upheld the "separate but equal" doctrine in *Plessy v. Ferguson* (1896) and, two years later, various disenfranchisement schemes in *Williams v. Mississippi* (1898). In his groundbreaking work, *The Strange Career of Jim Crow*, C. Vann Woodward argues that the entire country, not just the South, was complicit in this large-scale "capitulation to racism." He cites numerous factors that were operating at regional and national levels, "from the federal courts in numerous opinions, from Northern liberals eager to conciliate the South, from Southern conservatives who had abandoned their rare policy of moderation in their struggle against the Populists, from the Populists in their mood of disillusionment with their former Negro allies, and from a national temper suddenly expressed by imperialistic adventures and aggressions against colored peoples in distant lands" during the Spanish–American War.[9] The subsequent era of Jim Crow had arrived in the South and came to be defined by what the sociologist Aldon D. Morris refers to as the tripartite system of racial domination that was predicated upon personal, economic, and social levels of oppression.[10]

In terms of the two political parties, the situation that accompanied this rise of segregation and black disenfranchisement was a renewed Democratic dominance throughout all levels of southern politics. From the end of Reconstruction through much of the twentieth century, Republicans were *personae non gratae* in the region, and southern politics functioned under the umbrella of the Democratic Party at local, state, and national levels. Eric Foner's observation that "the Civil War generation of white Southerners was always likely to view the Republican Party as an alien embodiment of wartime defeat and black equality" could easily be extended to the children and grandchildren of the Confederacy as well.[11] As was the case during the antebellum years, southern Republican candidates often simply did not exist, and during presidential elections they were seldom seen on southern ballots. "By the dawn of the twentieth century, the Democratic Party was, to all intents and purposes, the South's sole functioning political party."[12] The party so thoroughly dominated regional politics that commentators began to refer to a "solid South" that was indivisibly loyal to the party. The term "yellow dog Democrat" also came into popular usage around this time to refer to white southerners who, so the expression went, were willing to vote a yellow dog into office—so long as the dog was a Democrat.

> From 1902 through 1950 all southern senators and almost all southern representatives were Democrats. Most Republicans who ran for federal office quickly learned, through unpleasant and humiliating experiences, that taking on a southern Democrat meant encountering a "massive inexorable force or object that crushes whatever is in its path."[13]

The identification of the white South with Democratic presidential candidates during the first half of the twentieth century is illustrated by the curious case of Al Smith, the Democratic governor of New York who ran for president in 1928. Smith was a widely unpopular candidate in light of his connections to the Tammany Hall political machinery of New York City, and especially because of his Catholicism, as many Protestant Americans held strong anti-Catholic prejudices—particularly in the South. In a phenomenon that would be repeated in 1948 and 1964 (although under different partisan configurations), Smith carried much of the South but was defeated in a national landslide, including in his home state of New York. He won only in Arkansas, Louisiana, Mississippi, Alabama, Georgia, and South Carolina—a state he carried with more than 90 percent of the popular vote. Despite southern anti-Catholicism and a feeling of general disdain for northern politicians—especially those from New York—Smith was able to achieve regional victory because of the southern perception that Herbert Hoover, his Republican opponent, was opposed to racial segregation. In short, the South's commitment to Jim Crow and its loyalty to the Democratic Party trumped not only its anti-Catholicism but also its anti-northern tendencies and more general questions about the overall viability of Smith's candidacy. Thus, for many decades, the South—especially the Deep South states of Louisiana, Mississippi, Alabama, Georgia, and South Carolina—was solidly Democratic and tended to vote as a unified bloc.

But as with all historical generalizations, the idea of a "solid South" is somewhat misleading because the region was never quite as socially or politically homogeneous as it appeared. V.O. Key, author of the classic *Southern Politics in State and Nation*, observed that

> The South, unlike most of the rest of the democratic world, really has no political parties ... A single party, the saying goes, dominates the South, but in reality the South has been Democratic only for external purposes, that is, presidential and congressional elections. The one-party system is purely an arrangement for national affairs."[14]

In other words, throughout the twentieth century the South was rife with political factionalism, class divisions, and competing ideas among various interest groups. Additionally, as history would show, even in the most solidly Democratic areas, southern whites were willing to break from the national party when it was perceived to be moving beyond the scope of their influence.

THE SOUTH AND THE NEW DEAL COALITION

Southern loyalty was only one aspect of the larger set of political and economic circumstances that would make the Democratic Party dominant at the national level during much of the twentieth century. When the New York Stock Exchange collapsed in October of 1929, it triggered a worldwide economic crisis that persisted throughout the following decade and created the social conditions that contributed to the rise of European fascism and the Second World War. In the United States, as in Europe, the Great Depression directly led to the restructuring of economic institutions and to the reorganization of the ideology and relative strength of the major political parties. In subsequent decades, the Democratic Party achieved a leading role in national politics largely as a reflection of the power of the "New Deal coalition," a contradictory set of economic, regional, and racial forces that supported the specific policies as well as the more general philosophy of government espoused by President Franklin D. Roosevelt. In addition to the "Solid South," where Democratic support had more to do with the legacies of the Civil War and white supremacy than with the immediate effects of the economic depression of the 1930s, northern blue-collar support for the Democratic Party was directly related to these post-1929 social and economic reforms.

Prior to the rise of the New Deal coalition, the Republicans had been enjoying their own period of dominance at the presidential level. But at the outset of the Depression, the Republican Herbert Hoover quickly became something of a public villain in light of his failure to provide economic relief for the growing numbers of desperate Americans: the unemployment rate had risen from 9 percent in 1930 to 23 percent by 1932. In some of the nation's industrial centers, it would reach more than 50 percent. Workers and citizens erected hundreds of "Hooverville" shantytowns and occupation settlements across the country, including in New York City's Central Park. Thus, the Republican Party increasingly perceived as being out of touch with the problems and concerns of ordinary Americans. The primary reason for this has to do with one of the central aspects of classical Republican economic ideology: free market, *laissez-faire* capitalism, known in a European context as "classical liberalism."

> **New Deal Coalition**
>
> The New Deal coalition refers to the diverse national amalgamation of voters who supported not only the specific social reforms of Franklin D. Roosevelt's New Deal during the Great Depression, but the Democratic Party. The coalition was composed of large segments of the northern working classes and southern whites. By today's standards, this unusually diverse group of voters underscores an important feature of the larger history of the two major political parties: for much of their existence, both the Republicans and Democrats were coalition-based rather than ideologically coherent entities. Today it is commonplace to characterize Republicans as "conservative" and Democrats as "liberal," but prior to the transformation of the two parties that occurred during the 1960s and 70s, this was not the case. Instead, both parties attracted a cross-section of what we would today call both "liberals" and "conservatives". Ideological debates tended to take place *within*, rather than *between* the parties.
>
> For example, the New Deal coalition contained northern union members whose economic interests favored state spending, government regulation, and other "liberal" policies, as well as southern segregationists who were undoubtedly "conservative" on social issues and who remained generally opposed to a strong federal government, particularly the "judicial activism" of the Supreme Court during the civil rights era. The New Deal coalition broke apart for complex reasons that historians continue to debate. In the South, white voters began to abandon their loyalty to the Democrats as the party became increasingly aligned with the civil rights movement and racial equality during the 1950s and 60s. Outside of the South, large segments of the industrial working classes also gradually abandoned their traditional Democratic loyalty over divisive social and cultural issues, including those of race and racism. This process of realignment culminated in the rise of the "Reagan Democrats" in the 1980 and 1984 presidential elections.

According to Michael W. Miles, "This doctrine was built on the foundations of English political economy which maintained that not only maximum efficiency and full production but the common good was served by the rational pursuit of self-interest in a competitive environment of free markets."[15] The basic premise of this ideology, championed by Herbert Hoover and a historic cornerstone of the Republican Party, was to minimize governmental involvement in the economy, including in a regulatory role. And it was this ideology that had been discredited by the collapse of the American economy in 1929, and the subsequent insolvency of countless banks—which had been operating without any significant oversight or consumer protections.

As a consequence of the party's relation to the economic crisis, in the 1930 congressional elections Republican leaders were voted out of office in large numbers. They lost 52 seats in the House of Representatives and eight more in the Senate. In subsequent years, Democratic control of Congress became particularly strong. This was especially true in the House of Representatives: with only two, two-year exceptions in 1947 and 1953, Democrats controlled the lower house without interruption during the 64-year period from 1930 to 1994. The Democratic Party would also come to dominate the presidency. In 1932, Hoover was crushed by Franklin D. Roosevelt and over the course of the next 36 years only a single Republican, General Dwight D. Eisenhower, would hold the office of the presidency.

During the 1930s, Roosevelt created a series of far-reaching social programs and new federal agencies that would attempt to rebuild the national economy and restore employment. The Federal Housing Authority (FHA) and the Social Security system were products of this era, as were a number of new banking regulations and protections such as the Federal Deposit Insurance Corporation (FDIC), which was created as a provision of the Glass-Steagall Act of 1933, and the Securities and Exchange Commission (SEC). These new agencies and regulations were part of a coordinated effort to make the economy less prone to the "boom and bust" cycles that had defined preceding eras. In sharp contrast to the *laissez-faire* doctrine of self-regulating capitalism, New Deal reforms gave the federal government a leading role in the economy, both in terms of oversight and through the creation of massive government-backed public projects that, in turn, created a base of employment that the private sector had failed to provide. New federal agencies such as the Tennessee Valley Authority (TVA), which "electrified the countryside," and the Works Progress Administration (WPA), "frankly and fully entered the business of hiring the American people to end the Great Depression."[16]

In short, under the presidency of FDR, the nation began to practice what the economist John Maynard Keynes was preaching (although Keynes personally thought New Deal reforms did not go far enough): increased economic regulation and deficit spending by the federal government could be used to create employment and bring stability to the economy. These policies made both FDR and the New Deal widely popular among American citizens, and although there remained a small constituency of Taft Republicans who opposed New Deal reforms, the assumption that the economy required a high degree of federal oversight and regulation was generally accepted by politicians of both parties. The diverse cross-section of American society that came to support the Democratic Party and its policies during this period were all part of the New Deal coalition: "union members, Roman Catholics, Jews, blacks, the poor, urban dwellers, and [white] southerners. The main issues that held the coalition together were a feeling that government had a responsibility for dealing with unemployment and that government could legitimately intervene in the economy."[17]

These premises of the New Deal remained dominant from their emergence in the 1930s, through the 1970s. Dwight Eisenhower, the lone Republican president of the era, also accepted the framework of state-led economic development, "having presided over the single greatest moment of state building in American history."[18] Most significantly, Eisenhower endorsed the National Highway Act of 1956, which created the interstate highway system, arguably the most ambitious and successful infrastructure project in American history. Kim Phillips-Fein has argued that "The Eisenhower administration did not simply tolerate the New Deal. It actively embraced the idea that government could play a positive role in society by transcending the narrow self-interest of economic classes and mediating conflicts between social groups."[19] But although the logic of the New Deal prevailed, there were several signals that suggested that as a political entity, the New Deal coalition was more fragile than it appeared.

As early as the 1940s, white support for the Democratic Party in the South began to wane in the face of new demands for black civil rights. During the immediate postwar years, there was widespread belief among southern Democrats that not only were they losing control over the national party, but that the traditional "southern way of life"—no longer defined by slavery but by Jim Crow—was coming under attack by the federal government. These fears were not without a sound basis. Indeed, the Supreme Court made several key interventions that began to undermine the legal and moral basis for Jim Crow, beginning with the ruling in *Smith v. Allwright* (1944), which declared unconstitutional the systematic exclusion of black southerners from southern primary elections. Prior to the ruling and in light of the region's one-party system, state primary elections often functioned in practice as elections themselves. And although southern blacks faced immediate threats of violence and even the lynch mob if they attempted to put the ruling into practice, the decision was a key victory for the National Association for the Advancement of Colored People (NAACP) during the early civil rights era. In 1946, President Truman began another series of efforts to address racial issues in the United States, with a focus on the South. The president ordered the formation of the Committee on Civil Rights, which was to draft a report on the state of racial issues. One year later, in October of 1947, the committee issued an outline of southern racial problems, from segregation to disenfranchisement to lynching. It also addressed the segregated United States Army and hiring discrimination within the federal government. The report, *To Secure These Rights*, argued that "The National Government of the United States must take the lead in safeguarding the civil rights of all

Americans."[20] The following year, in 1948, Truman issued Presidential Order 9981 to desegregate the Armed Forces.

Truman and the federal government were not motivated entirely by egalitarianism or a desire for social justice, but also because of more practical concerns about the economy, the military, and the global image of the United States. In this light, the increasing support given by the federal government to civil rights for black southerners was inherently related to the global developments of the Cold War and to the national independence movements developing in the "third world," those colonies of Europe that were slowly becoming nominally independent states after 1945. As the United States was vying against the Soviet Union for control over these new nation-states (which tended to be populated by people of color) the existence of *de jure* segregation, lynchings, and systematic disenfranchisement undercut the credibility of American foreign policy.[21] "In an era in which white colonialism was in retreat across the globe, the United States could simply not afford to repel the nonwhite governments of newly independent, postcolonial nations with continued examples of racism" in the South.[22] Although the Truman administration sought to maintain the balancing act between domestic and international civil rights on one hand and American geopolitical interests on the other, occasionally the balance tipped in favor of the latter, as was the case concerning American support for the National Party's apartheid government in South Africa, in what would become "the greatest political embarrassment to the United States" during the Cold War era.[23] As will be seen, Ronald Reagan too would have to face the issue of South African apartheid, and, like Truman, he would side with the National Party.

Regardless of these Cold War motivations, the southern wing of the Democratic Party was repulsed by the increasing federal support for black civil rights. During the months preceding the 1948 presidential election, southern Democrats broke away from the national party to form the States' Rights Democratic Party,

> On the occasion of Strom Thurmond's 100th birthday celebration (he was still an active senator!) on December 5, 2002, Trent Lott, the Republican Senator from Mississippi, unintentionally reminded the American public of the historical connections between the Dixiecrat movement and the conservatism of the contemporary Republican Party. He declared, "When Strom Thurmond ran for president, we voted for him. We're proud of it. And if the rest of the country had followed our lead, we wouldn't have had all these problems over the years." The apparent racial implication of "all these problems" triggered widespread criticism that forced Lott's resignation as Senate Majority Leader.

popularly known as the "Dixiecrats," and they selected as their presidential nominee Strom Thurmond, the hard-line segregationist from South Carolina who served in the United States Senate for nearly 50 years and whose racist past would haunt conservative leaders of subsequent generations. In their party platform the Dixiecrats did not mince words when it came to outlining their position on racial segregation:

> We stand for the segregation of races and the racial integrity of each race ... We oppose and condemn the action of the Democratic Convention in sponsoring a civil rights program calling for the elimination of segregation ... such a program would be utterly destructive of the social, economic and political life of the Southern people, and of other localities in which there may be differences in race, creed or national origin in appreciable numbers.[24]

Thus, the Dixiecrat movement was designed to protect the continuation of white political power in the South. As the historian Numan Bartley has argued, "The Dixiecrat vote coincided closely with the presence of large numbers of nonvoting Negroes. The Dixiecrat platform, while denouncing the President, the Supreme Court, and the national Democratic Party for all manner of real or imagined evils, clearly centered on opposition to civil rights."[25]

Although their platform spoke openly about upholding segregation, the Dixiecrats maintained that in its civil rights decisions the federal government was violating the rights of southern states by infringing upon their "traditional" ways of life. In that regard, one of the most significant contributions of the movement to the long-term shaping of a national conservative ideology was the revival of the Confederate notion of states' rights. For decades to come, particularly in the South, the phrase became the most important tactic to maintain the racial status quo and to thwart "outside interference" as the federal government gradually reversed its non-interventionist position on civil rights during the post-WWII period. Although states' rights ideology had an obvious southern Democratic heritage, it would be increasingly embraced by conservative Republicans in the context of a wide range of social, economic, and political issues. Furthermore, it would function as a coded appeal to attract white voters—both southern and non-southern—who were uneasy with civil rights and other racial issues.

Thus, the Dixiecrat revolt of 1948 offered the first clear signal that southern segregationists were a contradictory and ultimately fleeting element within the larger New Deal coalition. And as the rising tide of civil rights progressed throughout the South, and as the Democrats, who had dominated presidential politics since the Great Depression, came to be seen as inherently linked to the promotion of these goals, white southerners increasingly sought out political alternatives either in the form of third parties (as was the case with the Dixiecrats in 1948 and with the third party candidacy of George Wallace in 1968) or, as will be seen, ultimately in shifting their allegiance to an increasingly conservative Republican Party.

THE CIVIL RIGHTS MOVEMENT AND CONSERVATIVE REPUBLICANISM

The civil rights movement was multifaceted and found its strength at various levels of organization. At the top were the well-known figures such as Martin Luther King Jr., James Forman, Medgar Evers, and Bob Moses, each of whom powerfully articulated the movement's goals to a larger national and international audience. But on the ground it was the anonymous actions of the masses of black southerners that created social change through boycotts, marches, and sit-ins. These forces were coordinated through the existing institutional capacities of the southern black church, old civil rights legal institutions based in the North such as the NAACP, as well as new grassroots civil rights organizations such as the Montgomery Improvement Association, the Southern Christian Leadership Conference (SCLC), the Congress of Racial Equality (CORE), and the Student Nonviolent Coordinating Committee (SNCC), each of which had been designed, in different ways, to coordinate and to establish bonds between the "local movement centers."[26] Finally, the federal government, which played a key role in the rise of Jim Crow, slowly began to reverse its position regarding southern race relations in light of the larger historical context of the Cold War. In addition to the various pro-civil rights rulings of the Supreme Court in the landmark cases *Smith v. Allwright* (1944), *Brown v. Board of Education* (1954), and the reapportionment rulings in *Baker v. Carr* (1962) and *Reynolds v. Simms* (1964), the federal government would also contribute the Civil Rights Act of 1964 and the Voting Rights Act of 1965, the two legal capstones of the civil rights era.

For black southerners, the civil rights movement meant the coming of equal access to public education and other aspects of everyday life, such as municipal and interstate transportation, public facilities, and, perhaps most importantly, secured voting rights. But these changes had implications far beyond the lives of black southerners. Indeed, the civil rights movement reshaped the lives of all southerners, black *and* white, in ways that had been unthinkable in preceding decades. As Jason Sokol has written, white southerners experienced the changes of the civil rights era "just as deeply as, if much differently than, African-Americans."[27] Additionally, the movement would have profound implications for national politics because of its destabilizing effect on the coalitions that had historically composed the Democratic and Republican parties.

The process by which the civil rights movement transformed American politics and stimulated the formation of the American conservative movement was at once both simple and complex. At its most basic level, one of the primary consequences of the movement was the continued decoupling of southern segregationist politicians from the Democratic Party. The migration of conservative white southerners out of the Democratic and into the Republican Party took place in several phases, and can be explained by "push factors" having to do with the civil rights movement and black political activity that triggered many white southerners to leave the Democratic Party and seek out either third party candidates or, ultimately, to cast their lot with the conservative faction of the Republican Party. This transformation was also a consequence of the "pull factors" coming from Republican leaders and strategists who were attempting to establish new political and philosophical coalitions of conservatives on a national scale. In other words, the realignment of southern whites was not a "one-way street" whereby segregationists attempted to frame their own beliefs around a growing conservative ideology outside of the South. Instead, just as southern white conservatives identified with larger conservative causes, so too were non-southern politicians appealing for the hearts, minds, and—most importantly—the *votes* of the white South.

Because the Democratic Party was so historically embedded within southern political culture, when black southerners successfully gained the franchise during the 1960s, they did not form their own party or seek to join the Republicans—in light of the historical connections between Republicanism and black political interests, this may have appeared the more intuitive outcome (substantial numbers of black voters in the northern cities continued to support the Republican Party prior to the 1964 candidacy of Barry Goldwater). Instead, black southerners rejected the existing southern Democratic leadership and sought to exert their own influence within the structure of the party. This process occurred most memorably in Mississippi, as civil rights activists created an alternative delegation and sent the pro-civil rights Mississippi Freedom Democratic Party (MFDP) to the 1964 Democratic Convention in Atlantic City to challenge the legitimacy of the all-white Democratic Party "regulars." As Stokely Carmichael and Charles Hamilton recalled, the MFDP grew out of the organizing efforts of SNCC, and it came to adopt the "Democratic" name "because its objective was recognition by the national party ... as the official Democratic Party in the state."[28] In an attempt to pacify the MFDP, leaders of the national Democratic Party decided, in a compromise plan that satisfied neither the Freedom Democrats nor the regular Democrats, to allocate two seats "at large" to the civil rights activists, recognizing them not as Mississippians but as "special delegates." Despite the attempt at compromise, the state's white representatives were incensed and boycotted the remainder of the convention. The outcome:

> signaled to Mississippi [regular] Democrats that African Americans in Mississippi would be accepted into the party's ranks ... The game was up for segregationist Democrats ... Atlantic City signaled to traditional Mississippi Democrats that the Democratic Party had become the South's 'regional Negro party.' A Mississippi delegate walking out of the convention surmised, 'We didn't leave the national party. It left us.'[29]

This sentiment would be echoed by scores of white Americans in subsequent years, including Ronald Reagan, who used the line throughout his career in politics.

Thus, the civil rights movement had a direct impact on American politics and the conservative movement because it led to the fracturing of the New Deal coalition in the South by pushing segregationist southerners out of the Democratic Party. Strom Thurmond was perhaps the most well-known example of a southern segregationist who formally became a Republican in 1964, although he was only one of countless other southern politicians and citizens to make the change. This abrupt 1964 shift occurred primarily at the presidential level and does not, by itself, indicate a larger political transformation. But during the course of the ensuing years, white southerners also began to *identify* as Republicans. The political scientists Earl Black and Merle Black have referred to this as the two "great white switches" in southern politics. In an uneven process that would not become evident for several years, Goldwater's candidacy thus began something of a chain reaction that paved the way for the Reagan's success in the South and, later, for the Republican congressional "revolution" of 1994.[30]

But upon closer inspection, the civil rights movement and changing southern race relations had a deeper impact on American conservatism than in the simple terms of party identification. In addition to increasingly voting for Republican presidential candidates, many white southerners also changed the way they thought and talked about their convictions in a way that established ideological linkages with the larger conservative movement on a national scale. This ideological transformation took place as white southerners attempted to resist the social changes called for by civil rights activists. Of course, the most obvious way that the white South attempted to limit or otherwise subvert the movement was through violence. Civil rights activists ran up against harassment, threats, intimidation, beatings, and even death as they conducted freedom rides, boycotts, sit-ins, and voter registration drives. The names of 40 slain civil rights activists—including James Chaney, Andrew Goodman, and Michael Schwerner, who were killed in Philadelphia, Mississippi, where Reagan made his first stop on the 1980 campaign trail—have been etched in the Civil Rights Memorial in Montgomery, Alabama. The episodes of violence perpetrated by individual citizens and organizations like the Ku Klux Klan and White Citizens' Councils, often acting in conjunction with local and/or state-level law enforcement agencies, remain the most well-known form of white resistance to the civil rights movement. But aside from overt physical violence, white southerners also attempted to prevent civil rights progress through policies of "massive resistance" not only to the activists but against the federal government. The strategy of massive resistance reached its peak during the late-1950s, as southern governors such as Orval Faubus of Arkansas, J. Lindsay Almond of Virginia, and George Wallace of Alabama attempted to prevent the enrollment of black students in public schools and universities either through willfully defying federal court orders or simply by shutting down the public school systems altogether.

Although these methods of physical and often violent resistance to the civil rights movement were effective in delaying the movement's goals, they were not as significant to the larger development of the conservative movement as were the ideological weapons that grew out of the southern conflict. Indeed, the civil rights "backlash" was composed of important ideological dimensions that would form an important part of the platform of the contemporary conservative movement. By the early 1960s, despite George Wallace's vow to uphold "segregation now, segregation tomorrow, segregation forever," explicitly racist appeals to preserve segregation in the South were on the decline. This is not to imply that white southerners had reconciled or were somehow at peace with the civil rights movement and its goals, but that to a certain extent it had become unacceptable to use explicit racism as a basis of opposition to the movement. Instead, southern whites crafted what some historians have referred to as a more "color-blind" conservative ideology. The significance of this ideology lies in the ways in which southern conservatives created new buzzwords and coded linguistic appeals to symbolize their own opposition to racial equality without referring directly to race or by using explicitly racist or segregationist rhetoric. It is here, as white southerners revived old ideas—and invented some new ones too—that they made a direct and immediate contribution to the deepening of conservative ideology on a national scale.

George Wallace

George Wallace (1919–1998) began his political career as a racial moderate in Alabama, during a time in which moderation was not well received by southern voters. A former judge, Wallace was defeated in his bid to become governor by John Malcolm Patterson, a hard-line segregationist. Wallace recognized that the reason for his defeat was the unpopularity of his racial tolerance ("tolerance" that is, in the context of 1950s Alabama). After his loss, Wallace confided in one of his aides, "I was out-ni**ered by John Patterson; I'll never be out-ni**ered again!" True to his word, Wallace abandoned his moderation in order to win political power by appealing to the racism of Alabama voters. As he recalled in a later interview, "I began talking about ni**ers, and they stomped the floor [in approval]." Wallace made good on his 1963 promise to uphold "segregation forever" by physically blocking two black students, Vivian Jones and James Hood, from registering for classes at the University of Alabama. After the passage of the Civil Rights Act of 1964, he referred to it as "the most monstrous piece of legislation ever enacted by the United States Congress."

The larger significance of George Wallace is not limited to the South. After his "stand in the schoolhouse door," he became a nationally known figure and was inspired to run for president in the 1964 election. He made a strong showing in the primaries outside of the South, particularly in Indiana and Wisconsin, but he dropped out of the race after Barry Goldwater's candidacy signaled to his satisfaction that the Republicans had become a racially conservative party.[31] Wallace would run for the presidency again in 1968 as a candidate of the American Independent Party, winning 14 percent of the national popular vote and carrying the Deep South. Rather than campaigning on the lost cause of southern segregation, he became the "angry man's candidate" of the growing national backlash. He railed against the "bearded, pot-smokin', flower-carryin' demonstrators," and warned, "if one of them anarchists lies down in front of my automobile [in protest], it will be the last automobile he lies down in front of!"[32]

Wallace ran for president again in 1972 but was shot and paralyzed by Arthur Bremer during the campaign, thus forcing his withdrawal. Richard Nixon, Ronald Reagan, and George H.W. Bush would all attempt to win the so-called "Wallace vote" both within and outside of the South in subsequent elections. In his later years, Wallace would renounce his racism and beg the forgiveness of black civil rights leaders. He would also suspect that Richard Nixon and his notorious "dirty tricks" operatives played a role in his assassination attempt. Remarkably, Wallace was elected Governor of Alabama once more, serving from 1983 until 1987. In light of his instinctive anticipation of the growing national backlash, the historian Dan Carter describes George Wallace as "the most influential loser in twentieth-century American politics."[33]

For example, the Cold War context was a crucial factor in bolstering federal support for black civil rights in the South, but it was also a significant aspect of *opposition* to the civil rights movement. In other words, the Cold War had a contradictory effect on the civil rights movement. Whereas non-southern whites, including presidents Truman, Eisenhower, and Kennedy, tended to view black civil rights as an important step in winning the ideological battle against the Soviets, white southerners tended to see the conflict in exactly the opposite terms. For them, the civil rights movement and its leaders were characterized as participating in a communist-backed conspiracy. In addition to characterizing movement leaders as communistic, white southerners pointed to the "authoritarian" federal government that was imposing its policies on the region, much in the same way they imagined Stalin to impose his own tyrannical will upon the populations of Eastern Europe. Furthermore, white southerners were highly suspect of the egalitarian nature of the movement's goals, as well as of the ideological support that leftist and communist intellectuals gave it both within the United States and around the world.

In articulating their own opposition to racial equality in the language of the Cold War, white southerners began to formulate a key ideological development in the shaping of American conservatism, and in laying the groundwork for the ongoing controversy concerning the conservative movement's relationship to racism, particularly in the southern states. By presenting their own opposition to the civil rights movement as couched in the language of anticommunism, white southerners presented themselves not as "backward" southern racists, but as patriotic Americans who were simply acting out of a concern to preserve their own autonomy against communist (or "collectivist" or "socialist") influences:

> From a segregationist point of view, such language at least offered the white South the opportunity to recast ... a regional struggle to uphold racial segregation as a national battle against a foreign, totalitarian enemy ... it was possible to depict the region as the last bastion of true Americanism fighting against a single, un-American enemy.[34]

In this way segregationists effectively linked their own concerns with larger conservative causes on a national scale. The belief that "the civil rights movement was a communist conspiracy allowed whites to more easily justify their opposition. Since the enemy was not 'their Negroes' but a faceless red monolith, whites could picture themselves the defenders of America—and of freedom itself."[35] Thus, during the civil rights conflict, two of the three historic pillars of American conservatism—anticommunism and (racial) traditionalism—had become increasingly intertwined.

On top of these developments, conservative Republicans also began to realize the potential for a new alliance with white southern voters who had traditionally been loyal to the Democratic Party. In the 1952 and 1956 presidential elections, Dwight Eisenhower targeted the "outer South" metropolitan areas and carried Virginia, Tennessee, Texas, and Florida (he also won Louisiana in 1956), but his brand of "moderate" Republicanism was unable to make headway into the rural Deep South, where segregation and racism were paramount. Eisenhower's strong showings in the outer South came at a time when the Republican Party was a more moderate coalition that had largely made peace with the New Deal legacy. In terms of race, Eisenhower not only took further action to desegregate the American military, he also ordered federal troops to Little Rock, Arkansas, to maintain order during the crisis surrounding the desegregation of public schools in 1956—a move that triggered white southerners to speculate that the "second Reconstruction" was underway. Furthermore, not only was the conservative movement still in its infancy, but the civil rights movement, which would later apply unyielding pressure on the structure of southern politics, had also not yet reached maturity.

It was not until the late 1950s and early 1960s, as the conservative faction was gaining influence within the Republican Party and as it was becoming increasingly clear that white segregationists had a rapidly diminishing position in the Democratic Party, that conservatives began to reach out to southern segregationists for the purposes of bolstering a national conservative coalition. Leading conservatives outside of the South quickly realized they shared ideologically similar positions with the segregationists. In a 1957 article in *National Review*, entitled "Why the South Must Prevail," William Buckley addressed the question of black civil rights and its relation to his own philosophy. His conclusions celebrated the supposed cultural enlightenment of the white South:

> The central question that emerges . . . is whether the White community in the South is entitled to take such measures as are necessary to prevail, politically, socially, culturally, in areas in which it does not predominate numerically? The sobering answer is *Yes*—the white community is so entitled because, for the time being, it is the advanced race . . . it is a fact that obtrudes, one that cannot be hidden by ever-so-busy egalitarians and anthropologists.[36]

In an essay published six years later, also in *National Review*, "Crossroads for the GOP," William Rusher speculated that the nascent conservative movement could undermine the New Deal coalition and benefit politically from the inclusion of white segregationists who were increasingly marginalized in the Democratic Party. Rusher wrote that what was needed was to "galvanize the party in a vast new area, carry fresh scores and perhaps hundreds of Southern Republicans to unprecedented local victories [in order to] lay the foundation for a truly national Republican Party."[37]

Buckley and Rusher were not alone in laying the groundwork for the increasing association of national conservatism and southern racism. Barry Goldwater, the Republican presidential candidate of 1964, would also play a key role in the process. In Goldwater's 1960 breakthrough book, *Conscience of a Conservative*, the Arizona senator outlined what he thought should be the limitations of federal power. Goldwater based his views on an unchanging or static interpretation of the U.S. Constitution; this interpretation would be the basis for his controversial opposition to the 1964 Civil Rights Act. The Tenth Amendment to the Constitution reads, "powers not delegated to the United States by the Constitution, nor prohibited by it to the States, are reserved to the States respectively, or to the people." For Goldwater, the Constitution gave:

> reason for its reservation of States' Rights. Not only does it prevent the accumulation of power in a central government that is remote from the people and relatively immune from popular restrains; it also recognizes the principle that essentially local problems are best dealt with by the people most directly involved.[38]

This was a crucial point for Goldwater's position on civil rights because, in the South, the debate of federal authority versus "states' rights" was unfolding in concrete terms, in real time: on one side, black southerners who relied upon federal desegregation rulings and civil rights legislation, on the other, segregationists who relied upon "states' rights" to maintain the Jim Crow system.

While Goldwater believed that *voting* rights were valid "civil rights" and thus within the parameters of federal oversight and protection (based upon the Fifteenth Amendment), the same was not true for the sphere of education. For Goldwater, the federal government did not have constitutional authority to authorize or enforce the racial desegregation of public schools—or the racial segregation of private businesses or public parks. In reference to the *Brown* decision of 1954, he wrote:

> I am firmly convinced—not only that integrated schools are not required—but that the Constitution does not permit any

> interference whatsoever by the federal government in the field of education . . . I believe that it *is* both wise and just for negro children to attend the same schools as whites . . . I am not prepared to impose that judgment on the people of Mississippi or South Carolina . . . That is their business, not mine . . . the problem of race relations, like all social and cultural problems, is best handled by the people directly concerned.[39]

Thus, although Goldwater had a history of supporting civil rights initiatives in Arizona, his rhetoric concerning school desegregation was virtually indistinguishable from white southerners who maintained that Jim Crow arrangements were "local problems" not concerning the rest of the country—and certainly not concerning the federal government. Goldwater could not reconcile his theoretical support for civil rights with his practical adherence to a static interpretation of the Constitution.

Goldwater's position on civil rights was put to the test in June of 1964 during the run-up to the key California primary. In a move that enraged the Republican moderates, Goldwater, who had sought legal advice from William Rehnquist and Yale professor Robert Bork (Judge Rehnquist was appointed by President Nixon in 1972 to the Supreme Court and elevated to Chief Justice by President Reagan in 1986; Bork was nominated to the Supreme Court by Reagan in 1987 but failed to win confirmation), was one of only a handful of senate Republicans to join with the southern segregationist Democrats to vote against the Civil Rights Act of 1964. Speaking on the floor of the Senate just prior to his vote, Goldwater lamented that the bill would "require the creation of a federal police force of mammoth proportions" to patrol the southern states, which would then create an "informer psychology . . . neighbors spying on neighbors . . . who would harass their fellow citizens for selfish and narrow purposes. These . . . are the hallmarks of the police state and landmarks in the destruction of a free society." One of Goldwater's biographers, Rick Perlstein, has written of Goldwater's stunning hypocrisy concerning the southern racial issue that, "of the genuine police state in the nation's midst—Mississippi—[Goldwater] said nothing at all."[40] In other words, Goldwater's concern for his "fellow citizens" did not extend to black Americans who were suffering under the naked campaigns of terror perpetrated by Ku Klux Klan and Citizens' Councils in the Deep South. His rhetorical "color-blind" opposition to the bill that he characterized as an unconstitutional over-reach of federal authority did nothing to diminish the fact that his position supported the continuation of white rule and segregation in the South. Geoffrey Kabaservice argues that:

> Goldwater thereby put his stamp—and, by association, that of the Republican Party—on the side of Southern resistance to what was now the law of the land . . . only the sophistry of doctrinaire conservative ideology could produce the conclusion that the cause of freedom was best served by the maintenance of the South's apartheid regime.[41]

Less than two weeks after Goldwater's vote against the Civil Rights Act of 1964, the three civil rights workers James Chaney, Andrew Goodman, and Michael Schwerner were murdered in Philadelphia, Mississippi, as the Deep South continued to handle its civil rights problem "locally."

CONCLUSION

A large part of the answer to Congressman Todd Tiahrt's question concerning "why more African Americans aren't Republicans" can be found in the presidential politics of 1964 and the campaign of Barry Goldwater. The results, one of the worst landslide defeats for a presidential candidate in American history, seem to speak for themselves. In an outcome that appeared nearly as an exact replica of the 1928 and 1948 presidential contests—but in a perfect negative image, with the former Democrat/Dixiecrat states now supporting the Republican candidate—Goldwater won only his home state of Arizona and the Deep South states of Louisiana, Alabama, Georgia, South Carolina, and Mississippi, which he carried with nearly 90 percent of the popular vote. The conservative movement, through the candidacy of Barry Goldwater, rejected the notion of federal responsibility or authority in intervening in the racial affairs of the South. And as years passed, the Republican Party and the conservative leaders who would play an ever-increasing role in selecting the candidates, rhetoric, and platform of the party, continued to drive a wedge between the Republican Party and black Americans. As will be seen, Republicans would devise new strategies to benefit from the ongoing backlash not only in the South, but across the country, as racial conflict remained a divisive social issue—and an easy way to get votes.

In light of Goldwater's landslide defeat, the presidential election of 1964 seemed to signal that the conservative movement and its candidates had little appeal to the American people—and even to a Republican Party that was still deeply divided among its various factions. Goldwater had only narrowly defeated Nelson Rockefeller, the New York "modern" Republican, in the conflict-ridden primary elections. At the Republican National Convention in San Francisco in 1964, Rockefeller attempted to

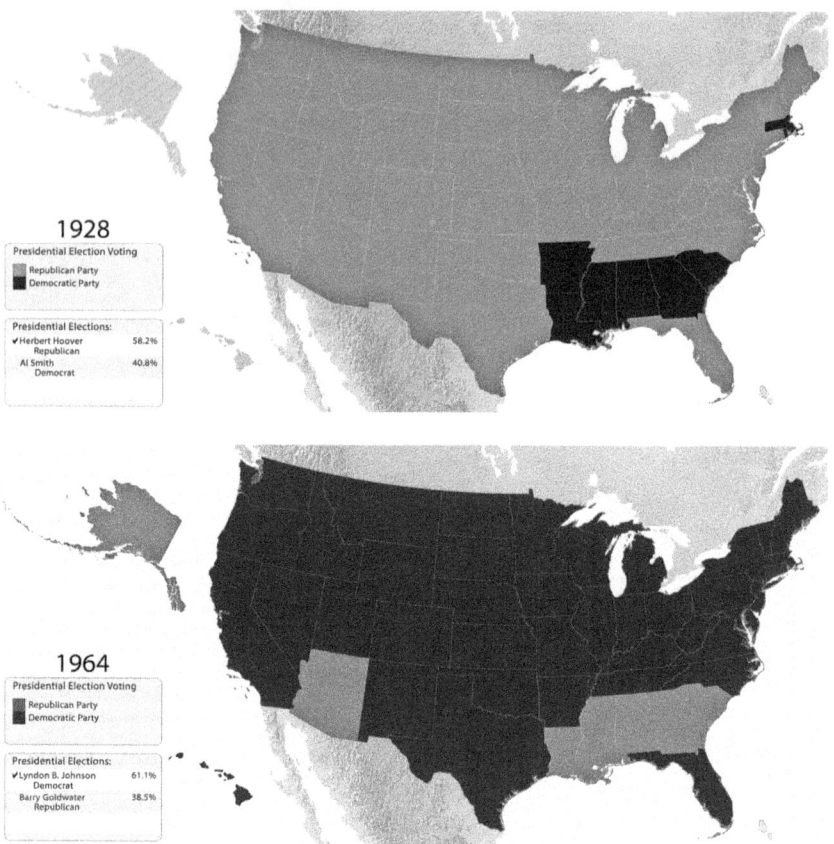

Figure 2.1 The heart of the "Solid South" was flipped inside out during the 1964 presidential election by the conservative candidacy of Barry Goldwater. The Republican "southern strategy" was a key component to the political success of the American conservative movement. Courtesy of "Voting America," Digital Scholarship Lab, University of Richmond, at http://dsl.richmond.edu/voting.

address the crowd on the dangers of the party becoming an "extremist" organization that appealed primarily to John Birch members, southern segregationists, and others on the far right wing of American politics. He was promptly and quite literally booed off the stage by the majoritarian conservative faction whose "boos, chants, jeers, hisses and catcalls made it impossible for him to be heard no matter how hard convention chair Senator Thurston Morton attempted to gavel the hall into silence."[42] The conservative faction had successfully captured control of the party, and their dismissal of Rockefeller's remarks foreshadowed the purging of other "modern" Republicans that would take place from within the party apparatus shortly thereafter. As Goldwater subsequently took the stage after Rockefeller, he brought the crowd to a state of euphoria. "I would like to remind you that extremism in the defense of liberty is no vice . . . and moderation in the pursuit of justice is no virtue!"

Even William Buckley acknowledged that the cause of American conservatism had a long way to go. Speaking two months prior to the 1964 election, Buckley delivered a lecture entitled "The Impending Defeat of Barry Goldwater" to the national convention of the Young Americans for Freedom:

> The glorious development of this year was the nomination of a man whose views have given the waiting community a choice . . . The successful fight to nominate Senator Goldwater has required the opinion makers to consider more seriously . . . the conservative alternative . . . The point is to win recruits whose attention we might never have attracted but for Barry Goldwater to win them not only for November 3 [the date of the election] but for future Novembers: to infuse the conservative spirit in enough people to entitle us to look about, on November 4, not at the ashes of defeat but at the well-planted seeds of hope, which will flower on the on a great November day in the future.[43]

Buckley's optimism would shortly prove not to have been unfounded.

Although the conservative movement was still in its infancy and could not yet forge a winning coalition on a national scale, Buckley and other movement leaders would not have to spend much time wallowing in the mire of defeat before one of their icons pulled off his own dramatic landslide victory. And it wouldn't be in the South, but in one of the supposedly most liberal states in the country. Indeed, the Goldwater catastrophe was not the end of the conservative movement, but the beginning—a shot across the bow of mainstream postwar consensus politics. And after Ronald Reagan was elected Governor of California two years later, it was clear that conservatism was a rising force in American life. After California, the events of the 1960s and 70s would push millions of Americans further to the political right, for a multiplicity of reasons, as the American conservative movement continued to gather momentum.

CHAPTER 3

The Social Backlash

Riots, Religion and Realignment

The outcome of the presidential election of 1964 was a comprehensive repudiation of Goldwater-style conservatism and a major blow to the Republican Party. By way of comparison, in his 1932 loss to Franklin Roosevelt during the crisis of the Great Depression, Herbert Hoover won more electoral votes, as well as a greater percentage of popular votes, than did Barry Goldwater in 1964. In addition to the presidential election, Republicans lost two seats in the Senate, 38 seats in the House of Representatives, and scores of state and local offices. The election results (with the glaring exception of the white South) indicated a rejection of an unpopular candidate, which Goldwater was, as well as the ideology for which he stood. In the wake of this electoral disaster, political commentators "seriously debated whether the Republicans might follow the Whigs into extinction," as "the surviving Republicans took stock of the disaster, like shivering survivors of a flood surveying the hideous transformation of a once-familiar landscape."[1] The results of the election underscored the fact that Goldwater and Reagan were ideologues: the ideas they propagated were far in advance of the actual strength of the conservative movement. In other words, in 1964, conservatism remained an ideological, rather than a populist political movement. But the social storms gathering on the horizon of American society would change everything. In two short years, Ronald Reagan would win the governorship of California by more than a million votes, and in subsequent years the nascent movement would continue to gather ideological and organizational momentum, as a growing number of Americans would find themselves taking the positions advocated by leading conservative activists and politicians.

The events that took place in the years following Goldwater's loss would necessitate a reinterpretation of the 1964 presidential election as an inauspicious start rather than a disastrous end to the conservative movement in the United States. During the period from the mid-1960s through the 1970s, conservatism would flourish. It did not come as a lightning bolt from the sky, but as a gradual and uneven social reaction to several interrelated historical factors. First and most importantly, conservatism found much fodder in the hostilities that surrounded what was arguably one of the most intense and divisive periods of domestic social conflict in the nation's history. The racial conflict in the American South became a protracted struggle on a national level, although the civil rights movement had achieved its most immediate goals by 1965 (an end to *de jure* segregation and the securing of voting rights). However, issues of racial inequality were hardly unique to the South, and new forms of intensified and explicit racial conflict would soon engulf the country, from Los Angeles to Detroit to Boston. Other social movements of the era that would provoke various conservative reactions can be understood, in part, as outgrowths of the southern black freedom struggle: demands for increased student freedom on university campuses, as well as women's liberation and gay rights, emerged as new fault lines in American society. These movements would be denounced by conservative politicians and grassroots activists for the ways they appeared to undercut traditional social relations and demonstrated the authoritarian power of the federal government. As will be seen, conservative leaders attempted to capitalize upon the widespread "backlash" against these various social pressures. New forms of politicized Christianity would also begin to play an important role in American social life, as the "religious right" would emerge during the 1970s as another related component of the rising traditionalist tide.

A second general factor that shaped the emerging conservative movement has to do with a more global context. In this sense, the role of the Vietnam War in the larger social conflicts of the 1960s and 70s cannot be overstated. The war contributed to the development of conservatism in a number of ways. Richard Nixon capitalized politically by appealing to the "silent majority"—the supposed mass of American society that outnumbered the more vocal protestors who were openly condemning the war and the more general rationale of American foreign policy. In addition to the nearly 60,000 American soldiers who lost their lives, the war would also come at a great financial cost, as it unrelentingly drained resources that might have otherwise been used to build social programs designed to combat social inequality. Thus, the war played a multifaceted role in shaping the conservative movement: it mobilized people who resented the perceived "anti-Americanism" of the antiwar protestors, and its staggering financial cost contributed to the larger cycle of protest and reaction that grew out of the deteriorating conditions in the nation's urban centers.

The increasing appeal of conservative ideology was also an outgrowth of the economic turmoil of the 1970s. These conditions will be discussed in greater detail in the following chapter, but suffice it to say that beginning in October of 1973, the Organization of Arab Petroleum Exporting Countries (OAPEC) oil embargo was the spark that led to a prolonged economic slump in the United States (and around the world), from which the American working class has arguably never recovered. Real wages (monetary earnings adjusted for inflation) in the United States declined for the first time in 1973, and would never again reach the peak they achieved in that year. Historically, economic conservatism had been an elite ideology that was disconnected from the masses of American people. But the economic turmoil of the 1970s functioned to give a more tangible rationale for the reduction of various government programs and, ultimately, for the deregulation of the economy—positions that had long since been championed by the libertarians. The deteriorating economic situation also put increasing pressure on traditional social relations such as the nuclear family, as more women began to enter the workplace, which in turn also fueled the conservative reaction. According to Thomas Borstelmann:

> The context of rising unemployment and inflation meant that white heterosexual men, the heart of the old American working class, experienced the increased public presence of women, gays, and people of color as competitors at a moment when the long-robust U.S. economy had stopped growing for the first time in a generation. This was a recipe for backlash.[2]

In sum, the related factors of domestic social conflict, the changing international context surrounding the war in Vietnam, as well as the economic "stagflation" of the 1970s, all contributed in different ways to the increasing strength of conservatism during the late 1960s and 1970s. One of the most significant outcomes of the social unrest and economic insecurity of these years was that it legitimized Goldwater/Reagan-style conservatism in the eyes of many Americans. And although there was no simple linear ascent of conservatism during this period, by the end of the 1970s, as a consequence of these general factors, the various conservative factions of traditionalism, libertarianism, and anticommunism would not only become strengthened on their own terms, they would also become increasingly interrelated.

THE EMERGENCE OF LAW AND ORDER

It is said that in the United States, the cultural winds blow from west to east. The same might be said for the development of conservative politics.

Although California conservatism has a longer postwar history and did not simply spring up overnight in 1965, in the immediate aftermath of Goldwater's defeat, several events quickly pushed the political mood of California voters to the right in a way that presaged larger changes that would soon envelop American society at large.

The "Freedom Summer" project of 1964 was in full swing in the southern states, as thousands of university students had traveled to the South to participate in civil rights protests and to give various forms of support to the movement. The students came from all around the country, including from California, whose state university system was one of the primary recruitment and training grounds for the young activists. At the campus in Berkeley, organizing efforts by CORE and SNCC for the Freedom Summer had been particularly strong. But in a stunning turn of events that caught the student activists by surprise, in the weeks prior to fall registration, university officials issued an order to ban all political activity on campus. This decision led to a series of conflicts between the university administration and state police on one hand, and students who attempted to assert their freedom of speech and assembly on the other. The "free speech movement" of 1964 and 1965 soon became one of the most visible and early examples of new left student organizing.

As the militancy of the student protests escalated, Pat Brown, the liberal governor of California and one of the primary targets of student criticism, was increasingly unable to reconcile his own political position in relation to a social group he had formerly perceived as part of his core constituency. Brown "only had a slight grasp of the issues involved in the controversy, and he could not understand why privileged elite attending the most prestigious collegiate institution in the state would launch a massive assault on the university that had given them such wonderful learning and life opportunities."[3] On the morning of December 4, 1964, after much hand-wringing on the matter, Brown spoke with the assistant prosecutor for Alameda

> Edwin Meese III would become a central and controversial figure in Ronald Reagan's political career. He played a leading role in the crackdown against student protesters throughout the 1960s, including in the conflict surrounding the creation of People's Park in Berkeley in 1969, at which time he was Chief of Staff to Governor Reagan. Meese later became a member of both Reagan's Presidential Cabinet and the National Security Council from 1981 to 1985, and would be embroiled in the Iran-contra affair. He became Attorney General of the United States in 1985 and resigned in 1988 over his role in the Wedtech scandal, a far-reaching conspiracy that involved the manipulation of Defense Department contracts.

County, Edwin Meese III, who requested permission from the governor to use police power to arrest the students who had occupied Sproul Hall, the main building of the university administration. Shortly after 3am, state police converged on the campus and arrested nearly 800 students, the largest single arrest in the history of California. The event drew the attention of political commentators across the country, including Ronald Reagan, who had been considering a campaign to run for governor following the success of "A Time for Choosing." In an ideological novelty that would become known as the philosophy of "law and order," Reagan reduced the issue of student protest to a legal question concerning whether the demonstrators had broken any laws in their occupation of the administration building. Through this tactic, Reagan was able to effectively:

> win over worried [white] Americans by condemning radical protests and "permissiveness" and by presenting himself as a defender of order and traditional American values. He attacked student radicals and promised to clean up the "mess at Berkeley" ... claiming the campus was dominated by a "minority of malcontents, beatniks, and filthy speech advocates," he bluntly warned radicals to "obey the rules or get out."[4]

Student unrest was not the only example of social conflict that was ripping American society apart during the 1960s.

California seemed an unlikely place for a colossal black uprising—particularly from the perspective of politicians and state officials, who were mostly white. During the course of the twentieth century, millions of black Americans had left the South for the cities of the North and of the West, and California was one of the primary destinations for those who embarked upon these "Great Migrations." From the point of view of Governor Brown, new generations of black Californians had much for which to be thankful. Not only was there an absence of the oppressive Jim Crow system that defined life in the southern states, but many black Californians seemed positioned to find opportunities—economic, social, and political—that had been unavailable in the South.

> Brown and his aides implemented affirmative action programs to bring more minorities into state government, promoted job training programs and a youth corps, and hailed California as a laboratory for social experiment and themselves as antipoverty trailblazers carving a progressive path for the rest of the nation ... The Urban League agreed with this assessment ... that Los Angeles was far and away the best for blacks.[5]

Thus, Brown's liberalism placed an emphasis on investment in various social services that were designed to narrow the gaps between blacks and whites, encourage upward mobility, and ultimately create a more equal society. For Brown and other liberals, events of the early 1960s appeared to indicate that he was on the right track: Jim Crow had fallen in the South, and the most explicit forms of racism had been defeated through the vanguard of civil rights activists and the begrudging support of the federal government. Of course, some conservatives were opposed to such government "interference" in matters with which it was not explicitly authorized by the U.S. Constitution, particularly in the realm of education. But in the context of the early 1960s, these arguments were not widely endorsed by the American people, as indicated by the results of the 1964 presidential election.

Unlike in the South, however, where issues of racial oppression seemed clearly defined and could be easily explained by the presence of explicit racism, liberals tended to be blind to racial oppression outside of the region. And unbeknownst to them, there were in fact many simmering grievances in black neighborhoods across the country—certainly in California, where among the many issues of concern perhaps none was more universal than the harassment, brutalization, and general mistreatment of black people at the hands of the police. The perception of social harmony and racial progress was shattered in the summer of 1965 in Watts, a predominantly black neighborhood of Los Angeles in the heart of Brown's "laboratory for social experiment." On the evening of August 11, 1965, a white policeman named Lee Minkus stopped and attempted to arrest Marquette Frye, whom he claimed he suspected of drunk driving. A crowd gathered, including Frye's mother, and within a couple of hours the standoff between black residents and the Los Angeles Police Department had escalated into an increasingly volatile situation. The next day, the city of Watts exploded. At the end of the "Watts Riots," property losses exceeded $200 million, more than 4,000 people had been arrested and 34 people had been killed.[6] Although these figures would be eclipsed a few years later by the civil insurrection in Detroit, the Watts Riots were, at the time, the largest such event in American history (with the possible exception of the New York City draft riots of 1863).

These two events, the student protests at Berkeley and the Watts Riots, set the tone for the 1966 California gubernatorial election. On one hand stood Brown and the California liberals, who were stunned by the student radicalism at Berkeley and by the unthinkable events in Watts. Brown himself was at a loss, and he struggled to make sense of what had taken place, "at various points . . . blam[ing] the riots on [Los Angeles Chief of Police] Parker's racist rhetoric, the blistering August heat, the legacy of

> The Watts Riots were only the first in a series of racial uprisings that ripped through nearly every major city in the United States between 1965 and 1968. Of the dozens of such events, the largest occurred in Newark and in Detroit, both in July of 1967 and both stemming from confrontations involving police harassment of black citizens. Many historians refer to these events as uprisings or rebellions rather than riots, as the latter term brings to mind random acts of violence instead of institutionalized social conflict. President Johnson launched an official investigation that resulted in the publication of the Report of the National Advisory Commission on Civil Disorders (commonly referred to as the Kerner Commission Report), which came to a blunt conclusion: the "racial disorders" had occurred because the United States was "moving toward two societies, one black, and one white—separate and unequal."

slavery, and poor police work in the ghettos, but mostly he argued that a slew of social ills lay at the heart of what ailed Watts."[7]

On the other hand stood Reagan and the conservatives. In contrast to Brown's equivocal explanation of the causes of the rioting, which were difficult to turn into concrete policy solutions, Reagan had a much more direct way of explaining the causes of the riots: instead of addressing the lack of jobs, bad schools, and police brutality—in short, conditions of institutionalized racism—Reagan quickly capitalized by repeating his analysis of the Berkeley protests. As with his earlier explanation of student protest, Reagan turned a blind eye to larger social issues and instead reduced the riots to a simple question of upholding the law. His position appealed to many white Californians who were increasingly resentful of what they perceived to be the failure of liberal programs designed to alleviate social and racial conflict.

Reagan was not the first politician to call for "law and order" in response to social conflict. In fact, Goldwater had attempted to invoke this strategy during his failed 1964 campaign. At the Republican National Convention in San Francisco, during the same speech in which he defended his own conservative "extremism," Goldwater warned his fellow party members in thinly veiled racist language that law and order would effectively balance the rising "license of the mob and of the jungle." A survey conducted among white ethnic voters in the New York City borough of Queens concluded that:

> the economic elements of the conservative program—"right-to-work" and voluntary social security—made an "almost universal negative impression" . . . But these could be trumped if the

Republicans changed their platform to capitalize on racial fears. And that's exactly what the Goldwater supporter suggested: "signs should not simply read 'vote Goldwater' but rather 'Make our neighborhood safe again. Vote Goldwater.'"[8]

Goldwater's campaign went on to release a short film entitled *Choice*, which depicted disorderly black mobs, drunken young people, and topless dancers assaulting traditional American values and sensibilities (Goldwater was incensed by the film and, upon seeing it for the first time, prohibited its further distribution). But in terms of winning votes, the main problem with Goldwater's rhetoric was that outside of the South there were not yet major social problems that legitimized a nationwide campaign based upon law and order. The intense social conflict of the 1960s (with the exception of the civil rights movement in the South) had not yet begun. In a sense, Goldwater had jumped the gun; his ideology was ahead of the realities on the ground from the perspective of most American voters.

Another reason Goldwater could not fully capitalize on the law and order strategy was his generally disagreeable demeanor: he embraced charges of extremism and oversaw the purging of the party moderates upon his 1964 primary victory over Nelson Rockefeller—but perhaps just as importantly, he did so in a polarizing and off-putting way. But where Goldwater had been ornery and divisive, Reagan was affable. "Law and order was a concept that Reagan latched on to instantly, and he did so in a way that seemed reasonable, not extremist . . . The candidate worked hard to avoid statements that could be construed as racist, and came across as too good natured a person to be a demagogue."[9] It was through this strategy of appealing to the anxieties of the white middle classes, largely through the rhetoric of law and order, that Reagan achieved his stunning victory over Brown. Subsequently, the ideology of law and order became the most important conservative catchall, presenting a clear alternative to the liberal solution to social problems, which generally entailed the expansion of government programs. The student protest at Berkeley and the rioting in Watts facilitated Reagan's transformation from a conservative ideologue into a practical politician. But in this transformation, it was not Reagan's rhetoric or his vision for the United States, but the social circumstances that had changed. In a sense, it was a case of good timing: these new conditions of social conflict worked to validate Reagan's philosophy, which, in light of contemporary events, was increasingly received by California voters as a pragmatic set of solutions to social problems rather than a shallow conservative ideology.

This transformation of California politics that paved the way for Reagan's ascent to the governorship can be understood as an early microcosm of national trends that would become clear in subsequent years. Several Republican governors would also adopt the rhetoric of law and order in the face of growing civil and racial unrest in the major cities of the United States. Among them was Spiro Agnew, Governor of Maryland from 1967 until he became Richard Nixon's Vice President in 1969. Indeed, there are striking similarities and differences between the political careers of Reagan and Agnew, and both men played important roles in shaping the new direction of the Republican Party. Like Reagan, Agnew was also a rising Republican star, although he was associated with the modern, rather than conservative Republican faction at the outset of his career. Agnew was also catapulted from being a relative outsider to the highest levels of political power in a very short amount of time. But *unlike* Reagan, Agnew's story would end in disgrace rather than in triumph. As Charles Holden and Zach Messitte have written, "in the history of American presidential politics no one has risen quite so far and fast (and then fallen quite so hard) as Spiro Agnew."[10]

Agnew had risen from chairman of the Baltimore County Appeals Board in 1961, to County Executive by 1962, to governor of Maryland by 1967, to Vice President of the United States under Richard Nixon after their 1968 election. His reputation had been that of a centrist, and he represented something of an ideological compromise between the moderate and conservative split in the Republican Party. In his early career, Agnew "did not want the party to move to the left any more than he wanted it to swing to the right. What he desired was a party devoid of almost any ideological tint whatsoever."[11] But by 1968, he had become increasingly associated with the reactionary politics of law and order. And like Reagan in California, issues of student rebellions and racial uprisings established the context for his rhetoric.

Agnew had witnessed prior racial conflict in Maryland that had shaped his emphasis on law and order, but it was the assassination of Martin Luther King Jr., on April 4, 1968, that directly led to his new political persona. There were riots in at least 37 American cities in the days after King's assassination. And despite its relatively mild history in terms of racial conflict, Baltimore also erupted in flames, perhaps because of a coincidental combination of events that effectively functioned to merge the grievances of student radicals and black Baltimoreans, in the process creating the rationale for a more hard-line conservative reaction that was equally holistic in its treatment of social disorder.

In the spring of 1968, students at the historically black Bowie State College had been boycotting classes and occupying the administration building for better campus facilities and increased state funding. As fate would have it, on April 3, 1968, the eve of King's assassination, a new and especially combative tone emerged in the campus discussions when it was rumored that Agnew planned to visit the predominantly white Towson State College campus to hear student grievances, after he refused to meet with black student protestors at Bowie. After hearing the news of Agnew's seemingly hypocritical concern for the white students, the black students at Bowie State organized a caravan to the state capital. By the time they arrived, news had broken that King had been assassinated. The black student protest converged with the public outrage over King's murder, and Baltimore was engulfed in a riot. By the end of the uprising in Baltimore over 5,600 people had been arrested, nearly all of them black. Although the two events—the Bowie State protests and King's assassination—only coincidently took place on the same day, the black riots and student protests were increasingly linked in the minds of many Americans as but two symptoms of a larger breakdown of respect for the law and order of society.

By all accounts, Agnew's response to the riots in Baltimore was harsh. In dealing with earlier social protests associated with the civil rights and black power movements (such as the small-scale rioting that occurred in Cambridge in 1967, during the "Brown Riot"), Agnew differentiated the moderate civil rights organizations from the radical black power activists and instances of public rioting. But following the rioting in Baltimore in 1968, he made no such distinction. On April 11, just days after Baltimore had stopped burning, the governor summoned a group of about 100 prominent black Baltimoreans to the state office building for what many had assumed would be an assessment of steps the city might take to prevent such uprisings in the future. Instead of articulating such plans, Agnew, who was surrounded by a phalanx of state troopers dressed in full military regalia, not only admonished the community leaders for failing to stop the rioting, he juxtaposed the goals of the civil rights movement with the lawlessness of looting, by criticizing the "perverted concept of race loyalty" that he thought existed in both the civil rights and black power movements. The governor's insulting words caused the majority of those in attendance to walk out before he had even finished speaking.

Agnew was roundly criticized by leading black Baltimoreans and by national civil rights activists. James Farmer of CORE immediately attacked Agnew's response:

> Many of the policies and utterances of Governor Agnew can be considered racist. For example, he speaks of law and order, without teaming it up with justice, and that is, in itself, racist. He speaks of shooting looters. And that would place property value above human life. And that, I think, in the American context is also racist.

A spokesman for the black caucus of the Maryland legislature claimed that Agnew had tried to divide the black community, and that his "actions are more in keeping with the slave system of a bygone era." "You talked to us like we are children," said state senator Verda F. Welcome, "So few white people understand black people." Many religious leaders in Baltimore, including from white and black churches, also rebuked him. For one black minister, "Governor Agnew's intemperate lecturing of the moderate Negro leadership hurts us deeply because it is an affront to men and women who have labored for many, many years to rid Baltimore of the evil effects of racism."[12]

Despite these criticisms, Agnew's response illustrated the growing backlash against the various forms of social unrest, particularly the student movement and the militant black movements in the nation's urban centers—whether in the form of civil rights initiatives, black power, or rioting, all of which were becoming increasingly linked in the minds of many white Americans. Further, in the aftermath of the riots that followed King's assassination, forces within the federal power structure intensified their ongoing efforts to criminalize the leaders of these movements. In the weeks prior to King's assassination, an aide gave his briefing to President Johnson:

> "We have permitted the Stokely Carmichaels, the Rap Browns, and the Martin Luther Kings to cloak themselves in an aura of respectability to which they are not entitled." King's civil disobedience was really "criminal disobedience," and . . . "I hope the President will publically unmask this type of conduct for what it really is."[13]

When President Johnson decided not to seek a second term as president amid the escalated war in Vietnam and in the face of tremendous domestic social conflict—whether political assassinations, antiwar protests, or rioting in the streets—it would be left to the next president to set the terms of the national discussion concerning the handling of the growing backlash and the issue of law and order. Richard Nixon would prove to be up for the task.

RICHARD NIXON AND THE SILENT MAJORITY

After serving as Vice President under Eisenhower from 1953 until 1961, Richard Nixon appeared destined to become a perpetual political loser. He lost the presidential election of 1960 to John F. Kennedy and then the California gubernatorial election of 1962 to Pat Brown, after which he sulkily told reporters that they "wouldn't have Nixon to kick around anymore, because, gentlemen, this is my last press conference." But Nixon would return to politics with his stunning comeback, winning a chaotic presidential election that was marked by the assassination of Robert Kennedy, brutal police suppression of demonstrators during the Democratic National Convention in Chicago, and the disruptive third-party candidacy of the southern demagogue George Wallace.[14]

Nixon remains something of an enigmatic figure in terms of the history of conservatism and the various Republican factions. Because of his role in the Eisenhower administration of the 1950s, his support for the Environmental Protection Agency (EPA), the Occupational Safety and Health Administration (OSHA), the Equal Rights Amendment (ERA), and especially his diplomatic opening to China, conservatives did not view Nixon as one of their own. But Nixon arguably did more to foster the politics of the divisive backlash, based largely upon the rhetoric of law and order, than any other political leader at the national level. The first signal that Nixon would attempt to seize upon the racial backlash came in his selection of his running mate Spiro Agnew, in light of Agnew's response to the rioting in Baltimore and because of the potential support he would receive in the South to offset the Wallace candidacy. In addition to his selection of Agnew, Nixon would also play to the white backlash through a more general application of the "southern strategy" for electoral success.

Many commentators and biographers have referred to something of a "dual" or "dichotomous" Nixon, implying that he is difficult to characterize, somehow torn between the competing forces of moderate and conservative Republicanism of the 1960s.[15] But Nixon's *modus operandi* might be referred to as "wedge politics": rather than a static "conservative" or "liberal" ideological approach, Nixon sought to create or inflame existing tensions in the coalitions of his rivals, and then to capitalize upon those "wedges" for his own political advantage. Occasionally, this would lead Nixon to pursue socially liberal policies, such as his backing of the "Philadelphia Plan" for racial hiring quotas in the construction industry. According to Chris Bonastia:

> Nixon viewed the Philadelphia Plan as a means of causing rifts between two core constituencies of the Democratic Party: African Americans and labor. Despite his pivotal role in establishing racial goals and timetables in employment, Nixon was able to label Democrats as the party of race and quotas in his 1972 re-election campaign.[16]

> ## Southern Strategy
>
> The "southern strategy" is a controversial aspect of the larger transformation of the Republican Party that occurred in the post-WWII decades as various politicians and strategists attempted to devise plans to break the historic loyalty of southern white voters to the Democratic Party. Although the moderate Republicans made early inroads in the South by appealing to the somewhat more liberal voters of the newly urban and suburbanizing areas, the southern strategy is more frequently associated with the campaign of Richard Nixon, particularly in 1972. The term was popularized through the work of Kevin Phillips, an advisor for Nixon in 1968 and whose subsequent 1969 book, *The Emerging Republican Majority*, articulated a plan to convert into Republicans the pro-segregationist southern whites who had voted for the third-party segregationist George Wallace in 1968. In a 1968 interview, Phillips infamously claimed that the key to politics is "knowing who hates who." In a 1970 interview, Phillips laid bare the strategy in its crudest form: "The more Negroes who register as Democrats in the South, the sooner the Negrophobe whites will quit the Democrats and become Republicans. That's where the votes are."[17]
>
> Nixon's strategy to encourage black southerners to join the Democratic Party—something they were already doing by 1968—in order to speed the "Republicanization" of southern whites, can be understood as part of Nixon's larger use of division as a general political strategy. Thus, there was a dual aspect of Nixon's "southern strategy": on one hand it refers to the political exploitation of racism in the South, on the other as a national application of the same strategy. Several observers interpreted Reagan's 1980 campaign speech in Neshoba, Mississippi, the symbolic epicenter of Deep South racism, as a continuation of this tactic.

Nixon would also come to realize that he could capitalize on the growing "ethnic revival" taking place among second- and third-generation European immigrants, who were increasingly asserting their identities as Italian-American, Polish-American, or Irish-American, in response to black in-migration and to the realization that it was possible to make political claims based on such identities.

These northern "ethnics" created a:

> nostalgic collage of memories of [Brooklyn] Dodgers pennants, pushcarts, stickball, mama's cooking, cries of *fuggedaboutit*, and other ethnic kitsch commemorating the city *ante-Negro*. In fights against scattered-site housing projects, expressways, and busing programs, ethnic revivalists transposed pastoral imagery of Old World peasant life to the urban landscape.[18]

Nixon would take advantage of this ethnic revival and

direct it toward conservative ends ... The [Republican Party] appealed to ethnic [working class] anxieties about blacks by supporting rollbacks of new civil rights policies, or by pushing 'law and order' ... the ethnic revival ... was both cause and symptom of the political, cultural, and economic fragmentation of the United States that was full-blown by 1980.[19]

It was here that the "southern strategy" seemed applicable to the northern states as well. Kevin Phillips had theorized that the ethnic factor of the New Deal coalition was a crucial element in the unfolding social conflicts in the northern urban centers that could potentially work to the advantage of the Republicans, provided the party take appropriate steps to capitalize upon it:

> The old bitterness toward Protestant Yankee Republicans that had for generations made Democrats out of the Irish, Italian and Eastern European immigrants had now shifted, among their children and grandchildren, to resentment of the new immigrants—Negroes and Latinos—and against the national Democratic Party, whose Great Society programs increasingly seemed to reflect favoritism for the new immigrants over the old.[20]

Indeed, it was these groups that Nixon saw as one of his greatest untapped bases of support. This key component of the New Deal coalition did not require much coaxing to join the reaction against the politics of protest taking place throughout American society, particularly in relation to the question of the war in Vietnam.

On November 3, 1969, in a televised address to the nation, Nixon called upon the "silent majority" of American citizens to back his plan for "Vietnamization" for the war effort, which entailed increased training and funding, while (he hoped) transferring the responsibility of the fighting to the South Vietnamese. In an effort to

> The "Great Society" plan of Lyndon Johnson was an audacious extension of the New Deal that created new federal agencies, programs, and laws designed to eradicate a variety of social problems including poverty (Office of Economic Opportunity), institutionalized racism (Civil Rights Act of 1964, Voting Rights Act of 1965), and access to health care (Social Security and Medicare). The programs were announced on the eve of a great period of social conflict in American society and many were targeted by the conservative movement as wasteful and unconstitutional. In addition to various forms of opposition, the potential of the Great Society programs was also limited by the financial cost and political energy usurped by the war in Vietnam.

build domestic support for the war and to encourage conservative opposition against the raging antiwar movement, in a pivotal nationwide telecast, Nixon proclaimed, "Let us be united for peace. Let us also be united against defeat. Because let us understand: North Vietnam cannot defeat or humiliate the United States. Only Americans can do that." Nixon's call for the silent majority to respond to the antiwar protests did not fall upon deaf ears. Less than six months after his address, on April 30, 1970, when Nixon announced an expansion of the war into Cambodia, he incensed the antiwar movement. Four days later, the Ohio National Guard opened fire on student demonstrators at Kent State University. The Guardsmen shot 13 students, including Dean Kahler, who was paralyzed from the waist down, and Allison Krause, Jeffrey Miller, Sandra Scheuer, and William Knox Schroeder, who were killed and subsequently immortalized in popular culture in "Ohio," the antiwar anthem of Crosby, Stills, Nash, and Young.

As a response to the killings at Kent State, antiwar protests continued to intensify around the country. In New York City, schools had been closed on the orders of the New York City Board of Education, and the moderate Republican mayor, John Lindsay, ordered American flags to be flown at half-mast. Thus, the stage was set for a large student-led antiwar rally to take place in the city on Friday, May 8, 1970, and a group of approximately 2,000 mostly high school and college students converged on Wall Street, the heart of the nation's financial center. They marched to protest the killings at Kent State and the ongoing war in Vietnam. During such protest marches, protesting students generally faced off against local authorities, or, as in Kent State, against the National Guard. But this particular rally would be different. As the students gathered on the corner of Broad and Wall Streets, they were surrounded by a group of several hundred construction workers wearing hardhats and overalls, who had converged on them from four directions in a coordinated attack. The workers charged through the students, beating them with their hardhats, crowbars, and lead pipes wrapped in American flags.

> The students chanted, "Peace now," and the workers shouted back, "Love it or leave it." Urged on by watching businessmen . . . with fists flying, they pummeled their way up the steps of the Subtreasury Building to raise a cluster of American flags on the statue of George Washington . . . "These hippies are getting what they deserve," said [a construction worker] . . . As he talked a co-worker standing with him yelled, "Damn straight," and punched a young man in a business suit who said he disagreed.[21]

After dispersing the student protestors to their satisfaction, the construction workers made their way to City Hall, assaulting anyone who looked like a protester or hippie. They fought past the thin layer of police and stormed into the building where they demanded that officials raise the American flag back to full-staff. As the flag was raised, the workers cheered in approval. But moments after the flag was raised, Sid Davidoff, an aide to the mayor, lowered it back down, at which point:

> The mob reacted in fury. Workers vaulted the police barricades, surged across the tops of parked cars and past half a dozen mounted policemen. Fists flailing they stormed through the policemen guarding the barred front doors. Uncertain whether they could contain the mob, the police asked city officials to raise the flag ... As the flag went up [a second time], the workers began singing "The Star-Spangled Banner."[22]

Another group of workers charged into Pace College across the street from the City Hall complex and seized a peace banner hanging from the building, brought it onto the street and set it on fire. Other workers smashed the windows of the building and beat up on-looking students.[23]

During the next two weeks, "hardhat rallies" took place throughout New York. On May 11, "upwards of 5,000 construction workers and longshoremen roamed through Lower Manhattan in organized bands, throwing punches at bystanders."[24] In the aftermath of these events Mayor Lindsay criticized the failure of the police to contain the rampaging workers and to protect the students. As a consequence, Lindsay—already a despised figure among the workers because of his order to lower the flag for the Kent State students—became an even bigger target for their wrath. On May 20, there was a massive hardhat parade in New York City, where an estimated crowd of 150,000 people marched through the streets, waving American flags and signs that denounced Lindsay as a communist sympathizer. Many of the marchers wore hardhats in support of the war effort in Vietnam and, by extension, for President Nixon. One of the marchers told a reporter, "We're part of the silent majority that's finally speaking—in answer to the creeps and the bums that have been hollering and marching against the President."[25]

The hardhat uprisings of May 1970 were an important new expression of working class populist conservatism and underscored the extent to which the "Old Left" would become politically unpredictable in the realigned politics of the Nixon era and beyond. But the hardhat uprising was not entirely spontaneous, nor did it necessarily spring directly from the grassroots of society. Following the clash that took place on May 8, *The Wall Street Journal* reported that several workers claimed to have been offered cash bonuses by their shop stewards or by their contractors if they agreed to "join the fray."[26] And the pro-Nixon hardhat parade had been

Figure 3.1 In a key moment in the development of working-class conservatism, hardhat workers demonstrate in New York City in May of 1970 in opposition to anti war protesters and the "red" mayor, the moderate Republican John Lindsay. Courtesy of the Estate of Garry Winogrand.

organized by the Building and Construction Trades Council of Greater New York, the labor group headed by Peter J. Brennan. Less than two weeks after the hardhat riots, President Nixon welcomed Brennan and other union leaders at the White House, where they presented him with a commemorative hardhat. After Nixon's landslide reelection in 1972, Brennan was confirmed as the United States Secretary of Labor.

For Nixon, it was an extraordinary coup. He had successfully capitalized upon the division between two segments of historically Democratic voters, and he would continue to use Brennan and other labor leaders to win increasing support from the ranks of organized labor. For Geoffrey Kabaservice:

> Nixon anticipated that he could use "the social issue" to appeal to white workers in much the same terms that he was trying to win over the Wallace voters in the South. Further, he believed that any appeals to blacks, students, intellectuals, or the establishment would cost him the support of the silent majority, including Southerners, white ethnics, blue collar workers, and "middle Americans."[27]

Inside the Oval Office, President Nixon proudly kept hardhats given to him by labor leaders from across the country to signify his political victory and the success of his "wedge politics." For Nixon, the hardhat was a political souvenir, a symbol of the growing power of the silent majority, the conservative middle classes who were increasingly raising their voices during the social conflict of the late 1960s and early 1970s.

The war in Vietnam was the most important, but not the only battle that awakened the silent majority. During the early 1970s, school desegregation had emerged as an equally divisive issue that led many Americans to become politically active in ways they had never considered. The Supreme Court had the South in its crosshairs when it issued the landmark *Brown v. Board of Education* decision in 1954 that overturned the "separate but equal" doctrine. The *Brown* decision was regionally specific: it targeted *de jure* segregation in the South, in Washington, D.C., and in ten other states that had legislation on the books allowing dual school systems for black and white children. But in the years that followed *Brown*, it became apparent that the nation's schools remained highly segregated, even if school boards did not explicitly assign students to schools based on their racial identity. Rather, it was in the suburbs, the white enclaves of residential space, where the battle over school desegregation would take a new form, motivating the increasingly not-so-silent majority to make up new political causes and forms of activism. In Boston, the busing issue of 1974–75 transformed a city once known for its abolitionism into a locus of bigotry centered in the working-class Irish neighborhood of South Boston, or "Southie." But it was the somewhat lesser-known busing conflict that took place in Louisville, Kentucky, in 1974, that perhaps best illustrated the ebb and flow of law and order ideology.

> The hardhat riots were reflected in popular culture through Merle Haggard's hit song of 1970, "The Fightin' Side of Me," which vilified antiwar protesters and threatened them with violence. Throughout the late-1960s and 70s, the genre of country music exploded in popularity as the social backlash gained momentum: in 1961, there were fewer than 90 country stations in the United States; by 1975, there were more than a thousand.[28] Unlike the counterculture of rock and roll, country music expressed themes of social traditionalism, patriotism, the docility of women, and thinly-veiled racism in such songs as Guy Drake's "Welfare Cadillac" (1970) and Tammy Wynette's "Don't Liberate Me, Love Me" (1971). The historian James N. Gregory has referred to country music as "the soundtrack for the revolt of the silent majority."[29]

Just as Louisville was implicated in the southern-oriented *Brown* ruling of 1954, it was also affected by *Swann v. Charlotte/Mecklenburg* (1971), which paved the way for the busing of students to achieve racial balance in cities where residential patterns determined the racial composition of schools. The merging of the Louisville and Jefferson County school districts was implemented on April 1, 1975, immediately establishing the newly unified district as one of the largest in the country. As a response to this ruling, Judge James F. Gordon called for a new busing system designed to bring racial balance to all Louisville schools, regardless of whether they were in racially homogeneous neighborhoods. Judge Gordon's order, which mandated the busing of suburban and rural white children into the various schools of Louisville's "inner city" (most of which had been historically black institutions), set off a wave of white reaction that intensified as the first day of the 1975–76 school year approached.

Opposition to the decisions included outspoken criticisms of "judicial activism" and fears of a "communist" tendency in the federal courts, while setting the stage for an increasing association between various forms of conservative expression. Clifford Sims, of Valley Station, Kentucky, linked the tax issue with trends he perceived to resemble totalitarian communism:

> We as taxpayers are paying for the schools in our communities, yet we are being forced to send our kids to other schools away from our own communities . . . We are being forced to do these things, I repeat: *forced*. This might be O.K. in Russia but this is the United States . . . Are we falling to communists?[30]

Other suburbanites framed their opposition to the busing order in terms of communism and in terms of their rights as taxpayers, and as in similar conflicts around the country, the rhetoric of the anti-busing movement in Louisville tended to emphasize white victimization and the loss of white "freedom." G.B. Nash, of Fairdale, Kentucky, feared that the busing decision was but one manifestation of the rising "new world order": "These are the kinds of laws and programs that the German people were forced to accept under Hitler . . . the anti-busing forces are not just fighting busing. We are fighting to save this nation and our freedom."[31] Another Louisville man argued, "This is not a black and white issue. It's a matter of our rights. I like education but I love freedom, and what good is education without freedom?"[32] Bill Kellerman, one of the leading figures in the anti-busing movement in Louisville, vainly attempted to convince Louisville blacks to join his protest. He found their lack of enthusiasm perplexing, "We want to ask blacks in this country, what the hell are you going to do when all of your rights are taken away from *you*?"[33]

As they criticized the federal courts, suburban whites seldom framed their opinions in explicitly racialized terms. Instead, in a farcical twist to the legacy of the civil rights movement, Louisville anti-busing demonstrators spoke defiantly about their own "rights" being violated by the "activism" of the Supreme Court and federal government. As Matthew Lassiter has argued, "While some far-right ideologues linked integration with communism and miscegenation, and conservative partisans frequently attacked civil rights groups and federal judges in strident terms, mainstream anti-busing sentiment [created] a fledgling rights-based language of middle class victimization."[34] This inversion of the civil rights narrative that cast middle-class suburban whites—*not blacks*—as the casualties of an unjust social system and authoritarian government was part of a larger transformation that was also crucial for the development of conservative ideology on a national scale.

One of the primary ways in which Louisville suburbanites displayed their protest was to boycott the public schools and businesses that did not explicitly condemn the busing policy; parents simply kept their children out of school. Throughout the city, the overwhelming extent of white opposition to busing quickly became apparent as the absenteeism that plagued the public schools also spread to area businesses. The Ford Motor Co. had to shut down production at its light truck assembly plant. One of the Ford workers was Red Cottrell, a former coal miner from "bloody" Harlan County, the scene of some of the most violent labor clashes in American history. Cottrell left the Harlan County coal fields to "escape the picket lines and violence," and ended up spearheading labor opposition to busing. "If they tried something like this in Harlan, they'd hang the judge," Cottrell said, "If [Judge] Gordon were here right now, they'd probably hang him from that very pole. I was born a racist but I'm not one now. I just don't want my kids being bused."[35] Work stoppages also took place at other major employers around Louisville: manufacturing operations were stopped at International Harvester Co., Brown Williamson Tobacco Corp., Phillips Morris Inc., and American Air Filter factories. A Louisville Chamber of Commerce official estimated that lost production in the city would total over $1 million.[36] As in the hardhat riots in New York City, the labor movement played a key role in Louisville. The workers soon formed United Labor Against Busing, which became a leading force in the anti-busing movement not only in Louisville but around the country, including in Boston.[37] On the second day of classes, suburban anti-busing aggression boiled over. Throughout the city, buses were set on fire and even run off the road while they were carrying children. At Fairdale High School, an anti-busing rally attracted more than 10,000 people. The mob set buses on fire and vandalized school property. By the end of the night, the police had arrested 135 suburban anti-busing demonstrators.

THE RELIGIOUS RIGHT AND THE CULTURE WARS

The historian Paul Boyer has written, "One cannot begin to understand the sea change in American political culture in the 1970s without grasping the centrality of religion to that transformation."[38] And the single most important event in the shaping of the political culture of the 1970s was, of course, the Watergate affair. In the early morning of June 17, 1972, five men were arrested at the Watergate in Washington, D.C., an office and residential complex that was, among other things, headquarters of the Democratic National Committee during the 1972 presidential campaign. The men caught breaking into the Democratic offices inexplicably carried large amounts of cash and, in the pages of the notebooks they carried, phone numbers of White House officials. It was later uncovered that some of them had ties to the CIA and to the anti-Castro Cuban-American community in Miami. Although the story initially had only a minor impact in the national media, the work of the political journalists Carl Bernstein and Bob Woodward helped lead to discoveries that President Nixon had been presiding over a White House that was a bastion of illegal activity: break-ins, money laundering, wiretaps, political sabotage—even shadowy connections to the attempted assassination of George Wallace.[39] As Nixon's heavy-handed paranoia was slowly coming to light, Lawrence F. O'Brien, the Democratic Party chairman, predicted, "I believe we are about to witness the ultimate test of an administration that so piously committed itself to a new era of law and order just four years ago."[40]

The resignation of Vice President Spiro Agnew in October 1973 in light of criminal charges of extortion and tax fraud, coupled with Nixon's own resignation less than one year later as a result of the investigations into Watergate, obliterated the notion of "law and order" that Nixon and Agnew had done so much to cultivate. Furthermore, Agnew's resignation and the Watergate conspiracy had a chaotic and disruptive effect on the growing conservatism in American politics and society. The resignations of Nixon and Agnew were initially a setback for the conservative movement and for the Republican Party, but ultimately, by strengthening the mistrust and resentment that an increasing number of Americans had toward the federal government, their resignations strengthened conservative ideology in the longer term.

There is a connection between the Watergate affair and the concomitant emergence of new forms of religious conservatism in American politics. One of Nixon's "dirty tricks" operatives was Charles "Chuck" Colson, a "tough-talking Washington lawyer whose methods more than matched his words."[41] Colson pled guilty to charges of obstruction of justice related to his role in the attempted Watergate cover-up and was sentenced to three years in federal prison. Because of his ruthless and cunning reputation (he once supposedly quipped that he would walk over his own grandmother to get Nixon reelected), when Colson was paroled in early 1975 and disclosed that while in prison he had undergone a personal religious conversion that entailed being "born again" as an evangelical Christian, "cynicism poured over him by the bucketful."[42] Colson openly recognized that during his years working for Nixon, as a true Machiavellian, he had helped to exploit religious sentiment in order to win political power for his boss. He spoke freely about his own role and that process:

> Sure, we used the prayer breakfasts and church services and all that for political ends . . . [Nixon] recognized that there were voting blocs that were enormously influenced by their religious leaders. He recognized that the blue-collar, white ethnic group in the North that had been a pivotal vote for Democratic majorities in the past was open to wooing by Republicans, that they were identifying with us on more social issues—the great 'Silent Majority' . . . We would bring [religious leaders] into the White House and they would be dazzled by the aura of the Oval Office, and I found them to be about the most pliable of any special interest group that we worked with.[43]

But in time, even the most cynical would be largely convinced that Colson's post-Watergate conversion was not entirely disingenuous. Indeed, Nixon's old "hatchet man," who had previously exploited the beliefs of religious voters for political gain, was now himself one of a growing number of Americans who would come to identify as having being "born again" as an evangelical Christian. Colson would become a leading voice of the "religious right," a somewhat ambiguous umbrella term that encompasses socially conservative Christians, usually outside of the mainline Protestant denominations, which would emerge as a social and political force during the 1970s.

There is of course a long history of intermingling between politics and religion in the United States. One of the tenets of "American exceptionalism" is the historic absence of a state-controlled church, which led to the flourishing of various Protestant groups in British North America during the seventeenth and eighteenth centuries:

> Unlike Europe, where proud monarchs and even learned theologians might consider themselves to be architects of

> momentous events ... the "City upon a Hill" that arose from the wilderness was entirely the work of God ... History convinced American Protestants that God favored their land by demonstrating his assistance in their countless struggles against the Catholic powers.[44]

During the American War of Independence, the authors of the Constitution debated to what extent the United States should become a "Christian nation," and what that term would imply for the policies of the new republic. Despite this longer history, it was not until much later that Protestantism in the United States would acquire the features that would make it relevant to the shaping of the American conservative movement.

In the early twentieth century, the various pressures stemming from industrialization and science inflamed tensions between religious faith on one hand and secular "modernism" on the other. While some Christians attempted to reconcile their faith in biblical teachings with advances in the natural and social sciences, others went in the opposite direction, establishing a set of rigid "fundamentals" for the Christian belief system. The term "fundamentalist" is derived from a series of essays by leading American and European Protestant theologians entitled *The Fundamentals*, published between 1910 and 1915, which defined the historical inerrancy of the Bible, the virgin birth and deity of Jesus, the doctrine of substitutionary atonement, the bodily resurrection of Jesus, and the genuineness of Jesus' miracles as constituting the *sine qua non* or "fundamentals" of Protestant Christianity.[45] Particularly because of its emphasis on the inerrancy of the Bible—that the Bible was a historical document to be interpreted literally—the fundamentalist movement was immediately and irrevocably at odds with various aspects of life in the United States. The early fundamentalist movement scored several political victories, including the national ban on the production, sale, and consumption of alcohol during the period of Prohibition (1920–1933). It was also successful in banning the teaching of evolution in public schools, particularly in the South, which led to the symbolic conviction of Tennessee high school biology teacher John Scopes during the infamous "Scopes monkey trial" of 1925.

From the inception of their movement, the fundamentalists were infused with a strong sense of religious nationalism. During the First World War, fundamentalist leaders "declared that Satan himself was directing the German war effort ... Modernism, they asserted, had turned Germany into a godless nation, and would do the same thing to America."[46] After the Second World War, the fundamentalists were attracted to the cause of anticommunism, as figures such as Carl McIntire and Billy James Hargis lent their support to the efforts of the John Birch Society and Joseph McCarthy, who was busy attempting to purge the nation of communists. In keeping with the conservative trends of the time, these fundamentalists tended to support southern segregation and were generally hostile toward the civil rights movement. Some of these religious leaders may have been simply racist from the outset, but for others, their racism was developed in conjunction with a conservative interpretation of the Bible, which, in various passages of the Old Testament, forbids what southern segregationists referred to as "miscegenation" or "racial mixing." In a 1965 sermon entitled "Ministers and Marches," a young pastor named Jerry Falwell criticized the efforts of Martin Luther King, James Forman, and other practitioners of the "social gospel"—the theological tradition of using biblical texts to bring about social change.

> It is very obvious that the Communists, as they do in all parts of the world, are taking advantage of a tense situation in our land, and are exploiting every incident to bring about violence and bloodshed . . . Preachers are not called to be politicians, but soul winners.[47]

At the time, Falwell believed religious leaders should focus their efforts on individual salvation rather than social or political issues.

In his attack on King and the social gospel of the civil rights movement, Falwell highlighted an important tension in the nascent religious right: the extent to which the movement should become actively involved in social and political issues. In fact, despite the early victories of the fundamentalist movement in bringing about Prohibition and in the anti-evolution crusade, many among them were hesitant to become too concerned with "worldly" affairs, instead opting to separate religion from politics. Billy Graham, another leading figure of the twentieth century religious resurgence, was also equivocal:

> [Graham] liked to say, and at times perhaps even believed that he was completely neutral in politics, but he freely admitted his fascination with the political realm . . . his overriding political concern was not the brand name of the party in power, but how that power was and could be used in the service of Christianity.[48]

By the end of the 1970s, this debate would effectively be settled, as fundamentalist evangelical Christians would become fully mobilized in the political realm and would constitute a leading role in the conservative movement.

Jerry Falwell and Pat Robertson

Concerning the question of political involvement, Jerry Falwell did not practice what he preached. Despite his excoriations of Martin Luther King Jr., in the 1960s, Falwell became a leading political organizer of evangelicals during the late-1970s, by which time he had already opened Lynchburg Baptist College (later renamed Liberty University) and was appearing on his own nationally syndicated television program, *Old Time Gospel Hour*. But Falwell cut his political teeth in a series of "I Love America" rallies in 1976, and in working alongside Anita Bryant in the anti-gay rights campaign in Miami in 1977, where he spoke at the "Christians for God and Decency" rally. Falwell focused his efforts on defeating what he perceived to be the related evils of abortion, pornography, and homosexuality, through local ballot initiatives and coordinated boycotts. After meetings with conservative activists including Paul Weyrich (who helped organize the Heritage Foundation in 1973) and Howard Phillips (a Nixon administration official and founder of the Conservative Caucus in 1974), in 1979 Falwell created the Moral Majority, a political action committee designed to endorse and fund conservative congressional candidates while preserving the tax-exempt status of his church ministry.

By 1980, "Republican Party leaders were treating [Falwell] like an influential lobbyist and the leader of an important swing constituency, rather than a small-town Baptist preacher that he had been only a few years earlier."[49] Falwell's rising stature appeared to be closely associated with the 1980 election of Ronald Reagan, but many movement leaders would come to lament that Reagan actually did very little for them other than to stage White House photo opportunities. Falwell closed the Moral Majority shortly after Reagan left office.

Although he waivered on the question of political involvement, Falwell never deviated from his attacks on gays, feminists, and abortionists. Two days after the terrorist attacks of September 11, 2001, he appeared on Pat Robertson's television program *The 700 Club*. Falwell said:

> The abortionists have got to bear some burden for this because God will not be mocked. And when we destroy 40 million little innocent babies, we make God mad ... the pagans, and the abortionists, and the feminists, and the gays and the lesbians who are actively trying to make that an alternative lifestyle, the ACLU, People For the American Way—all of them who have tried to secularize America—I point the finger in their face and say, you helped this happen.

Robertson replied, "Well, I totally concur, and the problem is we have adopted that agenda at the highest levels of our government."

In contrast to its association with conservatism in the South, during the 1960s, the growing "Jesus movement" (as it was known in the 1960s), particularly in California, was not nearly as socially conservative as it would eventually become. Instead, in this early phase, the movement came to adopt many of the characteristics of the youth counterculture, most notably through a greater informality in church services. The "Jesus freaks" advocated the use of upbeat contemporary-style music instead of traditional hymns, held outdoor concerts that resembled Woodstock more than a traditional church service, and congregants maintained a personal and casual relationship with the clergy. This new style of nondenominational Protestantism would come to flourish in American suburbs—a trend best illustrated by the Calvary Chapel Church of Costa Mesa, California, founded in 1965. "Emulating the model of proliferating fast-food franchises, some 800 Calvary Chapels had sprung up in the United States and abroad by 2000. Each, like its prototype, was theologically conservative; casual in style; and headed by a 'Pastor Dave,' 'Pastor Ron,' or 'Pastor Jim.'"[50] Although some of these leaders would occasionally address social issues, such as civil rights or the communist threat, by the end of the 1960s the evangelical movement had not yet become the religious right; it was not yet committed to direct involvement in party politics and its relation to the American conservative movement remained ambiguous.

It was against this complex and variegated historical landscape of American religion—the twentieth century fundamentalist movement, southern-style conservatism, anticommunism, and the counterculture of the 1960s—that established the general institutional and ideological background for the rise of the religious right. But it was not until the 1970s, in a series of cultural battles, that the movement became explicitly polarized and politicized through grassroots mobilizations and through the top-down engineering of powerful political interest groups. Through this process, the religious right would cement its co-constitutive relationship with the American conservative movement.

There were several important events for the growing politicization of the movement, including the ongoing issue of the teaching of evolution and sex education in public schools. But most importantly was the *Roe v. Wade* (1973) decision of the Supreme Court, which ensured women of the right to have an abortion. Prior to this decision, moral or political opposition to abortion had been largely confined to Catholic Americans—those politically valuable "white ethnics" that Nixon had so vigorously pursued—for whom biological reproduction was a long-standing issue in Church doctrine. Prior to 1973, "most non-Catholic conservative Republicans were in favor of abortion liberalization."[51] Indeed, abortion was simply not a widespread political issue in the late-1960s, and even in the immediate aftermath of the *Roe* decision, evangelical and fundamentalist groups did not offer a unified response. For the sociologist William Martin, this was partly related to the anti-Catholic prejudices that still existed in the minds of many Protestant Americans:

> Many liberal Protestants were uncomfortable with the massive numbers of abortions . . . but most affirmed a pro-choice position. Evangelical and fundamentalist Protestants, many of whom now consider abortion a litmus test of extraordinary importance, had little to say about it one way or the other . . . The fact that many Catholics were out in front caused many Protestants to keep a low profile.[52]

In fact, during his tenure as Governor of California, Ronald Reagan, albeit after some hesitation, signed into law the Therapeutic Abortion Act of 1967, the most liberal of all abortion laws in the United States (a point to which we will return in the concluding chapter).

Although the National Association of Evangelicals denounced the *Roe* decision in its magazine, other Protestant bodies—whether the doctrinally independent "Jesus movement" churches or the mainline Protestant organizations—were largely silent on the issue. Instead, certain key actors, who had previously sought to transform the United States into a nation that reflected their own interpretations of biblical principles, began to explore the possibilities of working with conservative politicians to mobilize support for the issue. The most important figure in that regard was Bill Bright, who founded the Campus Crusade for Christ in 1951 at the University of California, Los Angeles as an effort to "win the campus today and change the world tomorrow." Although Bright always had an interest in converting souls, it was the issue of abortion that led him to explore new ways to encourage Christians to become politically active. Bright sought the alliance of a fellow evangelical, John Conlan, the conservative Republican congressman from Arizona, and in 1974, they created Third Century Publishers for the purpose of circulating books designed to mobilize Christians politically. The mobilization effort was not designed on the basis of faith alone, but to promote a conservative worldview that was essentially a:

> voter mobilization effort for the conservative wing of the Republican Party . . . [Conlan] did not hesitate to ask pastors to endorse specific candidates or to set up voter registration tables on church property. He directed local Third Century chapters to screen born-again Christians who applied for training in political skills, and to turn away all who seemed politically liberal.[53]

The Equal Rights Amendment (ERA), a proposed amendment to the Constitution to outlaw gender-based discrimination, was another key aspect in the increasingly conservative orientation of American Protestants—although initially, like abortion, it hardly appeared to be a divisive issue. The idea of a constitutional amendment outlawing discrimination based upon one's gender was an old idea, having first been raised in 1921 by Alice Paul, the suffragist and leader of the National Woman's Party. With the rise of "second-wave" feminism in the 1960s, the issue once again gained momentum:

> The growth of women's rights organizations in the 1960s and 70s marked the emergence of feminism as a political force. With the foundation of the National Organization for Women (NOW) in 1967, the campaign to introduce the ERA was revived. NOW members also worked to raise women's consciousness, to reform sexist assumptions about gender roles and repeal restrictive abortion laws.[54]

When the ERA was introduced to Congress in late 1971 to begin the process of amending the Constitution, it did not appear to be a controversial issue. Instead, it received Democratic and Republican support from around the country: it passed by the overwhelming margin of 354 to 23 in the House of Representatives, 84 to 8 in the Senate, and was endorsed by an extraordinarily diverse group of politicians including Gerald Ford, George McGovern, Ted Kennedy, Richard Nixon, Spiro Agnew, Strom Thurmond, and George Wallace.

Following its early success, the ERA was passed to the state legislatures, where it needed to be ratified by 38 states in order to become a constitutional amendment. Initially, its momentum continued, and it was ratified in 30 states. But shortly thereafter, it hit a brick wall of conservative resistance, thanks primarily to the efforts of one woman, Phyllis Schlafly, a long-time conservative activist and operative within the Republican Party. Schlafly had run for congress in 1952 and 1970 and was the president of the National Federation of Republican Women (NFRW) from 1964 until 1967. Her book, *A Choice Not an Echo*, helped win the presidential nomination for Barry Goldwater in 1964. Schlafly had a tenuous relationship with the party moderates, and she was blocked from the presidency of the NFRW in 1967 by Nelson Rockefeller, after which she left the party and continued her political career outside of the party through her independent newsletter, the *Phyllis Schlafly Report*.

Like other conservative Republicans, Schlafly was not initially concerned with the ERA. Instead, a handful of readers of her newsletter wrote to her, requesting that she become involved in fighting the ERA and explaining its ramifications to American women. Thus, in the fall of 1972, she founded STOP ERA, an organization whose sole purpose was defeating the ratification the Equal Rights Amendment in the state legislatures. STOP was an acronym for "Stop Taking Our Privileges," and the massive campaign was based around the idea that the ERA would do the opposite of what it claimed: namely, it would strip women of their traditional privileges, thus *undermining* the position of women in society. In other words, as she herself paradoxically claimed, Schlafly opposed the Equal Rights Amendment because she *supported* women's rights:

> The ERA would deny a woman's existing legal right to be supported by her husband; privacy rights would be overturned and unisex public restrooms would be instituted; single sex schools and colleges would be outlawed; women would be drafted into the military and sent into combat alongside men; the ERA would challenge matrimonial preference in child custody cases; abortion rights and homosexual rights, including same sex marriage, would be upheld. [Schlafly] expressed the view that, far from being oppressed or victimized in a patriarchal society, American women were immensely privileged, while for feminists to plead for special pleading was demeaning.[55]

In 1975, Schlafly created the Eagle Forum, another organization that would act as an umbrella group to coordinate the activities of various grassroots efforts across the country.

As Marjorie J. Spruill has argued, the effort to stop the ratification of the ERA was inherently related to the increasing religious conservatism of the 1970s.

> Some, like Schlafly, were devout Catholics, many being active in "right-to-life" [anti-abortion] groups. By the mid-1970s, religious opponents of the feminist movements also included Mormons ... [and] evangelicals and fundamentalists—to whom denial of gender differences and separate, subordinate roles for women was not only erroneous but sacrilegious—who had previously eschewed politics as corrupting.[56]

These activists, through pressuring state legislators, completely turned the momentum of the ERA, which, in light of its bipartisan support at the highest levels of political power in 1972, appeared destined to become ratified as a constitutional amendment. But the ERA stalled, as the conservatives were rising and, conversely, the feminist groups, who were caught off guard by the sudden strength of the opposition, became increasingly fragmented. The ERA was ultimately defeated in 1982, when the extended deadline for ratification was reached without the requisite number of states supporting the amendment.

One of the related issues that divided the pro-ERA groups and spurred the conservative resistance was the perception of overlap between the issues of abortion and gay rights, particularly after the Stonewall riots of 1969 in New York City, which was a turning point in the recognition of the oppression of gays and lesbians in the United States. During the 1977 International Women's Year Conference that took place in Houston, Texas, which had been designed largely to rejuvenate the ERA effort in the state legislatures, the issue of gay rights became increasingly intertwined with the issue of gender equality more generally. And certainly the issues were intertwined in the minds of religious conservative activists, such as Jerry Falwell, who frequently spoke of abortionists, gays and lesbians, and feminists in the same breath.

In the aftermath of Stonewall and in the gradual but nevertheless increasing acceptance of gays and lesbians in American public life, a number of cities passed anti-discriminatory resolutions. But it was in Miami, a city hardly known for its conservatism (despite the influence of anti-Castro Cuban-Americans), where the highest profile effort to defeat the rising tide of gay rights took place. The political mobilization to repeal Miami's anti-discriminatory ordinance was led by Anita Bryant, whose efforts quickly gained national attention. Bryant would appear on stage with Ronald Reagan at the 1977 annual dinner of the Florida Conservative Union, as well as on the nationally syndicated television programs of Jerry Falwell and Pat Robertson. She would also foster linkages with the fight against the ERA, which was simultaneously being debated in the Florida state legislature. "For many social conservatives, the two causes [of the ERA and gay rights] were related, especially since Phyllis Schlafly insisted that the ERA would lead to the legalization of same-sex marriages."[57] On June 7, 1977, Bryant's efforts paid off: Miami's gay rights ordinance was repealed in spectacular fashion by a margin of more than two-to-one, in what was arguably the first major victory for social conservatism in the emerging "culture wars."

The historian Matthew D. Lassiter has argued that social conservatives, including the religious right, aided by a willing mainstream media, portrayed the "crisis of the American family" as a cultural, rather than economic phenomenon. During the 1970s, social conservatives successfully characterized the traditional American family—a working father with a nine-to-five job, a stay-at-home mother raising children in a tranquil suburban enclave—as being "under attack" from feminists, gay rights activists, and murderous doctors who performed abortions. In his analysis of these "culture wars," Lassiter points to the gap between dominant

> ## Anita Bryant
>
> Anita Bryant was a gospel singer and beauty pageant winner who became a leading opponent of the gay rights movement during the late 1970s, most notably in Miami in 1977, where her organization, Save Our Children, led efforts to repeal the city's anti-discriminatory ordinance. At the time, Bryant was also the spokesperson for the Florida Citrus Commission, and she regularly appeared in commercials to promote Florida tourism and orange juice consumption. Because of this association, gay bars across the country responded by leading the subsequent boycott of orange juice, replacing "screwdrivers" (a cocktail made with vodka and orange juice) with "Anita Bryants" (an alternative cocktail made with vodka and apple juice).
>
> One of the keys to the success of Save Our Children was the way in which the organization framed gay rights as an attack upon the traditional family. Bryant characterized gay rights as a direct threat to what she referred to as "family values." Gay men and lesbians, she argued, through their "gay lifestyles," were determined not only to destroy families, but to recruit (or to molest) children. In this sense, Bryant adopted the same strategy as Phyllis Schlafly, who had opposed the ERA on the grounds that it was an attack on womanhood. Indeed, social conservatives, particularly the religious right, had landed upon a winning framework—who, after all, wouldn't want to save children?
>
> Throughout the 1970s and into the 1980s, "family values" would become a rhetorical cornerstone of social conservatism. It was in this larger context that the work of child psychologist and evangelical Christian, James Dobson, would skyrocket in popularity. Dobson had published a number of books on the subject of child rearing through the use of strict discipline, and he went on to found Focus on the Family in 1977, which would blossom into a tax-exempt media empire. Dobson's lobby organization, the Family Research Council (founded in 1981), would also establish itself as a leading exponent of "family values" through promoting socially conservative policies and opposing the civil rights of gay Americans.

cultural explanations on one hand, versus the economic roots of the erosion of this family model on the other. He writes, "The ideological contradiction at the core of the 'pro-family movement' has always revolved around the inherent tension between the enthusiastic celebration of free-market capitalism and the simultaneous defense of traditional family values."[58] Sociologists have long realized that economic changes invariably lead to changes in the structure of society, including in the structure of families: as more would-be housewives enter the workplace in troubled economic times, family and gender relations will change as a consequence. And during the 1970s, social conservatives generally overlooked the connections between the eroding American economy and the breaking down of traditional social forms (such as the suburban family model), instead scapegoating the much easier targets of gays, lesbians, and feminists.

CONCLUSION

The campus protests at Berkeley and the various uprisings, riots, and revolts—whether in Watts, New York, Louisville, California, or Miami—can be used as guideposts to highlight the important changes taking place in conservative ideology, and the ways in which new segments of the American public were increasingly identifying with various aspects of conservatism in the post-Goldwater era. Initially, "law and order" was an important catchall for conservatives who disapproved of social protest. It was effectively used by a number of different politicians—including Goldwater, Reagan, Agnew, and Nixon—to rally patriotism in support of the war in Vietnam, and to condemn social protests and uprisings in poor black neighborhoods. During this period, from approximately 1964 to 1970, law and order functioned

> as a "bridge," enabling political leaders to tap into existing streams of conservatism . . . The rhetoric . . . mobilized grassroots conservatives, giving them the language of protest and a vocabulary of ideas with which to link troubling changes in their communities to broader developments in American society and culture.[59]

But in the hardhat riots, and later, in Louisville, it was the representatives of the silent majority who acted in a lawless and occasionally destructive way. Nixon, through his admiration for the hardhats and those who donned them, inadvertently undercut his earlier calls for law and order, and with Watergate, the era of law and order as a conservative mantra had ended. Later, in the various anti-busing protests around the country, suburban protestors also defied the notion of law and order in ways that indicated an increasingly hostile tone not only toward blacks and students, but toward the federal government.

Although the short-lived hardhat movement was a patriotic defense of the president and of the authority of political leaders in Washington, by the mid-1970s, Nixon's silent majority could no longer be counted on to support Washington or to act within the confines of "law and order." Instead of defending the president, anti-busing protestors had become sharply critical of the "political elites" in Washington and the decisions of the Supreme Court. Unlike in the New York hardhat riot, the resistance of the silent majority to busing had shifted the focus from a patriotic defense of the United States to a direct challenge to government policy. As Tracy K'Meyer has argued, "The blue collar component of the anti-busing movement [in Louisville] reflected . . . the defensive insecurity of working-class Americans, who felt . . . the federal government was helping others at their expense."[60] The religious right and traditionalists, such as Anita Bryant and Phyllis Schlafly emerged in this period to form an important cultural component of the American conservative movement. In subsequent years, as will be seen, their efforts would beconme increasingly linked to various aspects of economic conservatism, particularly issues related to state and federal taxes. It was this social and historical backdrop of rising conflict, increasing polarization, and uncertain alliances that set the stage for Ronald Reagan's ascension in national politics—a subject to which we now turn.

CHAPTER 4

Crises, Carter, and the Triumph of Ronald Reagan

By the middle of the 1970s, American conservatism was hardly confined to the ideologies of politicians such as Robert Taft or Barry Goldwater, or to conservative authors like William Buckley. The various developments that had emerged in American society over issues such as crime, rioting, patriotism and the Vietnam War, abortion and feminism, had both popularized and legitimized the rhetoric of the ideological conservatives, while also pointing toward new opportunities for politicians to capitalize upon the variegated cultural forms of conservative expression. Politics is often a case of timing: unlike 1964, where the ideology of Barry Goldwater was far beyond the sentiment of most of the American public, throughout the 1970s, the public mood would become increasingly receptive to conservatism in ways it had not been in the first half of the 1960s.

But the new problem for the conservative movement was one of leadership, as Nixon and Agnew, and by extension the Republican Party, had been largely discredited in light of the Watergate scandal. President Ford, who inherited the presidency, further damaged his own credibility and political future by pardoning Nixon from looming criminal charges and from the prospect of testifying at the Watergate hearings. Thus, in 1976, there was again an imbalance between political leadership and the conservative mood at the popular level of American society. But the disequilibrium had swung in the opposite direction: the Republican Party—although it still contained some liberal and "modern" residual elements—had become the organizational vehicle for harnessing conservatism on a national scale, but the prospects for the party actually winning political power at the presidential level remained dim.

But that did not stop Ronald Reagan from trying. Reagan, who had been out of public office for more than a year, was nearly successful in wresting the presidential nomination from President Ford through a campaign that showcased the ideas of the right wing of American politics. Reagan focused on slashing the national budget and transferring various responsibilities from the federal government to the states. In a speech before the Executive Club of Chicago in September 1975, he proposed cutting the federal budget by $90 billion and having the states make up the losses in terms of services and employment. The historian Sean Wilentz has written that Reagan's infamous "$90 billion plan" was "a wild idea that, if ever put into effect, would cause massive unemployment for public workers and force states to raise their taxes . . . The Ford campaign fully exploited the speech as evidence that Reagan was a pie-eyed extremist who literally didn't know what he was talking about."[1]

Reagan also attempted to rally American nationalism in light of the decline of the United States on the world stage, both politically and economically. During the 1970s, as it remains today, the United States *was* the world's most powerful military force, although a series of events, beginning with the defeat in Vietnam, contributed to the growing impression that American power was on the decline. The foreign policy issues that Reagan and other political leaders were debating in the late 1970s were important in establishing the underlying rationale of American foreign policy in the post-Vietnam era. For example, in 1976 the United States was considering the ratification of a new set of treaties with Panama that would shift control of the Canal Zone to the Panamanian government. For Reagan, it was the perfect illustration of how the United States was "giving away" its positions of strength. He took a hard-line on the issue and used it to win pockets of strong support. With the insistence, "We built it, we paid for it, it's ours!" he brought crowds to their feet, particularly in the South. Reagan's stance on the canal issue led him to victory in North Carolina, the first time a Republican incumbent president had been defeated in a state primary election. Reagan also won in Texas, Alabama, Georgia, Indiana, Nebraska, and California. Although he ultimately failed to win the nomination, he established himself as a frontrunner for the 1980 contest, despite the fact that if he were to win he would be one month shy of his 70th birthday upon taking office.

Rather than a setback, 1976 ultimately worked to the advantage of the Republican Party, the conservative movement, and Reagan personally. First, had Reagan won the party's nomination and entered the presidential election against Jimmy Carter in 1976, he most likely would have lost in light of the uphill battle facing the Republicans after Watergate (during the 1974 off-year elections, Democrats gained 52 seats in the House and four in the Senate). This would have made it difficult for Reagan to run again in 1980 and he most likely would have been forced to give up his quest for the presidency and retire from politics. Second, Reagan and the conservative movement were able to remain on the sidelines during the various crises of the late 1970s, during which time the nation's economy entered a deep recession. Thus, Reagan was unscathed by the economic storm. Reagan and the conservative movement also benefited from international developments that would unfold during the late 1970s: the revolts in Central America, the Iranian Revolution and the subsequent American hostage crisis, as well as the Soviet invasion of Afghanistan. Both the economic and international crises created the conditions inside the United States for an even greater receptivity to Reagan's ideas, particularly his persistent reliance upon a unique mixture of simplistic optimism, budget and tax cuts, and a restoration of American power around the world. Thus, as during the Great Depression and again after the Goldwater debacle, Ronald Reagan emerged from a tumultuous period in American history as his political rivals were left to pick up the pieces. Instead of Ronald Reagan, it was Jimmy Carter who would bear the brunt of the troubling developments.

As Frye Gaillard has written, "with the country reeling from the shame of Watergate and the endless agonies left by the Vietnam War, Carter offered hope for a new kind of pride."[2] The "hope" that Carter offered came from various sources. As a political outsider, he was far removed from the criminal treachery of the Nixon White House and from the associated stigma of Washington politics. A trained nuclear engineer, he brought a technocratic, rather than explicitly ideological approach to politics. He had a reputation of governing from the head rather than the heart. Furthermore, Carter was a centrist whose ideas were more in line with modern Republicans rather than the liberal faction of the Democratic Party. Importantly, he was also a southerner, and this worked to his advantage in temporarily limiting the "southernization" of the Republican Party, which had been ongoing since at least 1964. In a temporary reversal of recent trends in presidential elections, Carter carried every state of the former Confederacy, with the exception of Virginia. And as the first openly "born again" Christian president, he also appealed to the rising number of Americans who also identified as such.

From the outset of his 1976 campaign, Carter attempted to emphasize these various assets related to his personality and professional training through the presentation of his public image. At the 1976 national convention, the Democratic faithful were eagerly awaiting his acceptance of the party's presidential nomination, and all eyes were on the stage. But instead of stepping out from behind the curtain, Carter emerged from the rear of the hall "so he could walk through the crowd, touching hundreds and smiling at all, embodying his well-developed persona as an outsider, a humble man of the people who would emerge from their ranks to lead them on to higher ground."[3] Indeed, when Jimmy Carter was elected president, he appeared well positioned to lead the United States in a new direction, away from the politics of division that had defined the Nixon era, and to restore public confidence in the office of the presidency.

But instead of working to Carter's advantage, all of these factors—particularly his centrism—would contribute to his political downfall. Carter was habitually "caught in the middle" throughout his presidency, not only regularly facing the expected attacks from conservative Republicans, but from the liberal faction of the Democratic Party as well. Thus, by the end of his first and only term, Carter was "doubly" unpopular. Furthermore, his technocratic moderation was widely perceived as weakness, particularly in light of the deterioration of American economic and geopolitical power. As will be seen, all of this would directly work to the advantage of the conservatives and culminate in the election of Ronald Reagan in 1980.

THE ECONOMIC CRISIS OF THE CARTER ERA

The myriad of crises that emerged during the course of the late 1970s were deeply interconnected, although they can be divided into two general categories: economic and political. Both of these sets of crises would directly undermine Jimmy Carter, progressively destabilize American liberalism, and create the conditions for Reagan's 1980 victory and the political triumph of the American conservative movement.

The economic crisis that became particularly acute during the second half of Carter's presidency did not originate during his time in office, but with the Organization of Petroleum Exporting Countries (OPEC) oil embargo, which was launched in October of 1973 by the group's Arab members as retaliation against American support for Israel during the Yom Kippur War. The embargo came at a time when American oil production had already begun to decline, and thus the United States had become largely dependent on imported oil, which, by the early 1970s, was mostly coming from the Middle East. The embargo immediately caused oil prices to quadruple, sending shockwaves throughout the American (and global) economy. As Thomas Borstelmann has written,

> For two generations, Americans had considered easy access to inexpensive gasoline as almost a birthright, a defining feature of what it means to be American. In the 1920s, advertising executive and best-selling author Bruce Barton called gasoline "the juice of the fountain of youth," a symbol of American freedom. Now in the

1970s the fountain was drying up, leaving the nation thirsty and vulnerable.[4]

The resulting spike in energy prices continued long after the embargo ended in March of 1974, and it set the tone for a general price inflation that persisted throughout the remainder of the decade. This inflation was one side of the toxic mixture that plagued the American economy during much of Carter's presidency. The other side, the absence of economic growth and subsequent rising unemployment, was not supposed to coincide with price inflation—at least not according to Keynesian economic models, which predicted that inflation was associated with economic expansion rather than contraction. The resulting condition of "stagflation" would become a key rationale for launching massive economic reforms of subsequent years.

These conditions must be understood in the larger context of American economic decline. As the economist Gerald Epstein has argued,

> [A]lthough the causes of stagflation are not fully known, any analysis is doomed if it does not attempt to understand the implications of one central fact: the decline of United States power in the world economy since World War II. In the late 1940s, the United Stated produced 60 percent of the Western industrialized world's manufactures and 40 percent of the world's goods and services. By the late 1970s, both shares had been cut in half.[5]

The general American economic decline of the 1970s coincided with a number of factors that had already mobilized leading American corporations and their representatives into action. Throughout the decade these individuals and their newly formed organizations would work to convince the public of the merits of specific economic reforms and of the more general virtues of free market capitalism—a key component of Reagan's long-standing economic philosophy.

During the protests surrounding the Vietnam War, antiwar activists were targeting not only military recruiting stations and Reserve Officers' Training Corps (ROTC) facilities on university campuses, but by the early 1970s, they increasingly focused on boycotting and demonstrating against weapons manufacturers and what they described as other forms of war profiteering. The environmentalist movement was also a thorn in the side of business interests, and its efforts, among other things, had resulted in the creation of the Environmental Protection Agency (EPA) and the Occupational Safety and Health Administration (OSHA), both of which were signed into existence by Richard Nixon in 1970. Furthermore, consumer rights activists had also become a leading force in placing restrictions and regulations on corporations, including the attorney Ralph Nader, who burst on the scene with the publication of his 1965 book, *Unsafe at Any Speed: The Designed-In Dangers of the American Automobile*, prior to which things such as seatbelts were virtually unheard of in ordinary passenger automobiles. Nader's work drove American car manufactures to devote more attention—and money—to safety features designed to protect automobile consumers. Taken together, all of these efforts had pushed for a greater level of corporate accountability and reform over a wide range of issues during the 1960s and early 1970s.

As a consequence of these factors that had been applying pressure to the images and to the bottom lines of American corporations, business leaders began to push back through a series of organizational and ideological efforts. As Kim Phillips-Fein has shown, one of the first signs of this counter-offensive was launched through the U.S. Chamber of Commerce, in a 1971 memo entitled "The Attack on the Free Enterprise System," written by Lewis Powell, a former president of the American Bar Association and a board member of Philip Morris. Powell argued that although previous eras in American history had witnessed anarchist and communist efforts to overthrow American capitalism through armed revolt, "what concerns us now is quite new in the history of America. We are not dealing with episodic or isolated attacks from a relatively few extremists . . . Rather, the assault on the enterprise system is broadly based and consistently pursued. It is gaining momentum and converts." He noted that this assault was coming not only from "extremists on the left" but from "perfectly respectable elements of society: from the college campuses, the pulpit, the media, the intellectual and literary journals, the arts and sciences, and from politicians."[6] Although a small group of businessmen had been fighting the New Deal regulatory framework since the Great Depression of the 1930s, the 1970s marked a turning point in the concerted effort of business interests to reverse various regulations and laws ranging from consumer protections to environmental standards, and to convince the American public that they shared a common set of interests with the leading American corporations—in other words, what was good for Wall Street was good for Main Street. In this sense, in a historical parallel of the pro-business efforts of Lemuel Boulware, Reagan's old mentor at General Electric during the 1950s, the fight was on for the hearts and minds of the American public.

For Lewis Powell and for other business leaders, the thousands of university campuses across the country were the most important ideological battlefields, and during the 1970s nearly every leading American corporation increased their involvement in American higher education, for the purpose of guiding young people toward careers in business while attempting to convince them that capitalism was a righteous system—that for every advance of the free market, so too came an advance for the freedom of the individual. Through the use of new organizations such as "Students in Free Enterprise" (or SIFE, established in 1975), which was funded through corporate donations, campuses of American universities were gradually transformed from places that fomented critical thinking and political dissent into the training grounds of a new managerial and professional class of businesspeople. Building upon some of the counterculture ideas of self-expression and self-empowerment, new courses were integrated into university curriculums that glorified entrepreneurialism as an expression of freedom and individuality. As Bethany E. Morton writes,

> Here lay the answer to the postwar organization man, that otherdirected drone who, in the right light, looked disturbingly like his Soviet counterpart. Texts assigned in the new classes extolled the entrepreneur as a rare and special type, not content with the ordinary round of bureaucracy in corporate life. In this guise, the entrepreneur inherited the mantle of Jeffersonian virtue . . . a hero for the age of the mass office, a foil to sissified bureaucrats and the distant Shylocks of Wall Street.[7]

During the 1970s a new phenomenon was sweeping American universities: the business major. It was through this corporate push-back that the business suit came to challenge the tie-dye for dominance in the wardrobes of American university students. The massive increase of business administration programs in the nation's universities continued through the 1970s such that "by 1981, business majors outnumbered their classmates in all languages and literatures, the arts, philosophy, religion, the social sciences, and history combined," while non-business degrees were increasingly derided by a new type of university teacher, such as the Texas business instructor who chastised students who opted for the "sitting-under-a-tree-and-wondering-who-you-are routine."[8]

The corporate counterattack of the 1970s was not limited to the classroom. As a related component of this larger effort, the 1970s witnessed the emergence of several influential corporate-funded lobby groups, publishing houses, and "think tanks" geared toward generating support for conservative economic ideas as well as specific pieces of legislation. The new organizations also worked to establish alliances between business interests, intellectuals, politicians, and the American public. Some of them, such as the Heritage Foundation, were focused primarily on cultural

> ### Heritage Foundation
>
> During the 1970s, numerous organizations, foundations, research centers, and "think tanks" were created for the purpose of funding and supporting conservative ideas and their dissemination, including the Business Roundtable (1972), the Cato Institute (1974), the National Journalism Center (1977), and the Manhattan Institute for Policy Research (1978). The Heritage Foundation was created in 1973 by Republican congressional staffers Paul Weyrich and Edward Feulner and funded by the fortune of Joseph Coors (of Coors Brewing Company), with the self-expressed purpose to "formulate and promote conservative public policies based on the principles of free enterprise, limited government, individual freedom, traditional American values, and a strong national defense."
>
> One of the first significant efforts of the Heritage Foundation came in 1974, when it supplied financial and legal support to the parents of Kanawha County, West Virginia, home of West Virginia's capital and largest city, Charleston. Led by Alice Moore, Kanawha parents organized a boycott of the public schools and successfully worked to ban books that were associated with what they referred to as "secular humanism." Targeted books included those that taught sex education and biological evolution, as well as the works of black authors such as Nikki Giovanni, Alice Walker, and James Baldwin. The boycott was backed by the area's largest labor unions and received national media coverage.
>
> The Heritage Foundation capitalized on the grassroots social conservatism of the working class West Virginia parents, who were unlikely to be attracted to strictly economic forms of conservatism. James Moffett, a publisher of books that were banned by the Kanawha school board, noted,
>
> > Political conservatives don't have a lot of appeal on practical terms to the working class. They don't have much to offer them, and they know that ... They want to win them over, and the only way they can is through social or moral issues. [Liberals] leave themselves open by having nothing to offer people who want some kind of spiritual dimension and to whom liberals seem materialistic. Liberals have a big hole there and some adept conservatives are adept at taking advantage of it.[9]

issues, while others would set their sights directly on the economy. In terms of the latter, the most important was the Business Roundtable, a multifaceted organization designed to engage in pro-business public relations and lobbying efforts. The Business Roundtable was composed of the heads of the largest American corporations and focused on discrediting labor unions, cutting taxes (particularly for wealthy Americans), and rolling back government regulations on industry. But unlike the earlier efforts of Barry Goldwater, Ronald Reagan, and Lemuel Boulware, the Roundtable used dry and seemingly politically neutral concepts (such as "capital formation") rather than explicitly anti-labor or anticommunist rhetoric. The Roundtable argued that the "major problem of the American economy was a shortage of investment, [it] merely wanted to make policy changes that would encourage new economic growth ... No longer was the issue one of fundamental political principles or the rights of management; it was one merely of cost-benefit analysis."[10]

Toward this end, the Roundtable began to give support to what was, at the time, a relatively obscure set of ideas known as "supply-side" economics, which held that the main problem for the

> Arthur Laffer became synonymous with an idea that is closely tied to "supply-side" economics: the "Laffer curve," a visual representation of the idea that beyond a certain point, raising tax rates will *decrease* tax revenues because of the reduction in investment, jobs, and income caused by the tax increase. In other words, taxes tend to negate themselves. The idea is usually expressed in a simple graph, whose *x*-axis expresses the rate of taxation and whose *y*-axis shows the amount of potential tax revenue, the curve being an upside-down "u" shape. Reagan was enamored with the idea, and he used a similar simple graph to explain his rationale for lowering taxes during his July 27, 1981, televised address, which he delivered to promote the Kemp-Roth tax cut (see Figure 4.1).

American economy was the lack of investment in productive capacities, and that this deficiency could be overcome by a reduction of taxes, again, particularly for wealthy Americans. Supply-side economists argued that tax reduction would spur capital investment in such things as factories and new businesses, which would create jobs that would ultimately "trickle down" throughout the American class structure and lead to sustained economic growth. The idea was put into the language of scientific economic reasoning by Arthur Laffer, a professor of economics at the University of Chicago, and popularized in the pages of the *Wall Street Journal* by its associate editor, Jude Wanniski. Wanniski supposedly had a chance encounter with the Republican congressman Jack Kemp of New York in 1978, who was already a faithful reader of Wanniski's *Wall Street Journal* editorials. Kemp would soon co-sponsor legislation calling for an across-the-board tax reduction by an average of 30 percent.[11] A version of the bill, popularly known as the "Kemp-Roth tax cut," would be signed into law by Ronald Reagan as the Economic Recovery Tax Act of 1981 (this legislation will be discussed in greater detail in the concluding chapter), as "supply-side" ideology was perfectly consistent with the economic principles that Reagan had long advocated—namely, cutting taxes and eliminating government regulations of economic activity.

Figure 4.1 In an address from the Oval Office on July 27, 1981, President Reagan uses a cartoonish prop to explain the rationale and potential benefits of tax reduction. Courtesy of Ronald Reagan Library.

Thus, new organizations and ideas began to unify around efforts to reduce taxes and economic regulations, and these efforts would begin to find increasing resonance with the general public, who were also being squeezed between conditions of high unemployment and inflation. In one of the most striking events in the apparent unification of public "grassroots" anti-tax sentiment with the organizational and legislative efforts of the various ideas related to the development of supply-side economics, the 1978 "tax revolt" in California would once again show that the political winds in the United States tend to blow from west to east. Massive immigration into California, coupled with inflation, was driving a sharp increase in home prices. And because homeowners paid property taxes on the basis of the value of their homes, many California residents were facing situations in which their taxes were doubling or even tripling after the their homes were reassessed by the state. In some cases, residents were forced to sell their homes because they could not afford to live in them, even if they owned them outright. This situation led to the convergence of the public mood and the life's work of Howard Jarvis, a southern California industrialist who had once attempted to win the Republican nomination for the United States Senate in 1962. Since his failed bid for public office, Jarvis embarked on the crusade that would define the remainder of his life: opposition to taxes. Shortly after his failed 1962 Senate run, Jarvis created the United Organizations of Taxpayers (UOT), which unsuccessfully attempted to introduce tax limitation measures in 1968, 1971, and 1976, failing on all three occasions to gather the number of signatures required by California's ballot initiative process.

But beginning in 1977, Jarvis began to link the UOT to other organizations, such as the Los Angeles Apartment Owners Association, various chambers of commerce, and the People's Advocate, self-described as being "dedicated to educating the public regarding issues of taxation, government spending, financing, and local, state and national government structures," founded by Paul Gann. The People's Advocate would play a leading role in renewed efforts to gather signatures. Together, Jarvis and Gann authored another attempt to change the California constitution to place severe restrictions on property taxes. The resultant "People's Initiative to Limit Property Taxation," otherwise known as the Jarvis-Gann Initiative, proposed to restrict property taxes to only 1 percent of the value of a home and to return the values of all recently appraised properties to their 1975 levels. Furthermore, the initiative sought to make the process of raising taxes more difficult by increasing the required legislative majority from 50 percent to two-thirds, as well as limiting the condition under which the value of a property can be reassessed by the state. After Jarvis and Gann utilized "a phalanx of professional consultants to raise money and deliver Jarvis's message," the petition had the necessary number of signatures and the "People's Initiative to Limit Property Taxation" became Proposition 13, to be put before California voters.[12] Proposition 13 passed on June 6, 1978, by a two-to-one margin, with a 65 percent voter turnout rate. The victory for Jarvis and Gann resulted in an immediate 60 percent reduction in property taxes, effectively erasing the $6 billion California budget surplus.

In a televised press conference in the aftermath of his stunning victory, Howard Jarvis declared,

> We have a new revolution against the arrogant politicians and insensitive bureaucrats whose philosophy of tax, tax, tax, spend, spend, spend, and elect, and elect, and elect, is bankrupting we the American people, and the time has come to put a stop to it! ... The taxpayers have spoken. We have made clear our goals. Now we are watching you. It is your responsibility to [cut] the barrels of lard out of the government budget.

In language that calls to mind the rhetoric of conservative activists that would emerge some 30 years later in the context of the economic crisis of 2008 and the subsequent Obama presidency, after the passage of the measure, one supporter proclaimed, "I voted for Proposition 13 because I believe the taxpayers have just got to tell the government a message that we're mad as hell and we're not going to take anymore." Another Californian expressed a similar sentiment, "It's kind of like a Boston Tea Party. We're saying that we've had it!"[13]

Social scientists and politicians continue to debate the ramifications of the unprecedented slashing of the California property tax rate and massive reduction in the state's budget that took place after the passage of Proposition 13. The new legislation would have far-reaching implications for the balancing of California's budget, and would place an extraordinary pressure on publically funded institutions such as education and various social services. A common interpretation of the event is that it represented a "populist" and "grassroots" expression of anti-government and anti-tax conservatism that indicated an increasing appeal of libertarian economic ideas, such as those advocated by Ronald Reagan. However, Daniel A. Smith has argued that Proposition 13 was not at all a grassroots phenomenon, but an example of "faux populism," which he defines as "a populist-sounding message without the political mobilization of 'the people.' . . . Absent from faux populist movements is the active laboring and protest of the masses."[14] And in a way that would again bring to mind debates over the nature of the tea party movement during the Obama era, "While steeped in populist rhetoric, Prop 13 was centrally orchestrated, as Jarvis relied on large property interests for much of his financial and especially his organizational backing."[15]

Thus, Reagan was in a prime position to capitalize on the sentiment of Americans who saw the possibility of saving much-needed money through a reduction of taxes, as larger conservative forces that had long-advocated such goals were more than willing to lend their support. This series of political and ideological realignments that developed during the late 1970s was a unique moment in American social and economic history. Writing in 1980, Walter Dean Burnham argued, "It has never before happened in modern times that the Republicans have been able to take the offensive on bread-and-butter economic issues."[16]

In sum, the economic conditions of the late 1970s related to "stagflation" set in motion a conservative ideological and organizational response focused on wining the hearts and minds of the American public through educational programs in universities and high schools, as well as through new foundations and ideas such as supply-side economics. And regardless of whether such anti-tax expressions as the controversial

Proposition 13 initiative were truly "populist" or whether they were orchestrated expressions of elite interests, it was clear that by the end of the 1970s the ideas of the economic conservatives were taking hold among an increasing number of American citizens.

THE GEOPOLITICAL CRISIS OF THE CARTER ERA

In addition to the general economic crisis of the 1970s, there were several interrelated world events that appeared to indicate that the United States, the leading "superpower" since the end of the Second World War, was on a downward spiral in terms of its international influence. As with "stagflation," this geopolitical situation also created the conditions for the increased appeal of conservative ideology in the form of a renewed wave of anticommunism and militarism. And just as the economic problems of the 1970s undermined Carter's presidency, the perception that the United States had become "weak" would also work to ensure Reagan's victory in 1980.

The overriding theme of American foreign policy for much of the 1970s was a move in the direction of détente, a French word for "relaxation" used to describe the reduction in Cold War tension and a corresponding reliance upon internationalist and cooperative—rather than strictly militaristic—approaches to geopolitical conflict. The détente spirit was the result of several historical factors, but it most directly grew out of the American failure in Vietnam. As Howard Zinn has written, "From 1964 to 1972, the wealthiest and most powerful nation in the history of the world made a maximum military effort, with everything short of atomic bombs, to defeat a nationalist revolutionary movement in a tiny, peasant country—and failed."[17] This military failure combined with several other factors—the human and financial cost of the war and a general skepticism toward government that was also incubated during the Watergate affair—all of which led to a general reduction in the willingness of Americans to use military force around the world. Following a series of diplomatic meetings and negotiations between the United States, China, and Russia during the late 1960s and early 1970s, détente:

> promised to replace Cold War conflict with a peaceful international order ... the years between 1969 and 1977 witnessed no major foreign policy crises threatening war between the United States and either of its main Communist adversaries. The flow of trade, ideas, and people across societies increased by virtually all measures, especially in Europe and Asia.[18]

The spirit of détente was largely incomplete, but there is a general consensus among historians that during the 1970s, there was a reduction, rather than escalation of Cold War hostility. However, détente would prove to be but a fleeting moment of the Cold War era: it would come undone in light of several interconnected developments in Central America and the Middle East.

In this context, one of the first issues that destabilized détente was the fate of the Panama Canal, which had been under the control of the United States since it first opened in 1914. By the mid-1970s, there were several factors that had led the United States to consider the ratification of a new set of canal treaties that would cede control to the Panamanian government, including demonstrations for increased Panamanian autonomy as well as the prevalent "Vietnam syndrome" that balked at the possibility of another American military intervention, particularly in a "third world" country. The proposed treaties had widespread political support, not only from Presidents Ford and Carter, but from conservative leaders including Barry Goldwater and William Buckley. However, the public did not support a transfer of the Canal Zone to the Panamanian government, and several conservative organizations (including the Committee for the Survival of a Free Congress and Young Americans for Freedom) engaged in a series of high-profile criticisms of President Carter's efforts with the goal of preventing the treaties' ratification by Congress.

Jimmy Carter saw the treaties as a symbolically important gesture that would bolster the post-Vietnam image of the United States, as well as preserve regional stability in Central America. But for conservative activists, including Ronald Reagan, the treaties represented a capitulation to Panama's dictator, General Omar Torrijos, and a "giveaway" of American

> On January 13, 1978, Reagan appeared on a highly publicized episode of William Buckley's television program, *Firing Line*, to debate the issue of the Canal Zone treaties. Reagan and his debate partners, Pat Buchanan, Roger Fontaine, and Admiral John McCain Jr. (the father of John McCain III, the Arizona senator and 2008 Republican presidential candidate) opposed the treaties, while Buckley, James Burnham, George Will, and Admiral Elmo Zumwalt argued in support of their ratification. Years later, Buckley indicated that despite his public criticism of Reagan's position on the treaties, he had tacitly approved of it in light of the role he believed it played in leading to Reagan's 1980 victory. "My thesis was (and is) that if he had favored the treaty, he would have lost his hard initial conservative support. But if the treaty had *not* passed ... uprisings in Central America during the 1980 presidential campaign might have frustrated Reagan's hopes."[19]

geopolitical assets. Reagan roused his audiences with assertions that "We built it, we paid for it, it's ours, and we aren't going to give it away to some tinhorn dictator!" He also used the issue to argue that the Soviets would exploit the opportunity to further their interests in Central America. But conservative sentiment was never unified on the issue, and Reagan's position was criticized by both William Buckley and Barry Goldwater. Goldwater quipped that Reagan would also come to agree with his opponents on the issue, "if only he knew more about it." For Goldwater, Reagan simply misunderstood the situation, and he consistently demonstrated "a surprisingly dangerous state of mind, which is that he will not seek alternatives to military solutions when dealing with complex foreign policy issues."[20]

Another factor in the growing conservative reaction against détente had to do with the ongoing Nicaraguan Revolution, which was well underway when Carter took office in January of 1977. Nicaragua would serve as a prime testing ground for Carter's foreign policy, which placed an emphasis on the recognition of international human rights as well as the limitations of American military power. The Nicaraguan government had been a key American ally in Central America since the emergence of the Somoza dynasty in the 1930s. By the 1970s, it was Anastasio Somoza Debayle who ruled the country, and he was but one of several military autocrats who backed American political and economic interests throughout Latin America (and the world). Somoza's undemocratic regime was increasingly unpopular and had come under attack from several sources: the communist peasant revolutionaries of the Sandinista National Liberation Front, the Catholic clergy who practiced "liberation theology," as well as from union members and a coalition of anti-Somoza business interests.

As would be the case in other areas of his presidency, Carter was caught in the middle of the prevailing forces within party politics: his centrism satisfied neither the conservative Republicans nor the more liberal members of his own party. And in terms of global American power, Carter's emphasis on human rights was consistently faced with the realities of maintaining the country's geopolitical interests. In the case of Nicaragua, as Derek Buckaloo has argued, Carter sought to give a greater emphasis to human rights and democratic reforms without jeopardizing American economic interests. However, Carter's desire to support the opposition movements necessarily entailed the implicit recognition that it was the historic American backing for the Somoza regime that gave rise to the popular uprising in the first place. Buckaloo writes,

> Armed with human rights commitments and distaste for Somoza, the White House wanted to move Somoza toward an openness

> toward political change . . . without affecting the economic realities that underpinned both his regime and the revolution overtaking it . . . Thus, the White House remained caught between competing desires to apply human rights policies without fear and to avoid the revolutionary change that followed from those policies.[21]

After it became increasingly clear that Somoza's days were numbered, Carter sought to delay the revolution through dispatching a special peacekeeping force to supervise the transition to a new government. But after the Somoza regime fell to the Sandinista forces in July of 1979, Carter had little choice but to acknowledge the new democratic government.

> Left-wing liberals on Capitol Hill, still resentful of America's past support for Somoza, deplored Carter's initial efforts to forestall the Sandinistas' victory . . . Somoza's many American supporters, meanwhile, were furious at the administration's abandonment of an old ally. The idealist Jimmy Carter was left stranded, a hapless man in the middle.[22]

Thus, Carter struggled to reconcile his own supposed emphasis on human rights–oriented policies with the realities of American geopolitical interests as well as with the competing ideas of various political forces inside the United States—both liberal and conservative. But the uprisings in Latin America were only a precursor to the even graver challenges that would soon develop in the Middle East, where the United States would be forced to come to terms with a revolutionary force that was not only more fanatical and anti-American, but one that posed a direct threat to the American economy. Both the Iranian Revolution and the Soviet invasion of Afghanistan were two additional developments that would effectively seal Carter's fate and provide more fodder for Reagan and the conservatives.

As in Nicaragua, in Iran the United States had supported the totalitarian regime of the Shah, Reza Pahlavi, since the CIA-led coup of 1953, which overthrew the democratically elected Mohammad Mosaddegh after he implemented a program to nationalize the production of oil. In February of 1979, the Shah's regime came crashing down under the weight of a massive popular uprising that the American intelligence agencies entirely failed to see coming, believing at first that the Islamic fundamentalists were simply communist agents. In his history of the CIA, Tim Weiner argues:

> The idea that religion would prove to be a compelling political force in the late twentieth century was incomprehensible. Few at the CIA believed that an ancient cleric could seize power and proclaim Iran an Islamic republic. "We did not understand who

Khomeini was and the support his movement had," [Director of the Central Intelligence Agency, Admiral Stansfield] Turner said— or what his seventh-century view of the world might mean for the United States. "We were just plain asleep."[23]

With the fall of the Shah and the ascension of the fundamentalist Islamic cleric Ruhollah Musavi Khomeini, the United States had lost a cornerstone of its foreign policy in the Middle East and was faced with a potentially catastrophic threat to one of its primary sources of imported oil. On the heels of the revolution, OPEC nations exploited the chance to raise oil prices by nearly 20 percent, sending the American economy into yet another tailspin of rising prices and unemployment.

The anti-American sentiment of the Iranian Revolution of 1979 was always a feature in its development, although the various revolutionary factions were often in conflict. Shortly after the fall of the Shah, a group of Iranian leftist students raided the American embassy in Tehran and seized those who were working inside. To the relief of many Americans and certainly to Jimmy Carter, followers of the Ayatollah launched a quick rescue mission, expelling the students from the embassy and setting the Americans free. The CIA's Iran branch chief, stationed at the agency's headquarters in Langley, Virginia, was optimistic that the Islamic forces would generally act in line with American interests and as a bulwark against communist influence in Iran. "Don't worry about another embassy attack. The only thing that could trigger an attack would be if the Shah was let into the United States—and no one in this town is stupid enough to do that."[24] But as a consequence of his overthrow, the sickly Shah was sent into exile, where he made repeated requests to enter the United States to receive medical treatment. President Carter, who was fully cognizant of the dangers in admitting him, nevertheless caved in to political pressure and granted him permission to enter the United States on October 22, 1979. Two weeks later, on November 4 (exactly one year before the day of the 1980 presidential election) a mob of students loyal to Khomeini— not the leftists as before—again stormed the American embassy and captured 53 American hostages. The following day, Khomeini delivered a speech and declared that the United States was the "great Satan." The hostages were held for the remainder of the Carter presidency, for 444 days, and would play a crucial role in Ronald Reagan's 1980 victory.

In events that were in part related to the revolution in Iran, just to the east, in neighboring Afghanistan, the Soviet Union was on the brink of intervening in order to prop up the foundering pro-Soviet government, which had also come under threat by the rising influence of politicized Islam. Just as in Iran, American intelligence failed to anticipate the subsequent full-scale invasion of Afghanistan by the Soviet army that would take place in the concluding days of 1979. On December 19, a team of CIA specialists on the Soviet Union issued a report to President Carter that outlined why the Soviets were unlikely to invade; less than a week later, there were more than 100,000 Soviet troops on the ground in Afghanistan.[25] As Sean Wilentz has argued, "The motivations and intrigues behind the Soviet Union's entry into Afghanistan were always unclear." And despite later realizations that the invasion would be a leading factor in the disintegration of the Soviet Union, "at the time ... the overwhelming impression in Washington was that the invasion was a major and alarming escalation of Soviet militarism—a sign of the Kremlin's growing strength and ambition."[26]

Meanwhile, conservatives remained unwavering in their commitment to anticommunism and American military power. Carter's handling of the Nicaraguan and Iranian revolutions, as well as the Soviet invasion of Afghanistan, would set the stage for Reagan's calls for a return to a militarized approach to American foreign policy—an effort, as will be seen, that would culminate in massive new expenditures for the American military. But more immediately, Carter was again caught in the middle of competing forces within American politics, particularly within his own party. As a consequence of the Soviet invasion of Afghanistan, the president made a series of maneuvers that included pulling out of the Strategic Arms Limitation Treaty (SALT), cutting off American grain shipments to the Soviet Union, and boycotting the 1980 Olympic Games in Moscow. All of these efforts gave a short-term boost to his popularity, but also exasperated divisions within the Democratic Party on the eve of the 1980 election. In short, as Andrew Busch has argued:

> Carter was plagued by certain objective conditions. No campaign, no matter how well run, could change the inflation rate, undo the embassy seizure, or wish out of existence the decay of the Democratic coalition ... [or] write the conservative movement out of existence ... Campaigns, for the most part, must work with what they have. In 1980, Jimmy Carter didn't have much.[27]

The legacy of the Carter presidency can be encapsulated by two events of 1979. First, on April 24, after months of hand-wringing, Carter gave the order to attempt a dramatic rescue of the American hostages in Iran. They were to be saved by an invasion of Special Forces, who would descend by helicopter, free the hostages, and heroically return them to the United States. Instead, several of the helicopters had to turn around because of an uncooperative sandstorm, and after the mission had been aborted one of the helicopters crashed into a fuel plane, causing an explosion that killed eight American troops. Despite Carter's brief rise in popularity after his disclosure of the incident, for many, it was another sign of his incompetence in dealing with difficult international situations.

This perception would come to fruition in another televised address, less than three months later, as the president attempted to summarize the myriad of difficulties facing the United States. On July 15, he delivered his "Crisis of Confidence" speech (often referred to as the "Malaise Speech"), a disarmingly blunt message in which Carter concluded that:

> The new Iranian leaders, who despised Carter for his role in admitting the exiled Shah into the United States, were nevertheless pushed toward negotiations for the release of the American hostages in light of the Iraqi invasion of Iran that occurred in September of 1980, less than two months before the election. Reagan's team had become gripped by the realization that Carter might benefit from an "October surprise": a hostage release that would give him a sufficient boost to win reelection. The surprise never materialized, and instead the Iranians, in a final insult to Carter, released the remaining hostages on the day of Reagan's inauguration, January 20, 1981.

> all the legislation in the world can't fix what's wrong with America ... I want to talk to you right now about a fundamental threat to American democracy ... It is a crisis of confidence ... that strikes at the very heart and soul and spirit of our national will ... In a nation that was proud of hard work, strong families, close-knit communities, and our faith in God, too many of us now tend to worship self-indulgence and consumption.

In terms of the energy dimension of the crises, the president made specific proposals: he called upon Americans to limit their consumption by building "conservation into your homes and your lives at a cost you can afford," and he hoped that through massive federal investment ("money, a lot of money"), the United States would be able "to achieve the crucial goal of 20 percent of our energy coming from solar power by the year 2000." In essence, according to Jimmy Carter, the United States had lost its way. There were indeed crises, but they were not strictly economic or political. Instead, they ran "much deeper than gasoline lines or energy shortages, deeper even than inflation or recession." The heart of the problems in America was America itself. It was an unusually frank assessment for a president to make; it was an assessment that was not well received.

THE 1980 PRESIDENTIAL ELECTION

The 1980 presidential election was thus shaped by long-term developments in American politics and society as well as by those that were more immediately related to the crises of the 1970s. The ways in which these developments would come to influence the election can be seen both in the interparty contests that took place between Jimmy Carter, Ronald Reagan, and the Independent candidate, John Anderson, as well as in the intraparty battles to win the nominations. Although conservative dominance in the Republican Party was essentially complete by 1980, there still remained viable debates taking place among the candidates that would temper the party's conservative turn and present a challenge to Reagan's quest for the presidency. And before Jimmy Carter would be able to face his Republican opponent, he too would need to stave off challenges from within the ranks of his party.

As an indicator of his general unpopularity, Carter was challenged by Senator Edward Kennedy for the Democratic presidential nomination of 1980. Kennedy, the brother of a president and of a senator, both of whom had been assassinated, seemed an obvious choice. He had a well-established political network and high levels of popular support, both of which he utilized in order to strengthen his bid for the presidency. But Kennedy faced two difficulties, the first of which was personal: in addition to his notorious drinking habit, he was culpable in the 1969 death of Mary Jo Kopechne, a young woman who died in his car after he drove it off the side of a Chappaquiddick Island bridge and fled the scene. But perhaps more than this incident, Kennedy's 1980 challenge ultimately failed because, as a representative of the liberal wing of the Democratic Party, he essentially pinned his hopes on a revival of liberal ideology and the New Deal coalition. This was a losing proposition for two reasons.

First, as we have seen, the coalition that had held the New Deal in place since the 1930s was in tatters by the end of the 1970s: the break-up of the Solid South and the growing social conservatism of the American working class had undermined the extent to which many traditional Democratic voters still adhered to the basic tenets of American liberalism. Thus, Kennedy likely overestimated the extent to which the American people would support his calls for a national health care program, a key component of his agenda. Additionally, in light of the economic crises of 1970s, American business interests had also largely turned against the framework of the New Deal, as:

> business elites . . . were persuaded that the time had passed for the coalition Kennedy now championed . . . [and] continued social

spending impressed most businessmen as a luxury that needed to be abandoned. To them, accordingly, the preferred way out of the budgetary impasse was the *de facto* elimination of the Democratic party's mass constituency.[28]

In sum, although Kennedy remained personally popular, his candidacy received a lukewarm response from "ordinary Americans" as well as from business interests. After Kennedy announced his candidacy, Carter is said to have angrily quipped, "I'll whip his ass." Although he eventually *did*, the whipping was not as thorough as he would have liked. And the divisions within the Democratic Party did not bode well as Carter looked ahead to the prospects of his reelection in the general election.

Carter's handling of the 1970s crises displayed a technocratic realism (which many observers interpreted as pessimism) that called for a scaling-back of American ambitions and expectations. Carter's style played perfectly into Reagan's hands. Since his days at General Electric, Reagan had mastered the art of a sunny disposition and a simplistic oratory style that explained why things "are the way they are," and how they will certainly get better. Reagan bridled at the call for Americans to reduce their consumption, to pause for self-reflection, and to downsize their expectations. Reagan had not held public office since he left the governor's office in California in January of 1975, although he delivered his counterpoints to Carter's doom and gloom through speaking tours and through the use of the broadcasting medium that first launched his career as a public figure: radio.

During the five years that separated Reagan's governorship from his 1980 victory, he delivered more than a thousand radio commentaries that were broadcast across the country. Through these addresses, Reagan planted himself firmly in the center of the conservative nexus that included social, economic, and anticommunist forms. The commentaries ranged from light-hearted topics to more serious questions of foreign and domestic policy. Reagan offered his characteristically optimistic and simple solutions to complex social and economic problems: he defended free market capitalism by noting a high school classroom experiment involving the distribution of candy; he illustrated the virtue of work through his retelling of a children's story about an industrious hen and a goose that considered itself a minority and refused to work; he warned against the dangers of the Canal Zone "giveaway," which would lead to a Caribbean domino of communist expansion—or, as he said elsewhere, that the global communist conspiracy had been "extending its tentacles deep into Central America"—and he lamented the loss of God in the nation's public schools.[29] Reagan's messages were inextricably linked to the ideological and organizational breakthroughs in the development of American conservatism that had taken place in the United States since the 1950s, and it was his task to transform these developments into a winning presidential candidacy.

Although the election may have been Reagan's to lose, his road to the White House would not be without obstacles. Many commentators believed that Reagan, despite his grandfatherly demeanor and experience as the Governor of California, was still a dangerous extremist who possessed little if any substantive knowledge of government and world affairs. Like Carter, Reagan faced challenges from within his party, as the struggle between the moderates and conservatives shaped the battle for the Republican nomination. Although at the outset of the nomination process there were as many as seven candidates, including the former president Gerald Ford, by the summer of 1980 it had become clear that the contest was essentially going to be fought between Ronald Reagan on the conservative side, and George H.W. Bush representing the moderate tradition. Bush won the first big contest in the Iowa caucuses and established himself as the early favorite. Throughout the campaign, Bush attacked Reagan over his economic policies, charging that his "supply-side" theories were nothing less than "economic madness." Bush dubbed Reagan's proposals "voodoo economics," because the ways they would purportedly heal the American economy seemed magical rather than rational. Indeed, in 1980, Republicans were far from being united on economic and tax issues.

However, as with the failed candidacy of Edward Kennedy, Bush's momentum was largely undone by the fact that he represented the Northeastern moderates, a dying contingent within the party. As Gerald Pomper has argued, "Bush's strength was confined to the Northeast and the traditional liberal factions of the party. These results ... were unsatisfactory in a party that had been shifting its geographical base to the South and West, and its ideological center toward conservatism."[30] Reagan faced a second and lesser threat from John Anderson, one of the few remaining liberal Republicans in the House of Representatives. After Anderson failed to win the primary in his home state of Illinois (Reagan's place of birth), he had little hope of winning the Republican nomination. Shortly after his loss in Illinois, Anderson dropped out of the Republican contest and entered the race as an independent candidate. He would ultimately win slightly less than 7 percent of the popular vote, and although he may have taken some votes away from Carter, his candidacy proved to be a negligible factor in the election.

And so it was that Reagan won the Republican nomination, although his choice for vice president remained unknown. At the Republican

National Convention in Detroit, a rumor circulated that Reagan would choose Gerald Ford as his running mate, creating an unprecedented "super ticket" that would potentially result in two presidents occupying the White House—what some commentators referred to as a "co-presidency." But these rumors were short-lived as Reagan rejected the possibility on the grounds that it would create an unclear division of power. Instead, in a move that contrasted Barry Goldwater's purging of the moderates in 1964, Reagan selected George H.W. Bush, his political rival during the party primaries, to serve as his running mate. The selection provided two obvious benefits: it united the party behind Reagan's candidacy while adding to his appeal in the Northeastern states, the historic stronghold of moderate—not conservative—Republicanism.

Reagan and Carter were locked in a virtual dead heat in the summer of 1980, with various national polls conflicting in their predictions. Carter's chances had been hurt by the twin crises, although he benefited from the ongoing negotiations with Iran over the release of the hostages, the improvements in the economy, and a recent Senate report that exonerated his brother, Billy, from charges of "influence pedaling." Polls conducted by Reagan's campaign indicated that Carter had come back from his early deficit and held a narrow edge in the weeks leading up to the election. As a response, Reagan's strategists pushed for a last minute one-on-one debate. According to Sean Wilentz:

> Carter's counselors were divided on whether to go ahead. [Carter's consultant] Pat Caddell feared Reagan's ease and verbal skills, but the majority ... thought that ducking the debate would do the president great harm and that ... Carter's superior grasp of the issues would defeat Reagan's slick salesmanship. For once, Carter did not listen to Caddell—and his decision may have cost him the election.[31]

The debate between Carter and Reagan took place in Cleveland, Ohio, on October 28, only one week before the election, and indeed Reagan's responses to questions about various aspects of foreign and domestic policy appeared both confident and moderate, in contrast to Carter's more technical and stiff demeanor. After Carter launched an attack on Reagan's opposition to Medicare by listing his own proposals that would ensure "catastrophic health insurance" to prevent sick Americans from being "wiped out economically," Reagan delivered one of his iconic lines, "Well, there you go again." It was a response that exuded confidence and pointed to Carter's negativity and overly technical invective, echoing the perception of the president's "Crisis of Confidence" speech. Reagan deflected Carter's criticism through a rhetorical maneuver for which the president simply had no effective response. For Lou Cannon, "The response was funny, irrelevant—and thoroughly authentic. It did not answer Carter's point, but it revealed a functioning intellect. What was on display that October night in Cleveland, as in the Carter and Reagan presidencies, were different types of intelligence."[32] The encounter is widely believed to have eased public fears over Reagan's supposed extremism, giving him an advantage in the days just prior to the election. In the interpretation of Gerald Pomper, "Because Reagan showed himself to be competent, because he made no errors, and because he appeared pleasant and reasonable, he was able to settle any doubts raised during the campaign. By not losing, he won."[33]

Despite the general consensus that Reagan won the debate, no one predicted the overwhelming margin of his victory that occurred on November 4. Reagan received nearly nine million more popular votes than Carter, a margin of 51 percent to 41 percent. But the real landslide occurred in the Electoral College as Reagan won every state but six, running away with more than 90 percent of the electoral votes, a stunning 489 to 49 margin. In his introduction to the *New Right Papers*, Robert Whitaker summarizes the forces that gave Reagan his historic victory:

> The combination of voters which elected Ronald Reagan . . . consisted of two major elements. The first was the basic Republican presidential vote, about forty percent, which has suffered little in defection even in Democratic landslides. The second element, which turned the election into a rout, was made up of voters who, in earlier days, were overwhelmingly Democrats. These former Democrats are largely white southerners and blue-collar northerners.[34]

These "Reagan Democrats," as they would become known, did not appear out of the blue in 1980: their increasing conservatism had been shaped by the three branches of American conservatism since the end of the Second World War and was solidified by the social conflicts of the 1960s and 70s.

A closer inspection of the composition of Reagan voters in 1980 shows that he successfully tapped into blocs that had been historically loyal to the Democratic Party, particularly union members and southern whites. The results of the 1980 election can also be understood in light of the falling support for Carter, as the votes he received from a wide range of demographic groups plummeted in comparison to those he had received in 1976. Nearly 60 percent of voters who were members of a labor union (or who had a household member in a labor union) voted for Carter in

1976, but in 1980, he received only 47 percent of their votes to Reagan's 44 percent (Ford received 39 percent of the labor vote in 1976). Additionally, there was no single age bracket that voted for Carter in higher levels than they had in 1976, and among those between the ages of 30 to 44, his support fell dramatically from 49 percent to 37 percent. Rural, urban, *and* suburban voters also turned away from Carter in 1980. In the case of the latter, he received 53 percent of the suburban vote in 1976, but only 37 percent in 1980.

Additionally, with the exception of Carter's home state of Georgia, Reagan carried the South. In 1976 Carter's southern heritage had led him to victory in the region, although he narrowly failed to win a majority of southern white voters. In 1976, he won 46 percent of the southern white vote, and 54 percent of the total southern popular vote, but in 1980, both of these figures dropped significantly. In 1980, Reagan won 51 percent of the southern vote, and 60 percent of the southern white vote. In retrospect, Carter's 1976 success in the South, like the support he received from northern union members, was only temporary. In all, Reagan won significant support from nearly every demographic group in the country, with one glaring exception: black Americans, whose distaste for the Republican Party remained steady. Carter, as he had in 1976, received an overwhelming 82 percent of the black vote nationwide, with Reagan receiving only 14 percent.[35]

The results of the 1980 congressional elections were also striking for what they revealed about the rising power of conservative Republicanism. The party gained control of the Senate for the first time in nearly 30 years, as "156 years of [Democratic] senatorial seniority were washed out."[36] And in the House of Representatives, which had been a historic bastion of Democratic power since the New Deal, Republicans made substantial gains, winning 33 seats and reducing the Democratic majority to its lowest margin in the twentieth century (at the time). The 1980 House elections marked the end of the careers of a number of prominent Democratic congressional leaders, including several committee chairmen. According to Charles Jacob:

> The portentous lesson that should be drawn is that in 1980 the Republicans rediscovered the joys of party. That is, a concerted, centrally directed and funded national party campaign was conducted to persuade the electorate to "Vote Republican. For a Change." ... The strategy worked to a great extent, producing a large conservative minority and the promise of a conservative congressional majority [in the future].[37]

The outcome of the 1980 elections, both in Reagan's stunning victory and in the Republican gains in Congress, was an outcome for the party that exceeded even the most optimistic of expectations.

CONCLUSION

The Carter presidency, coming as it did in the aftermath of the Watergate affair, is best understood as a political anomaly, an outlier that does not conform to the larger conservative trends. In other words, Reagan's landslide victory solidified the rightward drift, which had been slowly developing in American politics and society since the end of the Second World War. In terms of the South and the "Republicanization" of the region, party strategists recognized this important point. In 1978, the Campaign Director of the Republican National Committee, Charles Black, concluded that:

> If Jimmy Carter had been from Wyoming, Ford would have carried the hell out of the South [in 1976]. Carter is a temporary phenomenon . . . Watergate hit us harder in the South in '74 than in any region—wiped us out locally. Then, the Carter phenomenon—we were delayed a decade, maybe, but long-term, things are looking up.[38]

Reagan had succeeded in bringing together the three forms of conservatism under the banner of the Republican Party, and he also benefited from the timing of the crises of the 1970s. But as he had done in his Cleveland debate against Carter, in his inaugural address Reagan presented himself as an inclusive moderate.

> It is not my intention to do away with government. It is rather to make it work—work with us, not over us; to stand by our side, not ride on our back. Government can and must provide opportunity, not smother it; foster productivity, not stifle it.

And indeed, it remained to be seen to what extent Reagan's presidency and legacy would match his image as an icon of the American conservative movement.

CHAPTER 5

The Image and Reality of Ronald Reagan and American Conservatism

For much of the twentieth century, Americans had the reputation of being uninterested in politics. In 1929, Robert and Helen Lynd published *Middletown*, an ethnographic account of a Midwestern town on the eve of the Great Depression. The citizens of "Middletown" showed little concern for political issues or with politics as a profession. "In view of the apathy or repugnance with which many Middletown residents have come to regard politics," they wrote, "it is perhaps not surprising that the 'best citizens' are no longer to be found among Middletown's public officials."[1] A generation later, the sociologist C. Wright Mills published *White Collar: The American Middle Classes*, his analysis of the increasingly professionalized and bureaucratic labor force—the "cheerful robots," as he came to call them. Mills saw the middle class as the basis of a larger political apathy prevalent in the United States during the so-called consensus era: "The most decisive comment that can be made about the state of [American] politics concerns the facts of widespread public indifference."[2]

The accuracy of these characterizations of earlier historical eras is debatable, but today few observers would likely describe Americans as being indifferent or apathetic when it comes to politics or to their political opinions. Since the end of the Second World War, politics in the United States has become increasingly polarized, and a major factor in this polarization has been the rise of the American conservative movement. The ideas that defined this marginal force of the 1950s continued to gather momentum during the 1960s and 70s to such an extent that conservatism would ultimately come to challenge—if not outright replace—liberalism as the dominant political ideology in the United States. This is not to imply that the rise of conservatism was a linear or absolute process, nor does it mean that an inflexible conservative vision remained unchanged over time. During these years there were many interacting and overlapping ideas put forward by politicians, businessmen, religious leaders, social activists, and ordinary citizens, all of which contributed to the ways in which an increasing number of Americans came to interpret the world around them. And the various streams of American conservatism would ultimately come together under the Republican Party, whose leadership, with varying degrees of commitment and success, had attempted to shepherd the movement for the purposes of creating "the conservative equivalent of the New Deal Coalition."[3] Although the new coalition was unprecedented in American history, it was composed of older traditions, the three historic tributaries of the American conservative movement: anticommunism, social conservatism, and libertarianism.

In this sense, the post-WWII decades can be understood as a time of broad realignment between the nascent conservative factions in American society and their reflection within the Republican Party. In 1964 for example, conservative activists took control of the party apparatus, although they—and their candidate, Barry Goldwater—remained far more conservative than the ordinary American voter. Later, during the late-1960s and early 70s, President Nixon made great strides in fostering the new coalition, through what he referred to as the "silent majority." But Nixon's conservatism was more cultural than economic. Instead of rolling back the New Deal, he generally expanded state regulation of the economy. As Meg Jacobs has written:

> [Nixon] appealed to millions of Americans who had taken a cultural turn to the right, believing it was time to reign in women's liberation, the sexual revolution, and the student protest movement against the Vietnam War . . . On the other hand, the idea that government should protect the public from corporate excesses, especially in hard times, still had a strong hold on American politics.[4]

Prior to Reagan's election, economic conservatism was not yet part of the winning Republican equation. The economic problems of the 1970s functioned to legitimize the economic component of American conservatism in the minds of many American people. Throughout the remainder of the decade, the conservative movement came into its full institutional and ideological fruition. Although its progenitors are to be found in the 1950s and 60s, as Bruce Schulman and Julian Zelizer have argued, it was the "Big Bang of the 1970s" that unleashed the various components of the movement as we know it today:

> The 1970s unlock the mysteries of today ... The policies, social movements, leaders, and institutional changes that emerged out of this decade fundamentally reshaped America by moving the nation out of the New Deal and Cold War period into a new era defined by the conservative movement.[5]

Thus, by 1980, a number of historical conjunctures had aligned to set the stage for Ronald Reagan's victory. Not only had the conservative movement reached its maturity, but the Republican Party had largely been on the sidelines during the political and economic crises of the late 1970s, after which it was poised to reclaim power in Washington, continuing several trends that were temporarily obscured during the aftermath of the Watergate scandal. Most significantly, the Unites States resumed its rightward drift in national politics. The alternation of Republican and Democratic hegemony is not simply a natural cycle of "back-and-forth" between the only two viable options in American politics. Rather, key elections have marked political turning points—such as what occurred in 1980, with another example being Roosevelt's election in 1932—that correspond to large-scale restructurings of American politics, economics, and society. In short, although every presidential election is certainly an important event in American history, it is also true that "some [presidential] elections are more important than others."[6] Indeed, the crises of the late-1970s had galvanized American conservatives, and just as in 1966 when he won the governorship on the heels of the Watts Riots and the Berkeley free speech movement, Reagan's positions, which had once been widely perceived as extremist, would morph into what a growing number of voters would see as practical solutions to a variety of social problems—and this transformation was achieved with only the slightest of modifications to Reagan's articulation of his views. In other words, Reagan did not retool his beliefs to fit the times; instead, the public became increasingly receptive to his peculiar brand of nostalgic and ecumenical conservatism that united the movement's diverse components.

But the apparent vindication of Reagan and his conservative ideas that took place in 1980 did not necessarily convince contemporary observers that his victory was a significant—let alone *critical*—moment in American history. Writing shortly after Reagan's election, in an essay entitled "The Meaning of the Election," the political scientist Wilson Carey McWilliams concluded bluntly that "It didn't mean much." He argued:

> The election of 1980 did not try our souls; it tried our patience. Reagan had a zealous following and there were some Carter loyalists, but most voters saw little to recommend either ...

> A good many voters marked their ballots in a mood of revulsion, and masses of citizens stayed home.[7]

In a similar vein, only three weeks after the election, the historian Richard Wade perhaps put it best: "This is no big cosmic thing; Carter was a lousy president."[8] These assessments are based upon an interpretation of the election that emphasizes the short-term frustration that arose during the context of the sudden crises of the late-1970s, and of the widespread dissatisfaction—both among conservatives *and* liberals—with the way in which Carter handled those crises. From this perspective, Americans merely "threw the bums out," as has happened countless times in democratic political systems around the world. And in this sense, Reagan's victory was quite unremarkable.

It is only after we are removed from the immediate events surrounding the 1980 presidential election that it becomes possible to appreciate the ways in which it represented a critical moment in American history. In order to absorb the significance of Reagan's victory, a wider historical point of view—one that incorporates the historical developments that occurred both before *and* after Reagan took office—is essential. Indeed, as the years have passed since 1980, historians and social scientists have increasingly recognized the centrality of Reagan's election not only to the conservative movement and to developments taking place within the United States, but to global processes of economic and political restructuring. David Harvey argues that Reagan's election was one of "several epicenters [from which] revolutionary impulses seemingly spread and reverberated to remake the world around us in a totally different image."[9] Likewise, the historian Andrew Busch concludes that "the election of 1980 is one of only a handful of twentieth-century elections that must be considered truly pivotal."[10] But Harvey, a prominent figure of the international left, and Busch, a conservative American historian, are unlikely to agree upon the defining features of the Reagan era, and why his victory was so important. This point can be extended beyond Harvey and Busch: although there is a growing recognition that Reagan's victory was somehow significant, there is no such consensus as to why this was so. Unsurprisingly, conservatives and those sympathetic to Reagan tend to highlight the restoration of global American power (symbolized by the apparent American "victory" in the Cold War that occurred shortly after Reagan left office), as well as strong spurts of domestic economic activity during the 1980s, particularly after 1982. On the other hand, those who are critical of Reagan—but who nevertheless recognize the importance of his presidency—tend to highlight economic deregulation and rising inequality, ballooning deficits, and an escalation of Cold War militarism as among the key features of his presidency. Both of these characterizations share an interpretation that places Reagan's election at the center of a larger set of changes taking place in American society.

Adding to the ideological difficulty of making an assessment of Reagan's election is the fact that his relationship to his own policies and to the events of his presidency is also a matter of dispute. Conservative authors not only tend to look favorably upon the Reagan administration, its policies, and the events that unfolded in light of those policies, they also assign a leading role to Reagan in formulating those policies and in shaping those events. As we will see, one of the best examples of this tendency is the characterization that places Reagan's policies as being central to the collapse of the Soviet Union. Conversely, Reagan's detractors have not only criticized the policies of his administration, they characterize Reagan himself as lacking substantive knowledge of government and world affairs, and as being distant from the formulation of the policies and subsequent events that occurred during his administration of the presidency. The Democratic advisor Clark Clifford once referred to Reagan as an "amiable dunce," personally friendly but professionally incompetent. Mike Royko, a journalist for the *Newark Star Ledger*, famously dubbed Reagan "the Ted Baxter of American politics"—a reference to the good natured yet dim-witted news anchorman character on the *Mary Tyler Moore Show*. Indeed, these sorts of charges have been so daunting that even authors who are sympathetic to Reagan have been compelled to defend his involvement in policy making and his intellect more generally. In one such recent book, the first chapter is entitled, "Was Reagan a Dummy?"[11] Instead of taking one or the other side in these various characterizations, it is possible to probe another aspect of Reagan's life and presidency, which can in turn add a deeper layer of meaning to his contribution to American history and to his relationship to the conservative movement.

RONALD REAGAN AND THE PRESENTATION OF REALITY

One of the most illuminating frameworks for coming to terms with Ronald Reagan has to do with the relationship between his background in the performing arts and the ways in which he used these skills to transcend the realities and limitations of himself as an individual and as a politician. In his founding work in the field of dramaturgical sociology, *The Presentation of Self in Everyday Life*, the Canadian sociologist Irving Goffman discusses how individuals willfully or subconsciously shape the impressions of others through the process of presenting a "definition of the situation" that constructs a "presentation of reality" specific to the audience with which they are interacting. Goffman used the metaphor of a stage performance to capture the ways individuals attempt to "play the part" that is expected of them. He noted that the performance of an "actor" may or may not correspond to objective reality. Despite this gap, the "audience"—and occasionally the "actors" themselves—can become "sincerely convinced that [their] impression of reality ... is the real reality."[12] Reagan studied sociology at Eureka College, and although he graduated more than 20 years before the publication of Goffman's work, this framework, which emphasizes how individuals "construct reality," is a useful one to explore some of the characteristics that defined Reagan's personal qualities, his presidency, and his relationship to the conservative movement.

Before Reagan became a politician, he was an actor. Through decades of scripted performance in radio, film, and public relations work for General Electric, he mastered the art of "presenting reality" to a wide range of audiences: sports fans, film patrons, General Electric employees, and ordinary citizens. His background in the performing arts allowed him to develop his renowned oratory skills, which, as we have seen, directly contributed to his stunning electoral landslide in 1980. Indeed, Reagan would earn the nickname the "great communicator." One of the primary strengths of Reagan's communication skills rested in his ability to use images, words, and dramatic physical settings to "present reality" much in the same way an actor uses props to support a production in the theatre or on screen. Occasionally, Reagan was astoundingly successful. Such was the case during his 1987 speech at the Brandenburg Gate, against the backdrop of the Berlin Wall, where he delivered one of the most memorable lines of his political career, "Mr. Gorbachev, tear down this wall!" Gil Troy has referred to this speech as "a great moment of political theater."[13] At other times, Reagan's staged presentations backfired, such as his highly orchestrated 1985 visit to a cemetery in Bitberg, Germany, a move that some interpreted as being sympathetic to Nazism.

Reagan himself was quite cognizant of the relationship between his careers as a performer and politician. He once remarked, "There have been times in this office when I've wondered how you could do the job if you *hadn't* been an actor."[14] Reagan habitually drew parallels between his career in Hollywood and the highest levels of global political power. As he attempted to interpret complex political problems, he often tried to "make them fit the experiences of Hollywood or Sacramento. Sometimes this worked. More often it produced bizarre results, such as [his] comparison of Soviet leaders to Hollywood producers with whom he had negotiated as head of the Screen Actors Guild."[15] Through similar juxtapositions of stagecraft and statecraft, Reagan often seemed to blur the boundaries between performance and authenticity; put somewhat differently, between image and reality. Indeed, many who spent significant time in his presence have remarked that it seemed impossible to know the "real Reagan," that "Reagan's inner life remained a mystery even to his friends."[16] It was as though Reagan *had* no private life, only the shell of a public image.

Reagan's background in performance dates to his high school days in Dixon, and it was through his early career in radio that he began to develop the art of presenting reality. One afternoon as Reagan was broadcasting a baseball game between the Chicago Cubs and St. Louis Cardinals for WHO, the communication feed was lost (it was common for radio announcers, who were not always physically present in the stadium, to receive a telegraph of the events of the game before embellishing them for their listening audience). Reagan was suddenly without any knowledge of what was happing in the game. In a testament to his quick thinking and improvisational abilities, he simply invented the details: for nearly eight minutes, he called foul balls and even described in detail an imaginary child who ran out onto the field. Reagan had

> a talent for turning any small incident into a colorful story in the retelling ... [A] good part of Dutch's enthusiasm ... was his ability to envelop himself in what he was doing. The astounding realness of his play-by-play came out of this skill. No one ever could have guessed that Dutch Reagan was not in the press box at the game in Chicago.[17]

This blurring of reality with the imaginary continued in Reagan's film career, as he tended to be cast essentially *as himself*. In his first film project as a professional actor, *Love is on the Air* (1937), Reagan, a former small town radio announcer, was cast as a character named Andy McLeod, who was, of all things, a radio announcer from a small town. Upon his first arrival on set, Reagan's co-stars thought he had been given a specialized outfit for the part, not realizing that he was in fact wearing his own clothing. "The rakish hat he brought from Des Moines, the polka-dot ties, the slightly rumpled three-piece suit, even the large Eureka class ring he wore looked so much like the part that Nick Grinde, the director, thought they had come from the wardrobe department."[18] Thus, as Michael Rogin observes, Reagan began his film career by "playing the role he had left behind to come to Hollywood."[19] Later in his career, during the Second World War, as he was involved in the production of army propaganda films such as *This is the Army* (1943) and *Rear Gunner*

(1943), Reagan, who was an enlisted soldier, played the part of a member of the American military. During the making of these films, civilians, who had been hired to appear as extras, were given costumes that were indistinguishable from the uniforms worn by actual members of the military. This led to farcical situations during off-screen production breaks, as enlisted soldiers would mistake the costumed civilians for actual officers, giving salutes where they were undeserved; some officers were dismayed by the lack of respect they were shown by their apparent subordinates, who were actually unsuspecting civilians.[20]

During the 1966 gubernatorial campaign in California, Sam Yorty, the conservative Democratic mayor of Los Angeles and political rival of Governor Pat Brown, did not believe that Reagan would make an effective politician because of the apparent ambiguity between his career in film and his political persona: "I must say in all truthfulness that I never feel sure whether he's acting out a part, or whether he really says these things himself . . . I always wonder if he's got a script writer, and he's playing on the stage."[21] Upon his election as Governor of California, Reagan—who readily admitted he knew little about how governments actually worked—was asked about his priorities, agenda, and the style with which he planned to govern. In a stunning reply, he said that he was unsure because "I've never played a governor before." Reagan was perhaps making a tongue-in-cheek reference to the charges of Governor Brown, who, in his television campaign, had tried to use Reagan's acting background against him: "Ronald Reagan has played many roles. This year he wants to play Governor. Can you afford the price of admission?"[22] Regardless of whether Reagan intended sarcasm, the quip appeared to underscore the extent to which he relied upon his training as an actor to inform his style as a politician and, to his detractors, to indicate that he was thoroughly unprepared for the responsibilities of the office. Even in defeat, Reagan's biographers have noted how his background as an actor shaped his disposition as a politician. In the context of his hard-fought battle with Gerald Ford in 1976, in which Reagan was defeated for a second time in his quest for the presidency, Gary Wills has written:

> Some might think Reagan takes defeat almost too well. He seems at best deferring, as he was the hero's friend in the movies . . . Unlike many actors, Reagan never wanted to become a director. He took direction well. He carried the same attitude into political performance.[23]

The porous boundaries between Reagan's actual biography and the roles he played on screen flowed in both directions. His enduring nickname, "the Gipper," was derived from a part he had played as an actor. In 1940, he was cast as George Gipp, an actual college football player for Notre Dame whose death inspired his team to victory. From his deathbed, Reagan, as Gipp, hoped that his teammates would remember him and "win just one for the Gipper." Reagan used the line throughout his political career, including at the 1988 Republican convention when he urged his vice president, George H.W. Bush, to "go out there and win one for the Gipper!" It may have been that Reagan simply enjoyed quoting from films, as he did during the 1980 Republican primary debate in New Hampshire. In a controversial move, he had attempted to include the other candidates, rather than to limit the debate to just him and Bush, a condition that had been agreed upon in advance. When one of the moderators threatened to turn off his microphone and effectively cancel the debate, Reagan stood up and thundered, "Mr. Green, I'm paying for this microphone!" The line was widely seen as a key to Reagan's success in the Republican primaries, although unbeknownst to most Americans at the time, it originated in a movie whose plot centered upon the story of a presidential candidate. In the 1948 film, *State of the Union*, Spencer Tracy portrayed a presidential hopeful who, at a contentious news conference, had come under verbal attack from the assembled members of the press. As the cameras were rolling, he commandeered the microphone and defiantly declared, "I paid for this broadcast!"

Elsewhere during the 1980 campaign, as Reagan was championing a renewed militarism in foreign policy, he embellished the respect given to the American military around the world. In order to make his point, Reagan recalled a newsreel he claimed to have seen of the Spanish Civil War, in which an American naval company was not fired upon as they marched through the streets of a Spanish port town after rescuing one of their own. It was not without good reason that military historians who heard Reagan's retelling of the story could not locate the particular event in the archives: their search led them instead to the 1938 film, *Blockade*, starring Henry Fonda, which depicted a nearly identical scene.[24] Reagan had either intentionally misled his audience to manufacture a patriotic sentiment, or he had simply confused a movie with actual history. Regardless, these were not isolated incidents, but part of a pattern in which Reagan tended to blur the boundaries between real and imaginary events.

Much has been made about the origins of Reagan's sudden announcement in 1983 that called for the creation of a space laser system that would function as a missile shield to protect the United States against a Soviet nuclear attack. The subsequent Strategic Defense Initiative of 1985 (SDI, more popularly known as the "Star Wars" program), is the most controversial defense initiative of Reagan's presidency. Not only has the program had a dubious record of success after nearly 30 years of continued funding, but Reagan's idea for the program, as several authors have argued, was not inspired by the realities of applied laboratory science, but the science fiction of Hollywood. In 1940, Reagan starred in *Murder in the Air*. In the film, he portrayed arguably his most well-known character, Brass Bancroft, who was "an American secret agent charged with protecting a newly invented super weapon, the 'Inertia Projector,' capable of paralyzing electrical currents and destroying all enemy planes." Fitzgerald goes on to note that Reagan's inspiration for the SDI shield may also have been rooted in the Alfred Hitchcock film, *Torn Curtain* (1966), "which revolves around an attempt to develop an anti-missile missile. In it Paul Newman declares, 'We will produce a defensive weapon that will make all nuclear weapons obsolete, and thereby abolish the terror of nuclear warfare.'"[25]

In his deconstruction of the simulacrum that surrounded Reagan's attempted assassination, Michael Rogin has taken this intersection of reality and imagery one step further. John Hinckley's motivation to assassinate President Reagan was inspired by the character portrayed by Robert De Niro in *Taxi Driver* (1976), and it was no coincidence that Hinckley attempted to carry out his sinister plan on the morning of the Academy Awards. Reagan had been scheduled to make a brief speech at the ceremony later that evening, and had pre-recorded his remarks several days earlier, so the attempted assassination did not preclude his appearance (as a response to the shootings, the awards were postponed for one day). Although Reagan had been shot and was clinging to life in a Washington hospital, he appeared on screen at the Academy Awards in good health. Rogin writes:

> On March 30, 1981, only two months into his presidency, a crazed gunman, John Hinckley Jr., shot Reagan outside of the Washington Hilton Hotel. Reagan nearly died, although the severity of his wounds was unknown to the public at the time. The shooting had a contradictory impact on the Reagan presidency: on one hand Reagan's popularity soared, while his newfound heroic status led his advisors to the conclusion that he was politically invincible. On the other hand, the assassination attempt was a major disruption during the period of Reagan's acclimation to the office of the presidency.

> The television audience watching a screen saw a Hollywood audience watch another screen. One audience saw the other applaud a taped image of a healthy Reagan, while the real president lay in a hospital bed. Reagan was president because of film, hospitalized because of film, and present as an undamaged image because of film.[26]

Just as there is a perpetual tension between the image and reality of Reagan as an actor and as a politician, there is a parallel ambiguity in what several authors have referred to his "mythological" status among conservative Americans and historians. Although Reagan's reputation and image is essentially synonymous with American conservatism, upon closer inspection he did not always reflect the values and philosophies of the movement he supposedly epitomizes. Indeed, Reagan's career as a politician, including his presidency, both conformed to the expectations of his conservative supporters while at the same time defying preexisting judgments that he was a rigid conservative ideologue. The continuities— as well as the cracks between Reagan's reputation and his record—can be seen in relation to the three dimensions of American conservatism: social conservatism, anticommunism, and libertarianism.

RONALD REAGAN AND SOCIAL CONSERVATISM

There were several forms of social conservatism that shaped the development of the larger conservative movement during the postwar decades. Of these various manifestations, two deserve special attention. The first is the role of race and racism. Racial issues, particularly though not exclusively in the southern states, played a key role in the transformation and growing success of the Republican Party during the postwar era. The second crucial form of social conservatism is the evangelical movement, or religious right, which also played an important part in mobilizing and expressing conservative sentiment, particularly during the 1970s in relation to many different issues. Understanding Reagan's association to these two forms of social conservatism is thus a first step in an examination of his overall relationship to the American conservative movement.

During his childhood, Reagan received a piece of wisdom from his father Jack, who forbade him to attend a screening of *The Birth of the Nation*, a 1915 film celebrating the Ku Klux Klan and depicting the supposed anarchic consequences of black political power in the South. In light of their anti-Catholicism, Reagan's father (who was Catholic) loathed the Klan and was unequivocally opposed to their activities. "The Klan's the Klan, and a sheet is a sheet, and any man who wears one over his head is a bum," his father once told him. Reagan's brother John developed a boyhood friendship with one of the relatively few black children in Dixon, Winston "Wink" McReynolds, who made frequent visits to the Reagan family home.[27] In his 1990 autobiography, Reagan asserted that "I'd grown up in a home where no sin was more grievous than racial bigotry."[28] After he moved to California, Reagan remained sympathetic to civil rights issues. In 1946 he narrated a radio program, "Operation Terror," in which he denounced racial violence and the Ku Klux Klan, proclaiming, "I have to stand and speak, to lift my face and shout that this must end, to fill my lungs to bursting with clean air, and so to cry out, stop the flogging, stop the terror, stop the murder."[29]

But despite this background, beginning in the late 1940s, at which time the anticommunist issue had become a leading concern of the Hollywood studios and of the federal government, Reagan began to distance himself from civil rights issues because he feared being suspected as a communist sympathizer. As Stephen Vaughn has argued, it was during Reagan's tenure as president of SAG that his views on race began to shift:

> Within the context of the Guild ... he was a liberal on race issues, to be sure. But in a broader sense his views underwent a transformation as he became increasingly anticommunist ... By the time he stepped down as president of the Guild [in 1952] he had become much less willing to challenge authority over discrimination than the NAACP and many others in the civil rights movement.[30]

Reagan's relationship to issues of racial equality was central to his entry into politics, which occurred in 1964 as he gave his support to Barry Goldwater. As we have seen, the single most important dynamic in Goldwater's failed campaign was his self-professed conservative "extremism," highlighted by his opposition to the Civil Rights Act of 1964. It was this factor that explains Goldwater's success in the Deep South—an unprecedented showing for a Republican presidential candidate—and which severed the historic association between black Americans and the Republican Party. This stunning development paved the way for future Republican success in the southern states, from Nixon's southern strategy of 1968 and 1972, to the later rise of the southern congressional conservatives during the 1980s and 90s. In a 1995 address at the Goldwater Institute, Nancy Reagan spoke of what she considered to be the direct lineage from Goldwater to Reagan, which set the stage for the "Republican revolution" of 1994 led by Next Gingrich, who had orchestrated the party's first majority in the House of Representatives in more than 40 years. She claimed:

> The dramatic movement of 1995 is an outgrowth of a much earlier crusade that goes back half a century. Barry Goldwater handed the torch to Ronnie, and in turn Ronnie turned that torch

over to Newt and the Republican members of Congress to keep that dream alive.³¹

Like Goldwater, Reagan opposed the Civil Rights Act of 1964 (Reagan also opposed the Voting Rights Act of 1965, which Goldwater supported). Also like Goldwater, Reagan claimed to oppose the civil rights legislation because of his commitment to constitutional principles, rather than on the grounds of racism.

Conservative political strategists long recognized that their success depended on linking the supporters of George Wallace and Barry Goldwater with a broader swath of conservative sentiment that was not overtly racist. Echoing the analysis of Kevin Phillips, Melvin Bradford argued in the pages of *National Review* during the contentious 1976 Republican primaries:

> Until it is possible for us as conservatives to bring the Wallace electorate and the 85 percent of Republicans who are conservative under one tent, without losing many from either company, and without defrauding either, we are condemned to be governed perpetually by the old familiar left-liberal coalition.³²

Reagan walked this tightrope very carefully. Throughout his 1976 challenge to Gerald Ford, he repeated a sensationalized anecdote about a "welfare queen" whose fraudulent entitlement claims had cheated the government—and by extension, more dutiful tax-paying Americans—out of their hard-earned money. Reagan presented the story to manufacture outrage among his white audience, and to lend support to his economic programs that would slash state spending. Through these sorts of appeals, which juxtaposed racial animosity and economic issues, Reagan successfully appealed to the "Wallace vote," but with a much lighter touch than did Goldwater or Wallace himself. In contrast to these earlier conservative extremists, Reagan was cordial, patient, and good humored, the "sunny salesman of the white backlash."³³

Despite the clear stylistic differences that distinguished Reagan from his conservative predecessors, his presidential candidacies nevertheless continued the process of realignment that was so deeply related to the issue of racism. Reagan's tenure as president did little to lessen criticisms that he was, at best, uninterested in the concerns of black Americans or black people around the world. As a consequence of Reagan's economic conservatism, which would strip federal funding of a range of services in poor communities, Walter Dean Burnham has argued that black Americans were "among the chief losers of the 1980 election."³⁴ Most significantly in the international arena, Reagan consistently defended white rule in South Africa and vetoed the Comprehensive Anti-Apartheid Act of 1986, which had widespread bipartisan support. The law eventually imposed numerous sanctions on the apartheid government after Reagan's veto was overridden by Congress (see Primary Document 12).

But by 1980, racial issues were no longer explicitly at the forefront of American electoral politics in the same way they had been in preceding decades, and Reagan only addressed them when he was pressed, tending instead to avoid them whenever possible. In this sense, by the time Reagan was elected president, he had successfully distanced himself from the white backlash, but his association with it was already a *fait accompli*. In terms of his "presentation of reality," Reagan appeared as a racially neutral candidate—even one who personally loathed racism. In his autobiography, he lamented, "the myth that has always bothered me most is that I am a bigot who somehow surreptitiously condones racial prejudice . . . for some reason, this myth stuck with me when I became president."[35] Reagan's political success was shaped by the important role race and racism played in the development of the conservative movement. Thus, Reagan was able to denounce racial prejudice while simultaneously relying upon the racism embedded within parts of the conservative movement. Unlike Wallace, the "angry man's candidate," or Goldwater "the extremist," Reagan's strength was in expanding the base of the conservative movement by capitalizing upon issues that might appeal to a cross section of diverse conservative interests, rather than to a more narrow subsection of conservative voters.

And so it was with the religious right, which had made great strides during the 1970s, during which time it emerged as another dimension of the social conservative faction. As William Martin has argued, Reagan was an unlikely candidate for the adoration of the newly politicized evangelicals for several reasons. "Divorced, remarried, and a subpar parent of children who were hardly models of piety, he first won fame in the movie and television industries, both regularly excoriated by conservative Christians for their contribution to moral decay."[36] During his tenure as Governor of California, Reagan had signed into law the Therapeutic Abortion Act of 1967, at the time the most liberal abortion law in the United States. Furthermore, in 1978, Reagan's opposition to California Proposition 8 (popularly known as the Briggs Amendment), was widely seen as one of the key factors in the defeat of the ordinance that would have banned gays and lesbians from working in the California public school systems. Adding to the difficulty of winning evangelical support in the context of the 1980 election, both of Reagan's opponents, Jimmy Carter and John Anderson, were self-professed "born again" Christians who "made concerted efforts to win the support of various evangelical groups."[37] When he was asked about his own beliefs during the 1976 campaign, Reagan did not know what it meant to be "born again." Chuck Colson recalled that "Reagan shrugged, like the fellow had landed from Mars. He didn't know what he meant."[38] But Reagan quickly learned to master "the code," the veiled messages and rhetoric of the evangelical right having to do with personal morality, abortion, and "family values":

> There were lots of ways in which, through direct access and perhaps through some code words, [Reagan] conveyed to them that he was one of them, and that they could count on him to deliver what they were looking for in their national and in their community life.[39]

Reagan, like Nixon, understood that evangelical support would be important both to his own election as well as to the conservative coalition on a national scale. After 1976, he increasingly addressed issues that were important to conservative evangelicals in his radio broadcasts, such as "Religion and Education" (see Primary Document 8), in which he criticized the federal "expulsion" of God from public schools, linking the issue with a more general sense of "government interference," which itself was a cornerstone in larger conservative economic and philosophical principles.

However, if Reagan's relationship to the evangelicals remained vague, during his ascent to the White House, he landed upon a specific issue that he could use to demonstrate his new identification with their movement. Because it wove together issues of civil rights, taxes, and federal regulation, the question of tax exemption for religious schools in the South was at the ideological nexus of the conservative coalition. At the heart of the issue was Bob Jones University, located in Greenville, South Carolina, which, along with countless other southern private schools, flourished after the desegregation rulings of the civil rights era. As Kim Phillips-Fein has written:

> [In] the early 1950s, there were fewer than 150 Christian schools in the country; by 1981 there were more than 18,000. It was very difficult to tell the Christian schools apart from those that had been founded solely in an attempt to evade racial integration, which actively refused to admit black students.[40]

Bob Jones University did not admit unmarried black students prior to 1975, after which time it continued to adhere to a rigid policy that forbad interracial dating (a policy that would remain in place until 2000). University administrators defended these policies—the exclusion of black students as well as the later ban on interracial dating—based on their interpretation of biblical passages that called for the separation of races. Because it was classified as an educational institution, Bob Jones also received an exemption from federal taxes. Towards the end of the 1960s, civil rights activists began to challenge the constitutionality and financial legality of these institutions, arguing that their discriminatory character should disqualify them from tax exemption. After a series of legal battles and continuing conflict throughout the 1970s during the Carter presidency, the Internal Revenue Service (IRS)—independent of the legislative or judicial branches of the federal government—began to institute new restrictions on tax exemption for institutions that were considered "segregation academies."

It was against this historical backdrop that the Republican Party had incorporated the tax exemption issue into its 1980 party platform, and Reagan frequently used it in his campaign literature, explicitly promising to "oppose the IRS's attempt to remove the tax-exempt status of private schools by administrative fiat."[41] Throughout his campaign, Reagan frequently spoke about other issues that were dear to the evangelical movement. These attempts reached a crescendo at the Religious Roundtable meeting in Dallas, on the eve of the 1980 election. On their way to the meeting, Pastor James Robison, "a televangelist and rising star of the Christian Right," prepared Reagan for his address:

> [He] suggested that Reagan make the statement, "I know this is nonpartisan, so you can't endorse me, but I want you to know that I endorse you." Reagan loved the line and he received an enthusiastic response when he repeated it to the 2,500 people in attendance. The quote became a signal to many politically conservative evangelicals and fundamentalists that Reagan was with them in heart and soul.[42]

In the same speech, Reagan promised to end the federal government's "unconstitutional regulatory vendetta" against religious schools. Cries of "Amen" and "God bless you Ronnie!" echoed throughout the auditorium. In a press conference after his brief remarks, Reagan was asked about the subject of Darwin's theory of evolution (in Dallas public schools during the 1970s, evolutionary science was presented alongside biblical creationism as an equally valid explanation of life on earth). Reagan replied, "I have a great many questions about evolution. And I think the recent discoveries over the years have pointed out great flaws in it."[43]

Thus, upon his victory, the stage was set for Reagan and his new administration (including a new IRS commissioner, Roscoe Egger, and a new Treasury secretary, Don Regan) to intervene in the situation as several court cases, including one specifically involving Bob Jones University, slowly made their way to the Supreme Court. In December of 1981, Senator Trent Lott sent a memo to President Reagan, requesting that he order the IRS to end its revocation of tax exemptions for southern religious schools, which Reagan promptly did. In a clear victory for the southern conservatives and the evangelicals, on January 8, 1982, the Treasury and Justice Departments announced that they had reversed the IRS decision and ordered the restoration of tax exempt status for Bob Jones University. But the victory proved to be short lived, as was Reagan's standing among many in the evangelical community.

The restoration of tax exemption for Bob Jones University set off a wave of protest from a diverse set of secular and religious leaders. Samuel Rabinove, the legal director of the American Jewish Congress, claimed that it was "appalling that the administration would allow this important benefit to institutions that are racially discriminatory." More than one hundred lawyers in the Civil Rights Division of the Justice Department:

> signed a letter of protest . . . declaring that the new policy "violates existing federal civil rights laws." When a Justice Department spokesman announced that anyone against the policy was "welcome to leave," over twenty lawyers resigned their positions . . . NAACP executive director Benjamin Hooks declared the decision . . . "opens the door to every racist element in the nation to discriminate . . . and to do it with a subsidy from the government's pocket."[44]

Reagan would quickly yield to the mounting political pressure. Four days after the Treasury and Justice Department announcements, the president declared he would send a bill to Congress outlawing tax exemptions for any racially discriminatory institution, essentially reversing his earlier position and implicitly acknowledging that Bob Jones University was not simply a religious school. Reagan's change of heart represented "a clear slap in the face to the Christian Right" only one year into his administration; Bob Jones III, president of Bob Jones University, declared that Reagan was a "traitor to God's people."[45]

There were other issues that would drive a wedge between Reagan and the evangelical movement. In 1981, he nominated Sandra Day O'Connor as the first woman to serve on the Supreme Court, fulfilling one of his campaign pledges. O'Connor's nomination was clearly inconsistent with the expectations of social conservatives, particularly the religious right, who strongly opposed O'Connor's nomination in light of her support for both abortion rights and the Equal Rights Amendment. Evangelical leaders were incensed. Paul Weyrich (of the Moral Majority and the Free Congress Foundation) and Pat Robertson (of the Religious Roundtable, at whose convention Reagan had delivered his "I endorse you" line just prior to the election) criticized the O'Connor nomination and claimed that by focusing on economic rather than social issues, Reagan was taking evangelical support for granted. According to Daniel Williams:

> [E]vangelicals quickly discovered that Reagan's actions did not always live up to his soaring oratory. While Reagan gave Christian Right activists warm endorsements whenever they met with him ... he showed only limited interest in making their causes a legislative priority.[46]

The religious right became disenchanted by the gap that existed between Reagan's rhetorical support for their movement and the fact that he rarely took concrete action in promoting their interests. David John Marley has argued that this gap between the image and reality of Reagan's dealings with the religious right had a bifurcating effect on the evangelical movement. On one hand, it lowered the expectations of leaders such as Jerry Falwell, who had remained loyal to Reagan throughout his presidency. Falwell and other faithful Republicans were satisfied with the symbolic support they received through White House visits and photo opportunities. After Reagan's presidency, Falwell dissolved the Moral Majority and became a fringe figure of American politics. On the other hand, Reagan's presidency redoubled the commitment of other evangelicals to become a stronger political force in Washington. For example, Pat Robertson was so alienated by Reagan's presidency—but inspired by the possibilities of wielding political power—that he founded various political action committees and lobby groups immediately after Reagan left office, including the Freedom Council and the Christian Coalition. Robertson himself ran for president in 1988 as a direct result of being left "out in the cold" by Reagan. Marley concludes:

> In the final analysis, the Christian Right was not nearly as important to Ronald Reagan as he was to them. He gave them legitimacy in the public square, and they gave him their votes and the status of a living saint. He made public statements supporting prayer in school and opposing abortion, but limited his political activity on those issues. Instead he held prayer breakfasts,

declared 1983 as the year of the Bible, and hoped such symbols would satisfy this particular constituency.[47]

Although the religious right was not satisfied by the symbolic support they received from Reagan, they nevertheless became what Paul Frymer refers to as a "captured group" of the Republican Party, which he defines as "any politically relevant group that votes overwhelmingly for one of the major political parties and subsequently finds the primary opposition party making little or no effort to appeal to its interests or attract its votes."[48]

RONALD REAGAN AND ANTICOMMUNISM

As with the gaps that separate the image from the reality of his relationship to social conservatism, there are similar disconnects that surround Reagan's anticommunism. As we have seen, more than any other single factor, anticommunism was the guiding force of Reagan's political evolution during the postwar period: it molded his distaste for the New Deal, which he had once supported, and soured him to civil rights issues, to which he had once been sympathetic. Indeed, Reagan's early liberal inclinations, however tenuous, crumpled under the weight of anticommunism during the late 1940s and 50s.

But this is not to imply that Reagan's anticommunism remained static following his break from liberalism, as two historical developments contributed to the shaping of this facet of his ideology, as well as the public perception of it, during the period surrounding his presidency. Prior to the 1980 election, the Cold War was being waged under the fragility of détente, a brief and unique moment in the larger history of American–Soviet relations. And by the conclusion of Reagan's presidency, the Soviet Union found itself in an economic and political crisis the severity of which became evident during the unforeseen implosion of the empire in the years immediately after Reagan left office. These conditions that served as bookends to the Reagan presidency—détente and the collapse of the Soviet Union—were significant for the shaping of Reagan's anticommunism for several reasons. First, the collapse of the Soviet Union, a dramatic event that was entirely unforeseen by foreign policy observers, has clouded perceptions of the nature of Reagan's anticommunism, particularly among conservative historians and citizens, who have tended to equate it with the triumphalism related to the American "victory" in the Cold War. For example, William F. Buckley has written that, "It was Ronald Reagan, history is certain to confirm, who suddenly forced the leaders of the Soviet Union to look in the mirror . . . soon after that, the rot began to take hold in the Soviet Union."[49]

> The Union of Soviet Socialist Republics began to rupture in light of the contradiction between internal democratic reforms, economic liberalization, and pressure for increased autonomy for the Soviet satellite states on one hand, coupled with the attempt to preserve the highly centralized and authoritarian political system on the other. After a failed military coup in August 1991, which sought to reassert the power of the Communist Party apparatus, Russian President Boris Yeltsin consolidated his leadership over populist democratic reform efforts, while the popularity of Mikhail Gorbachev plummeted. On December 7, 1991, Yeltsin convened with his Belarusian and Ukrainian counterparts and moved to abolish the Soviet Union and replace it with a decentralized confederacy of independent states. By the end of the month, most of the Soviet republics had voted to join this new political entity, the Commonwealth of Independent States (CIS). A short time later, on December 25, Gorbachev resigned as General Secretary of the Communist Party, effectively transferring power to Yeltsin and marking the end of the Soviet Union.

This interpretation is indicative of the larger conservative assessment that equates Reagan's approach to foreign policy—whether in his public statements or through the military buildup of the 1980s—as having pressured the leadership and resources of the Soviet Union to such as extent that it ultimately collapsed. Other authors have referred to this visionary strategy as Reagan's "grand design" to bring about the fall of the Soviet Union and the end of the Cold War. But there is no evidence that Reagan consciously advocated this strategy during his presidency, or that his advisors had envisioned increased American pressure as leading to the destruction of the Soviet Union. It was only *after* the Soviet Union collapsed that Reagan administration officials began to take credit for a strategy they had never publically articulated during the time that Reagan was in office. As Michael Schaller has pointed out, as Reagan was running for his second term in 1984, he actually moved away from his earlier hard-line posturing and adopted an outlook that emphasized coexistence, rather than "American victory" or Soviet collapse.[50]

In fact, Reagan's approach to the Soviet Union was fraught with contradiction and inconsistency. Initially, détente strengthened Reagan's resolve to take a confrontational approach with Soviet leadership. Immediately upon his inauguration, Reagan moved to reverse détente by:

> initiat[ing] one of the largest military buildups in American history. He also refused to conduct amicable relations with Soviet leaders

until they changed their behavior at home and abroad . . . Reagan believed reform would occur only when communist regimes faced forceful pressure, including threats of war.[51]

One of the primary ways Reagan confronted the Soviets was through a moralistic posturing and a religious-infused language. Speaking to the National Association of Evangelicals in March of 1983, for example, he famously asserted in his "Evil Empire" speech that in the Soviet Union, "Morality is entirely subordinate to the interests of class war . . . let us pray for those who live in totalitarian darkness . . . they are the focus of evil in the modern world." Reagan also pushed for a resumption of proxy wars against communist forces around the world, in what would become known as the "Reagan Doctrine."

Despite his hard-line public stance against the Soviets, Reagan's anticommunism was often marked, however, by a gap between public policies and rhetoric on one hand, and his personal desire to engage Soviet leaders on the other. For example, in his first press conference after taking office, Reagan openly "condemned détente and branded Soviet leaders as liars and criminals committed to world domination," but he also simultaneously worked to assure Soviet ministers that his comments were "not meant to offend anyone."[53] There was a similar disparity reflected in Reagan's general policies toward the Soviet Union. As James Graham Wilson argues, Reagan:

> spoke about eliminating nuclear weapons from the Earth yet also called for a massive buildup of America's nuclear arsenal. He publicly questioned the legitimacy of Soviet leaders just as he was making entreaties with them for peace. He advocated policies that would discriminate against the Soviet Union

Shortly after Reagan's 1985 State of the Union address, the journalist Charles Krauthammer coined the term "Reagan Doctrine," which he defined as the guiding principle of the president's foreign policy that "proclaims overt and unashamed American support for anti-Communist revolution."[52] Historians have debated the extent to which the "Reagan Doctrine" was an intended and consistent policy of the administration, although during the course of Reagan's presidency American military and logistical support was given to anticommunist fighters around the world, including in Afghanistan, Nicaragua, Mozambique, Angola, and Cambodia. These efforts marked a break with the "Vietnam syndrome" and with principles of détente fostered during the Nixon and Carter eras.

economically, but he also lifted a grain embargo his predecessor had imposed.[54]

Further, despite his bellicose appearance, upon his first personal encounter with Mikhail Gorbachev in November of 1985, Reagan engaged his new counterpart with what his advisors had dubbed his "little green men" speech. Reagan mused that peace would be easier to achieve "if there was a threat to this world from some other species, from another planet, outside this universe." If such an extraterrestrial threat materialized, Soviets and Americans would quickly "forget all the little local differences that we have between our countries and we would find out once and for all that we really are all human beings here on this Earth together."[55] Thus, on one hand, Reagan was consistently and sharply critical of Soviet communism in his public speeches. But his public admonitions were belied by his personal outreaches to Soviet leaders, as well as his increasing openness to various weapons reductions treaties to such as extent that he was even criticized by leading conservative writers such as William Buckley, who feared that Reagan was being manipulated by Gorbachev. A 1985 *National Review* editorial warned that Gorbachev is "humorous, well traveled, well educated, articulate, intelligent. We seldom trouble to remind ourselves that to the extent he is all these things, he is a more dangerous man than he otherwise would be." As Robert Samuel has argued, "Conservative intellectuals loathed arms-control talks with 'the Evil Empire' . . . [they] wanted to triumph over the Soviet Union, not make deals with them."[56] These ambiguities are indicative of a larger pattern in Reagan's approach to foreign policy defined by his occasional collapsing of the distinction between his personal desires and the policies of his administration. Reagan's failure to draw clear distinctions between "Reagan the president" and "Reagan the man" put him into contradictory and potentially vulnerable political positions, none more so than during the unfolding of the Iran-contra affair.

Shortly after the 52 American hostages were released from Iran, they were received at the White House in a televised "welcome home" ceremony. Although Reagan and his advisors intended the ceremony to mark a break with the Carter administration and to establish a more optimistic national mood, in fact, "by receiving [them] in the heart of the White House, Reagan, like Carter, elevated their welfare to the highest level of national concern."[57] And in the following years, the hostage issue in the Middle East continued to be a political headache for Reagan and his administration, as a number of Americans were kidnapped and would be held in Lebanon.

Iran–Contra Affair

In light of the top-secret espionage, the involvement of shadowy international arms merchants, and the document shredding that surrounded the public discovery of the scandal, its complete details remain unknown. However, journalists, historians, and congressional panels have established the main contours of the Iran-contra affair, a complex series of events and cover-ups that led to resignations and criminal charges for several Reagan administration officials, while raising the question of impeachment for President Reagan himself. At the center of the affair were two very different sets of circumstances: seven American hostages in Lebanon on one hand, and on the other, the ongoing American effort to supply weapons and funding for anticommunist militias in Central America known as the "contras" (short for *la contrarrevolución*, Spanish for "counter-revolution"), especially though not exclusively in Nicaragua.

Despite the congressional restrictions known as the Boland amendments, which explicitly forbad American support for the contras, Reagan administration officials secretly continued to send weapons and money through the CIA and a covert agent who worked as an aide at the National Security Council, a Marine named Oliver North. To circumvent the ban on funding the contras, North embarked on a national fundraising campaign in order to solicit private donations from wealthy anticommunists, including the beer magnate Joseph Coors.

The second half of the conspiracy grew out of the earlier hostage crisis in Iran (see Chapter 4), as President Reagan remained adamant that his own presidency would not be derailed by similar scenarios in the Middle East. To this extent, Reagan was committed to "do whatever it takes" to free the seven American hostages being held by a militant Shia faction in Lebanon. Following the unrelated hijacking of TWA flight 847 in June of 1985, the White House was increasingly open to pacifying terrorists to secure the release of the hostages. This led to a series of dramatic and illegal arms shipments from the United States, through Israeli proxies, to Iran, with the explicit purpose of trading the weapons for the hostages. At least one of the shipments, which occurred on November 25, 1985, had the written authorization of President Reagan.

During the summer of 1985, Oliver North landed upon what he later referred to as a "neat idea": to use the money generated by the weapons sales to Iran to fund the contras in Nicaragua, thus linking two illegal and covert operations on opposite sides of the world. North's "neat idea" ran smoothly for several months, but the affair slowly came to light simultaneously in the Middle East as a result of the ongoing large arms shipments, and in Nicaragua after a CIA plane loaded with weapons was shot down along the Costa Rican border on October 5, 1986.

By all accounts, Reagan experienced deep personal anguish at the thought of Americans being held captive. But the problem arose when he was torn between his personal concern for the hostages—particularly after having met with their families—and the policy of his own administration, which was explicitly *not* to negotiate with terrorists. "The danger was that if left to his own good intentions, the president would confuse human interest with national interest, mistaking gestures for policies, romantic themes for strategies, and immediate emotional gratification for long-term strategic gains."[58] Reagan officials and CIA operatives first began a series of private fundraisings to buy the freedom of seven American hostages being held in Lebanon, as a way around the contradiction between Reagan's personal desire to free the hostages and the formal policy of non-negotiation. However, this tactic soon gave way to more concerted—and progressively more illegal—administration efforts to work for their release. As the arms shipments to Iran (along with North's "neat idea" of diverting the proceeds of the sales to Central American anticommunists) came to light, Reagan was under immense pressure to clarify his role in the complex affair, something he appeared unable to do. Throughout several press conferences and televised addresses in November of 1986, Reagan could not specify which of the CIA "findings" (written authorizations by the president) he had signed, whether or not he had authorized arms shipments to the Iranian government, and what had been the role of Israel.

Months later, at the conclusion of the Tower Commission investigation, which had been organized to conduct a formal inquiry into the scandal, Reagan delivered a televised address from the Oval Office. Reagan spoke:

> A few months ago I told the American people I did not trade arms for hostages. My heart and my best intentions still tell me that's true, but the facts and the evidence tell me it is not . . . what began as a strategic opening to Iran deteriorated, in its implementation, into trading arms for hostages. This runs counter to my own beliefs, to administration policy, and to the original strategy we had in mind.

The president could not distinguish between his "heart," his "best intentions," and the "facts and evidence" from the "original strategy" he apparently formulated. Jane Mayer and Doyle McManus argued that "The Reagan qualities that the public had once found endearing—the relentless optimism, the impatience with the dry specifics of policy—now threatened to turn against him."[59] Indeed, President Reagan's dualistic approach to the office that had defined his approach to the Soviets—and in which he tended to separate the personal from policy—had become a direct threat to his presidency.

ECONOMIC CONSERVATISM AND "REAGANISM" AFTER REAGAN

Ultimately, the Iran-contra affair did not lead to Reagan's impeachment, and after the dramatic televised coverage of the congressional hearings, it was largely forgotten by the American public in light of the larger developments of the late 1980s. For many Americans, this period was marked by a renewed optimism that stemmed from two primary sources. The first had to do with a thawing of Cold War tensions, reflected in the blossoming relationship between Reagan and Gorbachev. In this sense, it was ironic that Reagan's role in Iran-contra, which grew out of his staunch opposition to communism, was overlooked because of an improvement in American–Soviet relations and Reagan's warm relationship with his Soviet counterpart. The second source of optimism was the improving economy, for which Reagan and his economic philosophy largely received credit.

As we have seen, the American economy began the 1980s under the shadow of inflation, unemployment, and low growth, otherwise known as "stagflation." For Reagan, the problems that plagued the American economy during the 1970s were simple: the excessive regulatory state and burdensome tax structure had shackled American productive capacities, which could only be liberated through tax cuts and various forms of deregulation. As he famously declared in his inaugural address, "In this present crisis, government is not the solution to our problem; government is the problem." The anti-government component of Reagan's ideology was a constant feature of his worldview; he had been emphasizing it since his first political speech in 1964 for Goldwater. Just as Reagan had overturned détente through the "Reagan Doctrine" and a renewed antagonism with the Soviets, so too would he begin to dismantle the policies and the prevailing wisdom of the New Deal by making efforts to substantially reverse nearly 50 years of the dominant economic thinking. Toward this end, Reagan made several important contributions in a number of economic areas, including a rolling back of various market regulations, a combative posture toward organized labor, as well as an issue that had been at the historic center of his personal libertarian convictions: taxes.

Shortly after his election, Reagan delivered upon one of his central campaign promises. On August 13, 1981, he signed into law the Economic Recovery Tax Act of 1981 (more popularly known as the Kemp-Roth

The PATCO Strike

The Professional Air Traffic Controllers Organization (PATCO) was formed during the late 1960s as a response to several factors: the growing popularity of commercial air travel and concomitant demands upon the air traffic controllers, the inability of existing unions to understand the highly technical aspects of the profession, the efforts of the Federal Aviation Administration to impose labor regulations on the controllers, as well as the larger surge in unionization among public sector workers throughout the decade.[60] The controllers were a unique labor union in light of their general background in the military. They tended to be somewhat more socially conservative and, as such, they were generally thought to constitute part of the silent majority cultivated by Nixon. As such, PATCO was one of only four labor unions that publically endorsed Reagan in the 1980 election.

Towards the end of the 1970s, PATCO members, like other American workers, were reeling under the weight of stagflation. But because they were federal employees, they did not have the legal right to bargain for higher wages. By the end of the decade, PATCO began to look toward the scheduled 1981 contract negotiations in order to secure improved working conditions and to make a push for supposedly nonnegotiable items, including higher salaries and a shortened workweek. PATCO leadership, in light of their endorsement of Reagan, believed that they would receive favorable treatment at the hands of the new administration, although negotiations began to break down in the spring of 1981, and PATCO called a strike on August 3.

In a televised address on the morning of the strike, President Reagan issued an ultimatum: the workers, by breaking the "no strike" oath in their contracts, had broken the law, thus forfeiting their jobs. He demanded they return to work within 48 hours. Reagan remained true to his word, and fired more than 11,000 workers who did not obey his order. The Federal Labor Relations Authority formally decertified PATCO as the official air trafficker's union on October 22, effectively dissolving the union. The strike marked a turning point in American labor history. As Joseph A. McCartin has written, "No strike in American history unfolded more visibly before the eyes of the American people or impressed itself more quickly onto the public consciousness . . . And no strike since the advent of the New Deal damaged the U.S. labor movement more."[61]

tax cut after its congressional sponsors, Jack Kemp and William Roth). The legislation was among the largest tax cuts in American history, creating a wide range of tax reductions and loopholes, from slashing personal tax rates (most significantly in lowering the federal income taxes of the wealthiest Americans from 70 percent to 28 percent) to raising the limits of gift and estate exemptions. This unprecedented move triggered an immediate loss of federal revenue and caused the budget deficit to jump from $78 billion in 1981 to more than $207 billion by 1983. The tax cut forced Reagan to backtrack on his commitment to tax reduction: he would sign tax increases in the next three successive years, including the Tax Equity and Fiscal Responsibility Act of 1982 (TEFRA) and the Deficit Reduction Act of 1984 (DEFRA). These acts represented a major reversal for the Reagan administration, and for the president himself. Although Reagan remained philosophically opposed to raising taxes, "obviously, there had been a retreat from the thinking that had supported the Economic Recovery Tax Act of 1981. The White House spin machine did not call these changes tax increases; it labeled them revisions in the tax code."[62]

Consistent with the attempted illusion of tax increases represented as tax code revisions, Reagan's greatest accomplishment in terms of conservative economic ideology was based more on appearance and perception than reality. For more than Reagan's policy accomplishments, which were substantial, his lasting contribution occurred through his reframing of the public discourse from one in which the government tended to act as a mediator between the working class and business interests, to one in which the federal government was perceived as antagonistic toward the interests of American citizens, regardless of their class position. In Reagan's telling, the capitalists of Wall Street and the blue-collar workers of Detroit were equally oppressed by the bureaucratic and revenue-crazed "big government." This shift in the perceived function of the government would have far-reaching implications that would not only affect politics and economics in the United States, but would reverberate around the world.

Indeed, one of the central questions that has occupied historians of American conservatism concerns why the economic policies of today's Republican Party—particularly policies that provide favorable conditions such as tax breaks for wealthy Americans—often receive support from the working classes. In his instant classic, *What's the Matter with Kansas?*, Thomas Frank describes precisely this issue, which he characterizes as "the preeminent question of our times." He recalls of his earlier political assumption:

> Businessmen were the working class, I reasoned, because they worked for a living. They were the producers. They paid taxes; they built the buildings; they bought the cars ... government on the other hand, lived by imposing taxation. It produced nothing; it interfered with real people's business and then arrogantly handed out their hard-earned money to a population of parasites. This, then, was the conflict: Workers versus government. Nature versus artifice. Humility versus pride.[63]

The New Deal alliance between the American working class and the Democratic Party, which was largely based upon the consensus that the federal government should act as an economic regulator and as a buffer between the interests of corporations and banks on one hand, and the masses of American citizens on the other, unraveled as a consequence of a long and complex set of changes during the post-WWII period involving race, class, gender, religion, and politics. It is a process that cannot be reduced to a single factor or even to a single decade. But Ronald Reagan, who never wavered in his ideological attacks on the federal government, contributed more to this development than any other politician. As Kim Phillips-Fein has written, "Reagan, like [his mentor at GE, Samuel] Boulware, was able to turn the idea of government as the servant and spokesman of the worker on its head, creating a universe in which the corporation was the liberator and the state the real oppressor of the working class."[64] In this sense, Reagan's anti-tax and anti-federal legacy have influenced newer generations of conservatives such as the tea party movement, which first appeared in the public eye on Tax Day (April 15), 2009.

But Reagan's ideas have not only come to influence the thinking of self-identified conservatives, but to the collapsing of the distance between the economic principles of the Republican and Democratic parties, effectively shifting the larger national discussion in the conservative direction. Reagan was not the progenitor of this process—but here again, he did more than any other individual politician to solidify these ideological shifts. This is a point that has been frequently overlooked by historians of American conservatism, who instead tend to highlight the differences that continued between the parties after Reagan left office. This is true for liberal as well as conservative authors, both of whom tend to overstate the distinctions between Reagan's "conservatism" from the perceived "liberalism" of Bill Clinton.

In his 1996 State of the Union address, President Clinton declared that "the era of big government is over," and in several ways Clinton realized Reagan's anti-federal ideology in ways that previous generations of Democratic leaders would have found unfathomable. Clinton's signing of the North American Free Trade Agreement (NAFTA) on December 8, 1993, created the largest free trade zone in the world by eliminating tariffs between Mexico, Canada, and the United States. Although the agreement originated with Reagan and would have been signed into law by President Bush if not for the expiration of various time limitations, it was indicative of a larger pattern in the Clinton presidency that closely followed the libertarian strains in American conservatism popularized by Reagan. Nowhere were these tendencies more evident than in Clinton's methodical efforts to deregulate the American economy, exemplified by the Financial Services Modernization Act of 1999 and the Commodity Futures Modernization Act of 2000, both of which paved the way for a number of factors widely credited with triggering the global financial crisis of 2008, including the creation of new banking conglomerates and the explosion of the unregulated "over the counter" derivatives market.

One of the ironies of several of the recent works on Ronald Reagan's legacy is that they downplay the extent to which Reagan's economic philosophies were embraced by the Democratic Party leadership of the 1990s, particularly by Clinton. On one hand, conservative historians tend to celebrate Reagan's economic philosophies and moral leadership in sharp contrast to those of Clinton. For example, in Gil Troy's *The Reagan Revolution* (2009), Clinton's presidency revived Reagan's place in the public imagination because of Clinton's immoral personal conduct. He writes:

> Ironically, the Democratic victory in 1992 helped resurrect Ronald Reagan's historical reputation. Bill Clinton's presidency triggered nostalgia for Reagan's ... Bill Clinton's moral sloppiness fed a yearning for an old-fashioned leader who never took off his suit jacket in the Oval Office ... As Ronald Reagan's memory faded, memories of his presidency became more vivid and positive.[65]

These sorts of characterizations, which draw distinctions rather than parallels between Reagan and Clinton, have been made not only by conservative historians but by liberals as well.

In *The Age of Reagan* (2008), the liberal historian Sean Wilentz also tends to neglect the bipartisan ideological impact of the ideas that Reagan advocated, instead presenting them as fundamentally incompatible with Democratic ideology. Wilentz restricts Clinton's pro-market philosophy largely to his support for NAFTA, emphasizing that Clinton maintained that the free trade agreement would likely "benefit American workers"—despite the fact that it was strongly opposed by organized labor.[66] Wilentz also demonstrates a lack of appreciation for the consistency between Reagan and Clinton through his repeated characterization of Clinton and his policies as "neoliberal." He uses the term to signify Clinton simply as a "new Democrat," an ambiguous reference to differences in style and a general centrism in contrast to the "old Democrats" of the New Deal era. However, the term "neoliberal," of course, also has a much wider meaning that refers to the global system of economic deregulation, privatization, and general reduction in the role of the state in favor of free market policies. In this sense, Wilentz's assessment of Reagan, like those made by conservative historians, also misses the larger significance of Reagan's legacy.

David Harvey has described the emergence of neoliberalism in England, which was largely implemented during the rule of Margaret Thatcher, a close confidante and ideological ally of Reagan. Since the conclusion of the Second World War, similar to the American New Deal, the English economy operated under a social democratic and state-led system. And like Reagan, Thatcher saw neoliberal solutions as a cure for the stagflation of the late 1970s. Upon her election in 1979, her reforms:

> entailed confronting trade union power . . . dismantling or rolling back the commitments of the welfare state, the privatization of public enterprises [and] reducing taxes . . . All forms of social solidarity were to be dissolved in favor of individualism, private property [and] personal responsibility.[67]

Although Clinton used rhetoric in his campaign that was critical of Reaganesque policies, he signaled his openness to libertarian thinking and to neoliberalism in this broader sense through his decision to keep Alan Greenspan, who had been appointed by Ronald Reagan in 1986, in his post as Chairman of the Federal Reserve Board "because he believed [Greenspan] could deliver rapid growth."[68] Greenspan and his like-minded colleagues in the Clinton administration, Robert Rubin and Lawrence Summers, were at the forefront of Clinton's larger neoliberal economic orientation, and were once labeled as the "Committee to Save the World" by *Time* magazine because of the continued profitability yielded by their efforts. By understanding Clinton and his administration as "neo-liberal" in this sense, rather than limiting the term to refer to a stylistic and vague "new Democrat," it becomes possible to appreciate the legacy of Ronald Reagan in a way that goes beyond partisan divisions. As Gregory Albo has argued, rather than reversing course, Clinton merely extended the logic of Reagan's neoliberal program. He writes:

> Following the financial meltdown of September 2008, the public perception of deregulation was profoundly transformed as even the most strident believers were forced to recognize the weaknesses of the free market economic model. Alan Greenspan, a leading voice for deregulation for more than 20 years, testified in front of a congressional committee investigating the causes of the economic collapse that he had discovered "a flaw in the model that I perceived [to be] the critical function and structure that defines how the world works, so to speak."

> The 1996 Welfare Reform Bill . . . turned over welfare responsibilities to the states, as initially proposed by Reagan's

1982 New Federalism speech . . . it placed two-year time limits for the able-bodied to be on welfare, effectively making employment even more a wholly individual responsibility . . . The New Deal and Keynesianism were dead in American politics, sent to the graveyard by Clinton's Democrats.[69]

In the contemporary and ongoing global financial crisis, it has become clear that Reagan's bipartisan legacy continues to play a central role in the politics and economics of the United States. Barack Obama, who was elected in 2008 on promises to reform the deregulatory trends that had defined Wall Street since the Reagan era, has also proven to be more in-line with Reagan's free market economic principles than many of his detractors—*and supporters*—often care to recognize. In appointing the Lawrence Summers protégé Timothy Geithner to Secretary of the Treasury, and in naming Gary Gensler, the former executive of Goldman Sachs—one of the leading profiteers of the deregulatory efforts of the Clinton era and beyond—to lead the Commodity Futures Trading Commission, Obama, like Clinton, has shown that Reagan's legacy, for better or worse, continues to remain a critical component of American history.

Figure 5.1 President Reagan shakes hands with Arkansas Governor Bill Clinton at the signing of the Welfare Reform Act of 1988. Clinton followed the ideas that Reagan advocated: welfare reform, the deregulation of business, and the downsizing of federal and state government agencies. Courtesy of Ronald Reagan Library.

Documents

DOCUMENT 1: C. WRIGHT MILLS, "LETTER TO THE NEW LEFT" (1960)

C. Wright Mills (1916–1962) was an American sociologist who wrote several influential books during his short life, including The Power Elite *(1956),* The Sociological Imagination *(1959), and* The Causes of World War Three *(1961). In this 1960 essay, designed as an "open letter," Mills takes issue with Daniel Bell's assertion that the United States had reached a period marked by the "end of ideology." For Bell, as for many other social scientists and commentators of the 1950s, American society had arrived at a "consensus" that was illustrated by the ideological similarity between the Democratic and Republican parties and by the institutionalized and relatively predictable relationship between labor unions and corporations (or, in Marxist terms, between the proletariat and bourgeoisie). In other words, American productive capacities had brought about prosperity and the end of class conflict, with no need for the ideologies of socialism and radical social change. In terms of the two political parties, the "modern" Republicans had come to accept the general premise of the Democratic New Deal. Furthermore, Republican positions on key aspects of foreign and domestic policy were largely indistinguishable from those of the Democrats.*

Mills recognized that the "Old Left" (the industrial working class) was no longer the "decisive political force" that would enact "the social and institutional means of structural change." Instead, he foresaw the potential for the "young intelligentsia" to become organized as a "new left." Mills' writing not only anticipated the rise of the antiwar student movement that rocked California during Reagan's governorship, but other social movements of the 1960s and 70s as well. Similar to the "Port Huron Statement" (see Document 3), Mills' essay is included here because it illustrates, by way of counterpoint, the ways in which the conservative movement was but one part of the larger reaction against the supposed consensus of postwar American society. Thus, it is no coincidence that the "Letter to the New Left" was written the same year as the "Sharon Statement" of the Young Americans for Freedom (see Document 2), which called for the mobilization of a "new right."

It is no exaggeration to say that since the end of World War II in Britain and the United States, smug conservatives, tired liberals and disillusioned radicals have carried on a very wearied discourse in which issues are blurred and potential debate muted; the sickness of complacency has prevailed, the bi-partisan banality flourished . . .

Many intellectual fashions . . . stand in the way of a release of the imagination—about the cold war, the Soviet bloc, the politics of peace, about any new beginnings at home and abroad. But the fashion I have in mind is the weariness of many NATO intellectuals with what they call "ideology," and their proclamations of "the end of ideology." So far as I know, this began in the mid-fifties, mainly in intellectual circles . . . since then, many cultural gossips have taken it up as a posture and an unexamined slogan. Does it amount to anything?

Ultimately, the-end-of-ideology is based upon a disillusionment with any real commitment to socialism in any recognizable form. *That* is the only "ideology" that has really ended for these writers. But with its ending, *all* ideology, they think, has ended. *That* ideology they talk about; their own ideological assumptions, they do not.

Underneath this style of observation and comment there is the assumption that in the West there are no more real issues or even problems of great seriousness. The mixed economy plus the welfare state plus prosperity—that is the formula. U.S. capitalism will continue to be workable, the welfare state will continue along the road to ever greater justice. In the meantime, things everywhere are very complex, let us not be careless, there are great risks.

This posture—one of "false consciousness" if there ever was one—stands in the way, I think, of considering with any chances of success what may be happening in the world.

First and above all, it does rest upon a simple provincialism. If the phrase "the end of ideology" has any meaning at all, it pertains to self-selected circles of intellectuals in the richer countries. It is in fact merely their own self-image. The total population of these countries is a fraction of mankind; the period during which such a posture has been assumed is very short indeed. To speak in such terms of much of Latin America, Africa, Asia, the Soviet bloc is merely ludicrous. Anyone who stands in front of audiences—intellectual or mass—in any of these places and talks in such terms will be shrugged off (if the audience is polite) or laughed at out loud (if the audience is more candid and knowledgeable). The end-of-ideology is a slogan of complacency, circulating among the prematurely middle-aged, centered in the present, and in the rich Western societies. In the final analysis, it also rests upon a disbelief in the shaping by men of their own futures—as history and as biography. It is a consensus of a few provincials about their own immediate and provincial situation.

Second, the end-of-ideology is of course itself an ideology—a fragmentary one, to be sure, and perhaps more a mood. The end-of-ideology is in reality the ideology of an ending; the ending of political reflection itself as a public fact. It is a weary know-it-all justification—by tone of voice rather than by explicit argument—of the cultural and political default of the NATO intellectuals . . .

But the most immediately important thing about the "end of ideology" is that it *is* merely a fashion, and fashions change. Already this one is on its way out . . .

The end-of-ideology is on the way out because it stands for the refusal to work out an explicit political philosophy. And alert men everywhere today do feel the need of such a philosophy. What we should do is to continue directly to confront this need. In doing so, it may be useful to keep in mind that to have a working political philosophy means to have a philosophy that enables you to work . . .

We have been frequently told by an assorted variety of dead-end people that the meanings of Left and Right are now liquidated, by history and by reason. I think we should answer them in some such way as this:

The Right, among other things, means—what you are doing, celebrating society as it is, a going concern. Left means, or ought to mean, just the opposite. It means: structural criticism and reportage and theories of society, which at some point or another are focused politically as demands and programs. These criticisms, demands, theories, programs are guided morally by the humanist and secular ideals of Western civilization—above all, reason and freedom and justice. To be "Left" means to connect up cultural with political criticism, and both with demands and programs. And it means all this inside *every* country of the world . . .

To take seriously the problem of the need for a political orientation is not of course to seek for A Fanatical and Apocalyptic Lever of Change, for Dogmatic Ideology, for A Startling New Rhetoric, for Treacherous Abstractions—and all the other bogeymen of the dead-enders. These are of course "the extremes," the straw-men, the red herrings, used by our political enemies as the polar opposite of where they think they stand.

They tell us, for example, that ordinary men can't always be political "heroes." Who said they could? But keep looking around you and why not search out the conditions of such heroism as men do and might display? They tell us we are too "impatient," that our "pretentious" theories are not well enough grounded. That is true, but neither are they trivial; why don't they get to work, refuting or grounding them? They tell us we "don't really understand" Russia—and China—today. That is true; we don't; neither do they; we are studying it. They tell us we are "ominous" in our formulations. That is true; we do have enough imagination to be frightened and we don't have to hide it: we are not afraid we'll panic. They tell us we "are grinding axes." Of course we are: we do have, among other points of view, morally grounded ones; and we are aware of them. They tell us, in their wisdom, we don't understand that The Struggle is Without End. True: we want to change its form, its focus, its object.

We are frequently accused of being "utopian"—in our criticisms and in our proposals; and along with this, of basing our hopes for a New Left *politics* "merely on reason," or more concretely, upon the intelligentsia in its broadest sense.

There is truth in these charges. But must we not ask: what now is really meant by utopian? And: Is not our utopianism a major source of our strength? "Utopian" nowadays I think refers to any criticism or proposal that transcends the up-close milieu of a scatter of individuals: the milieu which men and women can understand directly and which they can reasonably hope directly to change. In this exact sense, our theoretical work is indeed utopian—in my own case, at least, deliberately so. What needs to be understood, and what needs to be changed, is not merely first this and then that detail of some institution or policy. If there is to be a politics of a New Left, what needs to be analyzed is the *structure* of institutions, the *foundations* of policies. In this sense, both in its criticisms and in its proposals, our work is necessarily structural—and so, *for us*, just now—utopian.

Which brings us face to face with the most important issue of political reflections—and of political action—in our time: the problem of the historical agency of change, of the social and institutional means of structural change. There are several points about this problem I would like to put to you.

First, the historic agencies of change for liberals of the capitalist societies have been an array of voluntary associations, coming to a political climax in a parliamentary or congressional system. For socialists of almost all varieties, the historic agency has been the working class—and later the peasantry; also parties and unions variously composed of members of the working class or (to blur, for now, a great problem) of political parties acting in its name—"representing its interests."

I cannot avoid the view that in both cases, the historic agency (in the advanced capitalist countries) has either collapsed or become most ambiguous: so far as structural change is concerned, *these* don't seem to be at once available and effective as *our* agency any more. I know this is a debatable point among us, and among many others as well; I am by no means certain about it. But, surely the fact of it—if it be that—ought not to be taken as an excuse for moaning and withdrawal (as it is by some of those who have become involved with the end-of-ideology); it ought not to be bypassed (as it is by many Soviet scholars and publicists, who in their reflections upon the course of advanced capitalist societies simply refuse to admit the political condition and attitudes of the working class).

Is anything more certain than that in 1970—indeed this time next year—our situation will be quite different, and—the chances are high—decisively so? But of course, that isn't saying much. The seeming collapse of our historic agencies of change ought to be taken as a problem, an issue, a trouble—in fact, as *the* political problem which *we* must into [an] issue and trouble.

Second, is it not obvious that when we talk about the collapse of agencies of change, we cannot seriously mean that such agencies do not exist. On the contrary, the means of history-making—of decision and of the enforcement of decision—have never in world history been so enlarged and so available to such small circles of men on both sides of The Curtains as they now are. My own conception of the shape of power—the theory of the power elite—I feel no need to argue here. This theory has been fortunate in its critics, from the most diverse points of political view, and I have learned from several of these critics. But I have not seen, as of this date, any analysis of the idea that causes me to modify any of its essential features.

The point that is immediately relevant does seem obvious: what is utopian for us is not at all utopian for the president of the Central Committee in Moscow, or the higher circles of the Presidency in Washington, or—recent events make evident–for the men of SAC [Strategic Air Command] and CIA. The historic agencies of change that have collapsed are those which were at least thought to be open to *the left* inside the advanced Western nations, those who have wished for structural changes of these societies. Many things follow from this obvious fact; of many of them, I am sure, we are not yet adequately aware.

Third, what I do not quite understand about some New-Left writers is why they cling so mightily to "the working class" of the advanced capitalist societies as *the* historic agency, or even as the most important agency, in the face of the really historical evidence that now stands against this expectation.

Such a labor metaphysic, I think, is a legacy from Victorian Marxism that is now quite unrealistic. It is an historically specific idea that has been turned into an a-historical and unspecific hope.

The social and historical conditions under which industrial workers tend to become a class-for-themselves, and a decisive political force, must be fully and precisely elaborated. There have been, there are, there will be such conditions; of course these conditions vary according to national social structure and the exact phase of their economic and political development. Of course we can't "write off the working class." But we must *study* all that, and freshly. Where labor exists as an agency, of course we must work with it, but we must not treat it as The Necessary Lever—as nice old Labour Gentlemen in your country and elsewhere used to do . . .

It is with this problem of agency in mind that I have been studying, for several years now, the cultural apparatus, the intellectuals—as a possible, immediate, radical agency of change. For a long time, I was not much happier with this idea than were many of you; but it turns out now, in the spring of 1960, that it may be a very relevant idea indeed . . .

Who is it that is getting fed up? Who is it that is getting disgusted with what Marx called "all the old crap"? Who is it that is thinking and acting in radical ways? All over the world—in the bloc, outside the bloc and in between—the answer's the same: it is the young intelligentsia . . .

That's why *we've* got to study these new generations of intellectuals around the world as real live agencies of historic change. Forget Victorian Marxism, except whenever you need it; and read Lenin again (be careful)—Rosa Luxemburg, too.

"But it's just some kind of moral upsurge, isn't it?" Correct. But under it: no apathy. Much of it is direct non-violent action, and it seems to be working, here and there. Now we must learn from their practice and work out with them new forms of action . . .

Isn't all this, isn't it something of what we are trying to mean by the phrase "The New Left?" Let the old men ask sourly, "Out of Apathy—into what?" The Age of Complacency is ending. Let the old women complain wisely about "the end of ideology." We are beginning to move again.

DOCUMENT 2: YOUNG AMERICANS FOR FREEDOM, "SHARON STATEMENT" (1960)

This short document takes its name from the fact that it was drafted in Sharon, Connecticut, at the estate of the family of William F. Buckley Jr. It was written in 1960, the same year C. Wright Mills published his "Letter to the New Left" (see above), as young people on both the political right and left were beginning to rebel against the supposed consensus politics of the Eisenhower era. In contrast to the new left, which was alarmed by southern racism and the threat of nuclear war, the Sharon Statement emphasizes patriotism, market economics, and the desire to limit, rather than extend the power of the federal government over the issues of the civil rights movement.

The issue of states' rights was a key aspect of southern conservative ideology used by southern segregationists to resist federal "interference," particularly concerning the issue of school desegregation. Indeed, the U.S. Constitution does not specify federal authority concerning education, and therefore conservative leaders such as Buckley, Goldwater, and Reagan maintained various levels of opposition to civil rights legislation on constitutionalist grounds, claiming that the individual states, such as Mississippi and Alabama, were entitled to handle the issue of school desegregation and other aspects of civil rights internally, and that the federal government did not have the constitutional right to enforce civil rights legislation. However glaring the differences in the political positions that existed between the new left and new right, it is telling that both movements appeared at precisely the same historical moment. Throughout the 1960s, the social and political cleavage that existed between the two camps increased exponentially, and although the new right would become a dominant force in American politics, the new left would largely dissolve by the middle of the 1970s.

In this time of moral and political crisis, it is the responsibility of the youth of America to affirm certain eternal truths.

We, as young conservatives, believe:

- That foremost among the transcendent values is the individual's use of his God-given free will, whence derives his right to be free from the restrictions of arbitrary force;
- That liberty is indivisible, and that political freedom cannot long exist without economic freedom;
- That the purpose of government is to protect those freedoms through the preservation of internal order, the provision of national defense, and the administration of justice;
- That when government ventures beyond these rightful functions, it accumulates power, which tends to diminish order and liberty;
- That the Constitution of the United States is the best arrangement yet devised for empowering government to fulfill its proper role, while restraining it from the concentration and abuse of power;
- That the genius of the Constitution—the division of powers—is summed up in the clause that reserves primacy to the several states, or to the people in those spheres not specifically delegated to the Federal government;
- That the market economy, allocating resources by the free play of supply and demand, is the single economic system compatible with the requirements of personal freedom and constitutional government, and that it is at the same time the most productive supplier of human needs;
- That when government interferes with the work of the market economy, it tends to reduce the moral and physical strength of the nation, that when it takes from one to bestow on another, it diminishes the incentive of the first, the integrity of the second, and the moral autonomy of both;
- That we will be free only so long as the national sovereignty of the United States is secure; that history shows periods of freedom are rare, and can exist only when free citizens concertedly defend their rights against all enemies;

- That the forces of international Communism are, at present, the greatest single threat to these liberties;
- That the United States should stress victory over, rather than coexistence with this menace; and
- That American foreign policy must be judged by this criterion: does it serve the just interests of the United States?

DOCUMENT 3: STUDENTS FOR A DEMOCRATIC SOCIETY, "THE PORT HURON STATEMENT" (1962)

The "Port Huron Statement" was composed by members of Students for a Democratic Society (SDS) in Port Huron, Michigan, in June of 1962. It is arguably the most comprehensive blueprint and statement of ideology produced by any of the social movements that would constitute the American new left. The lengthy document (only a small portion of which is reprinted here) contains several sections that critically address a wide range of themes, including the civil rights movement, the nuclear arms race and the Cold War, social inequality, American universities, and the political system. The document anticipated several later developments in American politics, particularly within the Republican Party: the rising South (what Kevin Phillips would later refer to as the "sunbelt"; what others have referred to as the "southernization" of the United States), as well as the increasingly conservative direction of the party. The document is also notable because of the way it resembled what conservatives were saying about American society: there was a feeling of apathy that stemmed from the supposed "consensus" politics of the Eisenhower era. And in this sense, it is useful to note not only the differences but the similarities between the new left and the new right in terms of the criticisms and solutions both groups offered American society.

We are people of this generation, bred in at least modest comfort, housed now in universities, looking uncomfortably to the world we inherit.

When we were kids the United States was the wealthiest and strongest country in the world ... Freedom and equality for each individual, government of, by, and for the people—these American values we found good, principles by which we could live as men. Many of us began maturing in complacency.

As we grew, however, our comfort was penetrated by events too troubling to dismiss. First, the permeating and victimizing fact of human degradation, symbolized by the Southern struggle against racial bigotry, compelled most of us from silence to activism. Second, the enclosing fact of the Cold War, symbolized by the presence of the Bomb, brought awareness that we . . . might die at any time. We might deliberately ignore, or avoid, or fail to feel all other human problems, but not these two, for these were too immediate and crushing in their impact . . .

While these and other problems either directly oppressed us or rankled our consciences and became our own subjective concerns, we began to see complicated and disturbing paradoxes in our surrounding America. The declaration "all men are created equal" . . . rang hollow before the facts of Negro life in the South and the big cities of the North. The proclaimed peaceful intentions of the United States contradicted its economic and military investments in the Cold War status quo.

We witnessed, and continue to witness, other paradoxes. With nuclear energy whole cities can easily be powered, yet the dominant nation states seem more likely to unleash destruction greater than that incurred in all wars of human history. Although our own technology is destroying old and creating new forms of social organization, men still tolerate meaningless work and idleness. While two-thirds of mankind suffers undernourishment, our own upper classes revel amidst superfluous abundance. Although world population is expected to double in forty years, the nations still tolerate anarchy as a major principle of international conduct and uncontrolled exploitation governs the sapping of the earth's physical resources . . .

[W]e ourselves are imbued with urgency, yet the message of our society is that there is no viable alternative to the present. Beneath the reassuring tones of the politicians . . . is the pervading feeling that there simply are no alternatives, that our times have witnessed the exhaustion not only of Utopias, but of any new departures as well . . . The fact that each individual sees apathy in his fellows perpetuates the common reluctance to organize for change. The dominant institutions are complex enough to blunt the minds of their potential critics, and entrenched enough to swiftly dissipate or entirely repel the energies of protest and reform, thus limiting human expectancies . . .

Some would have us believe that Americans feel contentment amidst prosperity—but might it not better be called a glaze above deeply felt anxieties about their role in the new world? And if these anxieties produce a developed indifference to human affairs, do they not as well produce a yearning to believe there is an alternative to the present, that something can be done to change circumstances in the school, the workplaces, the bureaucracies, the government? It is to this latter yearning, at once the spark and engine of change, that we direct our present appeal. The search for truly democratic alternatives to the present, and a commitment to social experimentation with them, is a worthy and fulfilling human enterprise, one which moves us and, we hope, others today. On such a basis do we offer this document of our convictions and analysis: as an effort in understanding and changing the conditions of humanity in the late twentieth century, an effort rooted in the ancient, still unfulfilled conception of man attaining determining influence over his circumstances of life . . .

As a social system we seek the establishment of a democracy of individual participation, governed by two central aims: that the individual share in those social decisions determining the quality and direction of his life; that society be organized to encourage independence in men and provide the media for their common participation.

In a participatory democracy, the political life would be based in several root principles:

- that decision-making of basic social consequence be carried on by public groupings;
- that politics be seen positively, as the art of collectively creating an acceptable pattern of social relations;
- that politics has the function of bringing people out of isolation and into community, thus being a necessary, though not sufficient, means of finding meaning in personal life;
- that the political order should serve to clarify problems in a way instrumental to their solution; it should provide outlets for the expression of personal grievance and aspiration; opposing views should be organized so as to illuminate choices and to facilitate the attainment of goals; channels should be commonly available to relate men to knowledge and to power so that private problems—from bad recreation facilities to personal alienation—are formulated as general issues.

The economic sphere would have as its basis the principles:

- that work should involve incentives worthier than money or survival. It should be educative, not stultifying; creative, not mechanical; self-directed, not manipulated; encouraging independence, a respect for others, a sense of dignity and a willingness to accept social responsibility, since it is this experience that has crucial influence on habits, perceptions and individual ethics;
- that the economic experience is so personally decisive that the individual must share in its full determination;
- that the economy itself is of such social importance that its major resources and means of production should be open to democratic participation and subject to democratic social regulation.

Like the political and economic ones, major social institutions—cultural, education, rehabilitative, and others—should be generally organized with the well-being and dignity of man as the essential measure of success.

In social change or interchange, we find violence to be abhorrent because it requires generally the transformation of the target, be it a human being or a community of people, into a depersonalized object of hate. It is imperative that the means of violence be abolished and the institutions—local, national, international—that encourage nonviolence as a condition of conflict be developed.

These are our central values, in skeletal form. It remains vital to understand their denial or attainment in the context of the modern world.

The Students

In the last few years, thousands of American students demonstrated that they at least felt the urgency of the times. They moved actively and directly against racial injustices, the threat of war, violations of individual rights of conscience and, less frequently, against economic manipulation. They succeeded in restoring a small measure of controversy to the campuses after the stillness of the McCarthy period. They succeeded, too, in gaining some concessions from the people and institutions they opposed, especially in the fight against racial bigotry.

The significance of these scattered movements lies not in their success or failure in gaining objectives—at least not yet . . . The significance is in the fact the students are breaking the crust of apathy and overcoming the inner alienation that remain the defining characteristics of American college life.

If student movements for change are rarities still on the campus scene, what is commonplace there? . . . It is a place of commitment to business-as-usual, getting ahead, playing it cool. It is a place of mass affirmation of the Twist, but mass reluctance toward the controversial public stance . . .

Almost no students value activity as a citizen . . . Attention is being paid to social status (the quality of shirt collars, meeting people, getting wives or husbands, making solid contacts for later on); much too, is paid to academic status (grades, honors, the med school rat-race). But neglected generally is real intellectual status, the personal cultivation of the mind.

"Students don't even give a damn about the apathy," one has said. Apathy toward apathy begets a privately constructed universe, a place of systematic study schedules, two nights each week for beer, a girl or two, and early marriage . . . Under these conditions university life loses all relevance to some . . .

The Society Beyond

Some regard this national doldrums as a sign of healthy approval of the established order—but is it approval by consent or manipulated acquiescence? Others declare that the people are withdrawn because compelling issues are fast disappearing–perhaps there are fewer breadlines in America, but is Jim Crow gone, is there enough work and work more fulfilling, is world war a diminishing threat, and what of the revolutionary new peoples?

There are no convincing apologies for the contemporary malaise. While the world tumbles toward the final war, while men in other nations are trying desperately to alter events, while the very future qua future is uncertain—America is without community, impulse, without the inner momentum necessary for an age when societies cannot successfully perpetuate themselves by their military weapons, when democracy must be viable because of its quality of life, not its quantity of rockets.

The very isolation of the individual—from power and community and ability to aspire—means the rise of a democracy without publics. With the great mass of people structurally remote and psychologically hesitant with respect to democratic institutions, those institutions themselves attenuate and become, in the fashion of the vicious circle, progressively less accessible to those few who aspire to serious participation in social affairs. The vital democratic connection between community and leadership, between the mass and the several elites, has been so wrenched and perverted that disastrous policies go unchallenged time and again.

Politics without Publics

The American political system is not the democratic model of which its glorifiers speak. In actuality it frustrates democracy by confusing the individual citizen, paralyzing policy discussion, and consolidating the irresponsible power of military and business interests.

A crucial feature of the political apparatus in America is that greater differences are harbored within each major party than the differences existing between them. Instead of two parties presenting distinctive and significant differences of approach, what dominates the system if a natural interlocking of Democrats from Southern states with the more conservative elements of the Republican party. This arrangement of forces is blessed by the seniority system of Congress which guarantees congressional committee domination by conservatives—10 of 17 committees in the Senate and 13 of 21 in House of Representatives are chaired currently by Dixiecrats.

The party overlap, however, is not the only structural antagonist of democracy in politics. First, the localized nature of the party system does not encourage discussion of national and international issues: thus problems are not raised by and for people, and political representatives usually are unfettered from any responsibilities to the general public except those regarding parochial matters. Second, whole constituencies are divested of the full political power they might have: many Negroes in the South are prevented from voting, migrant workers are disenfranchised by various residence requirements, some urban and suburban dwellers are victimized by gerrymandering, and poor people are too often without the power to obtain political representation. Third, the focus of political attention is significantly distorted by the enormous lobby force, composed predominantly of business interests, spending hundreds of millions each year in an attempt to conform facts about productivity, agriculture, defense, and social services, to the wants of private economic groupings.

What emerges from the party contradictions and insulation of privately held power is the organized political stalemate: calcification dominates flexibility as the principle of parliamentary organization, frustration is the expectancy of legislators intending liberal reform, and Congress becomes less and less central to national decision-making, especially in the area of foreign policy. In this context, confusion and blurring is built into the formulation of issues, long-range priorities are not discussed in the rational manner needed for policymaking, the politics of personality and "image" become a more important mechanism than the construction of issues in a way that affords each voter a challenging and real option. The American voter is buffeted from all directions by pseudo-problems, by the structurally initiated sense that nothing political is subject to human mastery. Worried by his mundane problems which never get solved, but constrained by the common belief that politics is an agonizingly slow accommodation of views, he quits all pretense of bothering.

A most alarming fact is that few, if any, politicians are calling for changes in these conditions. Only a handful even are calling on the President to "live up to" platform pledges; no one is demanding structural changes, such as the shuttling of Southern Democrats out of the Democratic Party. Rather than protesting the state of politics, most politicians are reinforcing and aggravating that state. While in practice they rig public opinion to suit their own interests, in word and ritual they enshrine "the sovereign public" and call for more and more letters. Their speeches and campaign actions are banal, based on a degrading conception of what people want to hear. They respond not to dialogue, but to pressure: and knowing this, the ordinary citizen sees even greater inclination to shun the political sphere . . .

In such a setting of status quo politics, where most if not all government activity is rationalized in Cold War anti-communist terms, it is somewhat natural that discontented, super-patriotic groups would emerge through political channels and explain their ultra-conservatism as the best means of Victory over Communism. They have become a politically influential force within the Republican Party, at a national level through Senator Goldwater, and at a local level through their important social and economic roles. Their political views are defined generally as the opposite of the supposed views of communists: complete individual freedom in the economic sphere, non-participation by the government in the machinery of production. But actually "anticommunism" becomes an umbrella by which to protest liberalism, internationalism, welfarism, the active civil rights and labor movements. It is to the disgrace of the United States that such a movement should become a prominent kind of public participation in the modern world—but, ironically, it is somewhat to the interests of the United States that such a movement should be a public constituency pointed toward realignment of the political parties, demanding a conservative Republican Party in the South and an exclusion of the "leftist" elements of the national GOP.

The Economy

American capitalism today advertises itself as the Welfare State. Many of us comfortably expect pensions, medical care, unemployment compensation, and other social services in our lifetimes. Even with one-fourth of our productive capacity unused, the majority of Americans are living in relative comfort—although their nagging incentive to "keep up" makes them continually dissatisfied with their possessions . . .

We live amidst a national celebration of economic prosperity while poverty and deprivation remain an unbreakable way of life for millions in the "affluent society," including many of our own generation. We hear glib reference to the "welfare state," "free enterprise," and "shareholder's democracy" while military defense is the main item of "public" spending and obvious oligopoly and other forms of minority rule defy real individual initiative or popular control. Work, too, is often unfulfilling and victimizing, accepted as a channel to status or plenty, if not a way to pay the bills, rarely as a means of understanding and controlling self and events. In work and leisure the individual is regulated as part of the system, a consuming unit, bombarded by hard-sell soft-sell, lies and semi-true appeals, and his basest drives. He is always told what he is supposed to enjoy while being told, too, that he is a "free" man because of "free enterprise."

The Remote Control Economy

We are subject to a remote control economy, which excludes the mass of individual "units"—the people—from basic decisions affecting the nature and organization of work, rewards, and opportunities. The modern concentration of wealth is fantastic. The wealthiest one percent of Americans own more than 80 percent of all personal shares of stock. From World War II until the mid-Fifties, the 50 biggest corporations increased their manufacturing production from 17 to 23 percent of the national total, and the share of the largest 200 companies rose from 30 to 37 percent. To regard the various decisions of these elites as purely economic is short-sighted: their decisions affect in a momentous way the entire fabric of social life in America. Foreign investments influence political policies in under-developed areas—and our efforts to build a "profitable" capitalist world blind our foreign policy to mankind's needs and destiny. The drive for sales spurs phenomenal advertising efforts; the ethical drug industry, for instance, spent more than $750 million on promotions in 1960, nearly four times the amount available to all American medical schools for their educational programs. The arts, too, are organized substantially according to their commercial appeal; aesthetic values are subordinated to exchange values, and writers swiftly learn to consider the commercial market as much as the humanistic marketplace of ideas. The tendency to over-production, to gluts of surplus commodities, encourages "market research" techniques to deliberately create pseudo-needs in consumers—we learn to buy "smart" things, regardless of their utility—and introduces wasteful "planned obsolescence" as a permanent feature of business strategy. While real social needs accumulate as rapidly as profits, it becomes evident that Money, instead of dignity of character, remains a pivotal American value, and Profitability, instead of social use, a pivotal standard in determining priorities of resource allocation.

Within existing arrangements, the American business community cannot be said to encourage a democratic process nationally. Economic minorities not responsible to a public in any democratic fashion make decisions of a more profound importance than even those made by Congress . . .

In short, the theory of government "countervailing" business neglects the extent to which government influence is marginal to the basic production decisions, the basic decision-making environment of society, the basic structure or distribution and allocation which is still determined by major corporations with power and wealth concentrated among the few. A conscious conspiracy—as in the case of price-rigging in the electrical industry—is by no means generally or continuously operative but power undeniably does rest in comparative insulation from the public and its political representatives.

The Military-Industrial Complex

The most spectacular and important creation of the authoritarian and oligopolistic structure of economic decision-making in America is the institution called "the military-industrial complex" by former President Eisenhower, the powerful congruence of interest and structure among military and business elites which affects so much of our development and destiny. Not only is ours the first generation to live with the possibility of world-wide cataclysm—it is the first to experience the actual social preparation for cataclysm, the general militarization of American society. In 1948 Congress established Universal Military Training, the first peacetime conscription. The military became a permanent institution. Four years earlier, General Motor's Charles E. Wilson had heralded the creation of what he called the "permanent war economy," the continuous use of military spending as a solution to economic problems . . .

Automation, Abundance, and Challenge

But while the economy remains relatively static in its setting of priorities and allocation of resources, new conditions are emerging with enormous implications: the revolution of automation, and the replacement of scarcity by the potential of material abundance.

Automation, the process of machines replacing men in performing sensory, motoric and complex logical tasks, is transforming society in ways that are scarcely comprehensible . . . Automation is destroying whole categories of work—impersonal thinkers have efficiently labeled this "structural unemployment"—in blue-collar, service, and even middle management occupations. In addition it is eliminating employment opportunities for a youth force . . . and rendering work far more difficult both to find and do for people in the forties and up. The consequences of this economic drama, strengthened by the force of post-war recessions, are momentous: five million becomes an acceptable unemployment tabulation, and misery, up-rootedness and anxiety become the lot of increasing numbers of Americans . . .

The Stance of Labor

Amidst all this, what of organized labor, the historic institutional representative of the exploited, the presumed "countervailing power" against the excesses of Big Business? The contemporary social assault on the labor movement is of crisis proportions. To the average American, "big labor" is a growing cancer equal in impact to Big Business—nothing could be more distorted, even granting a sizable union bureaucracy. But in addition to public exaggerations, the labor crisis can be measured in several ways. First, the high expectations of the newborn AFL-CIO of 30 million members by 1965 are suffering a reverse unimaginable five years ago. The demise of the dream of "organizing the unorganized" is dramatically reflected in the AFL-CIO decision, just two years after its creation, to slash its organizing staff in half. From 15 million members when the AFL and the CIO merged, the total has slipped to 13.5 million. During the post-war generation, union membership nationally has increased by four million—but the total number of workers has jumped by 13 million. Today only 40 percent of all non-agricultural workers are protected by any form or organization. Second, organizing conditions are going to worsen. Where labor now is strongest—in industries—automation is leading to an attrition of available work. As the number of jobs dwindles, so does labor's power of bargaining, since management can handle a strike in an automated plant more easily than the older mass-operated ones.

More important perhaps, the American economy has changed radically in the last decade, as suddenly the number of workers producing goods became fewer than the number in "nonproductive" areas—government, trade, finance, services, utilities, transportation. Since World War II "white collar" and "service" jobs have grown twice as fast as have "blue collar" production jobs. Labor has almost no organization in the expanding occupational areas of the new economy, but almost all of its entrenched strength in contracting areas. As big government hires more, as business seeks more office workers and skilled technicians, and as growing commercial America demands new hotels, service stations and the like, the conditions will become graver still. Further, there is continuing hostility to labor by the Southern states and their industrial interests— meaning "runaway plants," cheap labor threatening the organized trade union movement, and opposition from Dixiecrats to favorable labor legislation in Congress. Finally, there is indication that Big Business, for the sake of public relations if nothing more, has acknowledged labor's "right" to exist, but has deliberately tried to contain labor at its present strength, preventing strong unions from helping weaker ones or from spreading to unorganized sectors of the economy. Business is aided in its efforts by proliferation of "right-to-work" laws at state levels (especially in areas where labor is without organizing strength to begin with), and anti-labor legislation in Congress . . .

Anti-Communism

An unreasoning anti-communism has become a major social problem for those who want to construct a more democratic America. McCarthyism and other forms of exaggerated and conservative anti-communism seriously weaken democratic institutions and spawn movements contrary to the interests of basic freedoms and peace. In such an atmosphere even the most intelligent of Americans fear to join political organizations, sign petitions, speak out on serious issues. Militaristic policies are easily "sold" to a public fearful of a democratic enemy. Political debate is restricted, thought is standardized, action is inhibited by the demands of "unity" and "oneness" in the face of the declared danger. Even many liberals and socialists share static and repetitious participation in the anti-communist crusade and often discourage tentative, inquiring discussion about "the Russian question" within their ranks—often by employing "stalinist," "stalinoid," "trotskyite" and other epithets in an oversimplifying way to discredit opposition.

Thus much of the American anti-communism takes on the characteristics of paranoia. Not only does it lead to the perversion of democracy and to the political stagnation of a warfare society, but it also has the unintended consequence of preventing an honest and effective approach to the issues. Such an approach would require public analysis and debate of world politics. But almost nowhere in politics is such a rational analysis possible to make . . .

Communism and Foreign Policy

As democrats we are in basic opposition to the communist system. The Soviet Union, as a system, rests on the total suppression of organized opposition, as well as on a vision of the future in the name of which much human life has been sacrificed, and numerous small and large denials of human dignity rationalized. The Communist Party has equated falsely the "triumph of true socialism" with centralized bureaucracy. The Soviet state lacks independent labor organizations and other liberties we consider basic. And despite certain reforms, the system remains almost totally divorced from the image officially promulgated by the Party. Communist parties throughout the rest of the world are generally undemocratic in internal structure and mode of action. Moreover, in most cases they subordinate radical programs to requirements of Soviet foreign policy. The communist movement has failed, in every sense, to achieve its stated intentions of leading a worldwide movement for human emancipation.

But present trends in American anti-communism are not sufficient for the creation of appropriate policies with which to relate to and counter communist movements in the world. In no instance is this better illustrated than in our basic national policy-making assumption that the Soviet Union is inherently expansionist and aggressive, prepared to dominate the rest of the world by military means. On this assumption rests the monstrous

American structure of military "preparedness"; because of it we sacrifice values and social programs to the alleged needs of military power . . .

Our paranoia about the Soviet Union has made us incapable of achieving agreements absolutely necessary for disarmament and the preservation of peace. We are hardly able to see the possibility that the Soviet Union, though not "peace loving," may be seriously interested in disarmament.

Discrimination

To avoid conflict with the Dixiecrat-Republican alliance, President Kennedy has developed a civil rights philosophy of "enforcement, not enactment," implying that existing statutory tools are sufficient to change the lot of the Negro. So far he has employed executive power usefully to appoint Negroes to various offices, and seems interested in seeing the Southern Negro registered to vote . . . Only two civil rights bills, one to abolish the poll tax in five states and another to prevent unfair use of literacy tests in registration, have been proposed—the President giving active support to neither. But even this legislation, lethargically supported, then defeated, was intended to extend only to Federal elections. More important, the Kennedy interest in voter registration has not been supplemented with interest in giving the Southern Negro the economic protection that only trade unions can provide. It seems evident that the President is attempting to win the Negro permanently to the Democratic Party without basically disturbing the reactionary one-party oligarchy in the South. Moreover, the administration is decidedly "cool" (a phrase of Robert Kennedy's) toward mass nonviolent movements in the South, though by the support of racist Dixiecrats the Administration makes impossible gradual action through conventional channels. The Federal Bureau of Investigation in the South is composed of Southerners and their intervention in situations of racial tension is always after the incident, not before. Kennedy has refused to "enforce" the legal prerogative to keep Federal marshals active in Southern areas before, during and after any "situations" (this would invite Negroes to exercise their rights and it would infuriate the Southerners in Congress because of its "insulting" features).

What is Needed?

How to end the Cold War? How to increase democracy in America? These are the decisive issues confronting liberal and socialist forces today. To us, the issues are intimately related, the struggle for one invariably being a struggle for the other. What policy and structural alternatives are needed to obtain these ends?

Universal controlled disarmament must replace deterrence and arms control as the national defense goal. The strategy of mutual threat can only temporarily prevent thermonuclear war, and it cannot but erode democratic institutions here while consolidating oppressive institutions in the Soviet Union . . . The symmetry of threat and counter-threat lead not to stability but to the edge of hell . . .

Experiments in disengagement and demilitarization must be conducted as part of the total disarming process. These "disarmament experiments" can be of several kinds, so long as they are consistent with the principles of containing the arms race and isolating specific sectors of the world from the Cold War power-play. First, it is imperative that no more nations be supplied with, or locally produce, nuclear weapons . . . This would involve not only declarations of "denuclearization" in whole areas of Latin America, Africa, Asia and Europe, but would attempt to create inspection machinery to guarantee the peaceful use of atomic energy.

The Industrialization of the World

Many Americans are prone to think of the industrialization of the newly developed countries as a modern form of American noblesse, undertaken sacrificially for the benefit of others. On the contrary, the task of world industrialization, of eliminating the disparity between have and have-not nations, is as important as any issue facing America. The colonial revolution signals the end of an era for the old Western powers and a time of new beginnings for most of the people of the earth. In the course of these upheavals, many problems will emerge: American policies must be revised or accelerated in several ways.

The United States' principal goal should be creating a world where hunger, poverty, disease, ignorance, violence, and exploitation are replaced as central features by abundance, reason, love, and international cooperation. To many this will seem the product of juvenile hallucination: but we insist it is a more realistic goal than is a world of nuclear stalemate. Some will say this is a hope beyond all bounds: but is far better to us to have positive vision than a "hard headed" resignation. Some will sympathize, but claim it is impossible: if so, then, we, not Fate, are the responsible ones, for we have the means at our disposal. We should not give up the attempt for fear of failure . . .

Towards American Democracy

Every effort to end the Cold War and expand the process of world industrialization is an effort hostile to people and institutions whose interests lie in perpetuation of the East-West military threat and the postponement of change in the "have not" nations of the world. Every such effort, too, is bound to establish greater democracy in America. The major goals of a domestic effort would be:

America must abolish its political party stalemate . . . It has long been argued that the very overlapping of American parties guarantees that issues will be considered responsibly, that progress will be gradual instead of intemperate, and that therefore America will remain stable instead of torn by class strife. On the contrary: the enormous party overlap itself confuses issues and makes responsible presentation of choice to the electorate impossible, that guarantees Congressional listlessness and the drift of power to military and economic bureaucracies, that directs attention away from the more fundamental causes of social stability, such as a huge middle class, Keynesian economic techniques and Madison Avenue advertising . . . What is desirable is sufficient party disagreement to dramatize major issues, yet sufficient party overlap to guarantee stable transitions from administration to administration . . .

Institutions and practices which stifle dissent should be abolished, and the promotion of peaceful dissent should be actively promoted. The first Amendment freedoms of speech, assembly, thought, religion and press should be seen as guarantees, not threats, to national security. While society has the right to prevent active subversion of its laws and institutions, it has the duty as well to promote open discussion of all issues—otherwise it will be in fact promoting real subversion as the only means to implementing ideas. To eliminate the fears and apathy from national life it is necessary that the institutions bred by fear and apathy be rooted out: the House Un-American Activities Committee, the Senate Internal Security Committee, the loyalty oaths on Federal loans, the Attorney General's list of subversive organizations, the Smith and McCarren Acts. The process of eliminating these blighting institutions is the process of restoring democratic participation. Their existence is a sign of the decomposition and atrophy of the participation.

Corporations must be made publicly responsible. It is not possible to believe that true democracy can exist where a minority utterly controls enormous wealth and power. The influence of corporate elites on foreign policy is neither reliable nor democratic; a way must be found to be subordinate private American foreign investment to a democratically constructed foreign policy. The influence of the same giants on domestic life is intolerable as well; a way must be found to direct our economic resources to genuine human needs, not the private needs of corporations nor the rigged needs of maneuvered citizenry.

The allocation of resources must be based on social needs. A truly "public sector" must be established, and its nature debated and planned. At present the majority of America's "public sector," the largest part of our public spending, is for the military. When great social needs are so pressing, our concept of "government spending" is wrapped up in the "permanent war economy."

In fact, if war is to be avoided, the "permanent war economy" must be seen as an "interim war economy." At some point, America must return to other mechanisms of economic growth besides public military spending. We must plan economically in peace . . .

The University and Social Change

There is perhaps little reason to be optimistic about the above analysis. True, the Dixiecrat-GOP coalition is the weakest point in the dominating complex of corporate, military and political power. But the civil rights and peace and student movements are too poor and socially slighted, and the labor movement too quiescent, to be counted with enthusiasm. From where else can power and vision be summoned? We believe that the universities are an overlooked seat of influence.

First, the university is located in a permanent position of social influence. Its educational function makes it indispensable and automatically makes it a crucial institution in the formation of social attitudes. Second, in an unbelievably complicated world, it is the central institution for organizing, evaluating, and transmitting knowledge. Third, the extent to which academic resources presently are used to buttress immoral social practice is revealed first, by the extent to which defense contracts make the universities engineers of the arms race. Too, the use of modern social science as a manipulative tool reveals itself in the "human relations" consultants to the modern corporation, who introduce trivial sops to give laborers feelings of "participation" or "belonging," while actually deluding them in order to further exploit their labor. And, of course, the use of motivational research is already infamous as a manipulative aspect of American politics. But these social uses of the universities' resources also demonstrate the unchangeable reliance by men of power on the men and storehouses of knowledge: this makes the university functionally tied to society in new ways, revealing new potentialities, new levers for change. Fourth, the university is the only mainstream institution that is open to participation by individuals of nearly any viewpoint . . .

These, at least, are facts, no matter how dull the teaching, how paternalistic the rules, how irrelevant the research that goes on. Social relevance, the accessibility to knowledge, and internal openness. These together make the university a potential base and agency in a movement of social change.

Any new left in America must be, in large measure, a left with real intellectual skills, committed to deliberativeness, honesty, reflection as working tools. The university permits the political life to be an adjunct to the academic one, and action to be informed by reason.

A new left must be distributed in significant social roles throughout the country. The universities are distributed in such a manner.

A new left must consist of younger people who matured in the postwar world, and partially be directed to the recruitment of younger people. The university is an obvious beginning point.

A new left must include liberals and socialists, the former for their relevance, the latter for their sense of thoroughgoing reforms in the system. The university is a more sensible place than a political party for these two traditions to begin to discuss their differences and look for political synthesis.

A new left must start controversy across the land, if national policies and national apathy are to be reversed. The ideal university is a community of controversy, within itself and in its effects on communities beyond.

A new left must transform modern complexity into issues that can be understood and felt close-up by every human being. It must give form to the feelings of helplessness and indifference, so that people may see the political, social and economic sources of their private troubles and organize to change society. In a time of supposed prosperity, moral complacency and political manipulation, a new left cannot rely on only aching stomachs to be the engine force of social reform. The case for change, for alternatives that will involve uncomfortable personal efforts, must be argued as never before. The university is a relevant place for all of these activities.

But we need not indulge in allusions: the university system cannot complete a movement of ordinary people making demands for a better life. From its schools and colleges across the nation, a militant left might awaken its allies, and by beginning the process towards peace, civil rights, and labor struggles, reinsert theory and idealism where too often reign confusion and political barter. The power of students and faculty united is not only potential; it has shown its actuality in the South, and in the reform movements of the North.

The bridge to political power, though, will be built through genuine cooperation, locally, nationally, and internationally, between a new left of young people, and an awakening community of allies. In each community we must look within the university and act with confidence that we can be powerful, but we must look outwards to the less exotic but more lasting struggles for justice.

To turn these possibilities into realities will involve national efforts at university reform by an alliance of students and faculty. They must wrest control of the educational process from the administrative bureaucracy. They must make fraternal and functional contact with allies in labor, civil rights, and other liberal forces outside the campus. They must import major public issues into the curriculum—research and teaching on problems of war and peace is an outstanding example. They must make debate and controversy, not dull pedantic cant, the common style for educational life. They must consciously build a base for their assault upon the loci of power.

As students, for a democratic society, we are committed to stimulating this kind of social movement, this kind of vision and program is campus and community across the country. If we appear to seek the unattainable, it has been said, then let it be known that we do so to avoid the unimaginable.

DOCUMENT 4: RONALD REAGAN, "A TIME FOR CHOOSING" (1964)

The following made-for-television speech, broadcast on October 27, 1964, marked the entry of Ronald Reagan into party politics. Reagan gave his remarks in support of Barry Goldwater, who was running as the first presidential candidate of the nascent conservative movement. Many of Goldwater's advisors initially resisted the idea of using Reagan because of his connections to "extremist" conservative organizations and individuals, including the John Birch Society. Much to their relief, the speech was a smashing success. Although Goldwater went on to lose one of the most overwhelming electoral landslides in the history of American presidential elections, the conservative movement continued to gain strength, particularly in California, and although he lacked any previous experience in government, Reagan was elected governor of California two years later.

In this speech, Reagan gave the same message he had delivered countless times on behalf of General Electric during the 1950s and early 60s. He united anticommunism, social conservatism, and the benefits of unrestrained free market capitalism—the three ideological pillars of postwar conservatism in the United States. Throughout his masterful demonstration of persuasive speaking, Reagan also displayed one of the hallmarks of his rhetorical strategy: the use of anecdotes from unsubstantiated and often dubious sources (for example, "two friends of mine were talking to a Cuban refugee . . . ," or "Not too long ago, a judge called me . . ."). Reagan never deviated from the political and economic agenda implicit in this speech: promoting free markets, dismantling the New Deal framework, and fighting what he perceived to be the forces of communism, whether in the United States or around the world.

Thank you and good evening. The sponsor has been identified, but unlike most television programs, the performer hasn't been provided with a script. As a matter of fact, I have been permitted to choose my own words and discuss my own ideas regarding the choice that we face in the next few weeks.

I have spent most of my life as a Democrat. I recently have seen fit to follow another course. I believe that the issues confronting us cross party lines. Now, one side in this campaign has been telling us that the issues of this election are the maintenance of peace and prosperity. The line has been used, "We've never had it so good." But I have an uncomfortable feeling that this prosperity isn't something on which we can base our hopes for the future. No nation in history has ever survived a tax burden that reached a third of its national income. Today, 37 cents out of every dollar earned in this country is the tax collector's share, and yet our government continues to spend 17 million dollars a day more than the government takes in. We haven't balanced our budget 28 out of the last 34 years. We've raised our debt limit three times in the last twelve months, and now our national debt is one and a half times bigger than all the combined debts of all the nations of the world. We have 15 billion dollars in gold in our treasury; we don't own an ounce. Foreign dollar claims are 27.3 billion dollars. And we've just had announced that the dollar of 1939 will now purchase 45 cents in its total value.

As for the peace that we would preserve, I wonder who among us would like to approach the wife or mother whose husband or son has died in South Vietnam and ask them if they think this is a peace that should be maintained indefinitely. Do they mean peace, or do they mean we just want to be left in peace? There can be no real peace while one American is dying some place in the world for the rest of us. We're at war with the most dangerous enemy that has ever faced mankind in his long climb from the swamp to the stars, and it's been said if we lose that war, and in so doing lose this way of freedom of ours, history will record with the greatest astonishment that those who had the most to lose did the least to prevent its happening. Well I think it's time we ask ourselves if we still know the freedoms that were intended for us by the founding fathers.

Not too long ago, two friends of mine were talking to a Cuban refugee, a businessman who had escaped from Castro, and in the midst of his story one of my friends turned to the other and said, "We don't know how lucky we are." And the Cuban stopped and said, "How lucky you are? I had someplace to escape to." And in that sentence he told us the entire story. If we lose freedom here, there's no place to escape to. This is the last stand on earth.

And this idea that government is beholden to the people, that it has no other source of power except the sovereign people, is still the newest and the most unique idea in all the long history of man's relation to man.

This is the issue of this [1964 presidential] election: whether we believe in our capacity for self-government or whether we abandon the American Revolution and confess that a little intellectual elite in a far distant capitol can plan our lives for us better than we can plan them ourselves.

You and I are told increasingly we have to choose between a left or right. Well I'd like to suggest there is no such thing as a left or right. There's only an up or down: [up] man's old-aged dream, the ultimate in individual freedom consistent with law and order, or down to the ant heap of totalitarianism. And regardless of their sincerity, their humanitarian motives, those who would trade our freedom for security have embarked on this downward course.

In this vote-harvesting time, they use terms like the "Great Society," or as we were told a few days ago by the president, we must accept a greater government activity in the affairs of the people. But they've been a little more explicit in the past and among themselves; and all of the things I now will quote have appeared in print. These are not Republican accusations. For example, they have voices that say, "The cold war will end through our acceptance of a not undemocratic socialism." Another voice says, "The profit motive has become outmoded. It must be replaced by the incentives of the welfare state." Or, "Our traditional system of individual freedom is incapable of solving the complex problems of the twentieth century." Senator Fulbright has said at Stanford University that the Constitution is outmoded. He referred to the President as "our moral teacher and our leader," and he says he is "hobbled in his task by the restrictions of power imposed on him by this antiquated document." He must be freed so that he can do for us what he knows is best. And Senator Clark of Pennsylvania, another articulate spokesman, defines liberalism as meeting the material needs of the masses through the full power of centralized government.

Well, I, for one, resent it when a representative of the people refers to you and me, the free men and women of this country, as "the masses." This is a term we haven't applied to ourselves in America. But beyond that, "the full power of centralized government"—this was the very thing the Founding Fathers sought to minimize. They knew that governments don't control things. A government can't control the economy without controlling people. And they know when a government sets out to do that, it must use force and coercion to achieve its purpose. They also knew, those Founding Fathers, that outside of its legitimate functions, government does nothing as well or as economically as the private sector of the economy.

Now, we have no better example of this than government's involvement in the farm economy over the last 30 years. Since 1955, the cost of this program has nearly doubled. One-fourth of farming in America is responsible for 85 percent of the farm surplus. Three-fourths of farming is out on the free market and has known a 21 percent increase in the per capita consumption of all its produce. You see, that one-fourth of farming —that's regulated and controlled by the federal government. In the last three years we've spent 43 dollars in the feed grain program for every dollar bushel of corn we don't grow.

Senator Humphrey last week charged that Barry Goldwater, as President, would seek to eliminate farmers. He should do his homework a little better, because he'll find out that we've had a decline of 5 million in the farm population under these government programs. He'll also find that the Democratic administration has sought to get from Congress [an] extension of the farm program to include that three-fourths that is now free. He'll find that they've also asked for the right to imprison farmers who wouldn't keep books as prescribed by the federal government. The Secretary of Agriculture asked for the right to seize farms through condemnation and resell them to other individuals. And contained in that same program was a provision that would have allowed the federal government to remove 2 million farmers from the soil. At the same time, there's been an increase in the Department of Agriculture employees. There's now one for every 30 farms in the United States, and still they can't tell us how 66 shiploads of grain headed for Austria disappeared without a trace and Billie Sol Estes [an American businessman with ties to President Johnson and convicted of fraud in 1964] never left shore.

Every responsible farmer and farm organization has repeatedly asked the government to free the farm economy, but how—who are farmers to know what's best for them? The wheat farmers voted against a wheat program. The government passed it anyway. Now the price of bread goes up; the price of wheat to the farmer goes down . . . They've just declared Rice County, Kansas, a depressed area. Rice County, Kansas, has two hundred oil wells, and the 14,000 people there have over 30 million dollars on deposit in personal savings in their banks. And when the government tells you you're depressed, lie down and be depressed.

We have so many people who can't see a fat man standing beside a thin one without coming to the conclusion the fat man got that way by taking advantage of the thin one. So they're going to solve all the problems of human misery through government and government planning. Well, now, if government planning and welfare had the answer—and they've had almost 30 years of it—shouldn't we expect government to read the score to us once in a while? Shouldn't they be telling us about the decline each year in the number of people needing help? The reduction in the need for public housing? But the reverse is true. Each year the need grows greater; the program grows greater. We were told four years ago that 17 million people went to bed hungry each night. Well that was probably true. They were all on a diet.

But now we're told that 9.3 million families in this country are poverty-stricken on the basis of earning less than 3,000 dollars a year. Welfare spending is 10 times greater than in the dark depths of the Depression. We're spending 45 billion dollars on welfare. Now do a little arithmetic, and you'll find that if we divided the 45 billion dollars up equally among those 9 million poor families, we'd be able to give each family 4,600 dollars a year. And this added to their present income should eliminate poverty. Direct aid to the poor, however, is only running about 600 dollars per family. It would seem that someplace there must be some overhead . . . Now do they honestly expect us to believe that if we add 1 billion dollars to the 45 billion we're spending, one more program to the 30-odd we have—and remember, this new program doesn't replace any, it just duplicates existing programs—do they believe that poverty is suddenly going to disappear by magic?

Well, in all fairness I should explain there is one part of the new program that isn't duplicated. This is the youth feature. We're now going to solve the dropout problem, juvenile delinquency, by reinstituting something like the old CCC [Civilian Conservation Corps] camps, and we're going to put our young people in these camps. But again we do some arithmetic, and we find that we're going to spend each year just on room and board for each young person we help 4,700 dollars a year. We can send them to Harvard for 2,700! Course, don't get me wrong. I'm not suggesting Harvard is the answer to juvenile delinquency.

But seriously, what are we doing to those we seek to help? Not too long ago, a judge called me here in Los Angeles. He told me of a young woman who'd come before him for a divorce. She had six children, was pregnant with her seventh. Under his questioning, she revealed her husband was a laborer earning 250 dollars a month. She wanted a divorce to get an 80 dollar raise. She's eligible for 330 dollars a month in the Aid to Dependent Children Program. She got the idea from two women in her neighborhood who had already done that very thing. Yet anytime you and I question the schemes of the do-gooders, we're denounced as being against their humanitarian goals. They say we're always against things—we're never for anything. Well, the trouble with our liberal friends is not that they're ignorant; it's just that they know so much that isn't so.

Now—we're for a provision that destitution should not follow unemployment by reason of old age, and to that end we've accepted Social

Security as a step toward meeting the problem. But we're against those entrusted with this program when they practice deception regarding its fiscal shortcomings, when they charge that any criticism of the program means that we want to end payments to those people who depend on them for a livelihood. They've called it "insurance" to us in a hundred million pieces of literature. But then they appeared before the Supreme Court and they testified it was a welfare program. They only use the term "insurance" to sell it to the people. And they said Social Security dues are a tax for the general use of the government, and the government has used that tax. There is no fund, because Robert Byers, the actuarial head, appeared before a congressional committee and admitted that Social Security as of this moment is 298 billion dollars in the hole. But he said there should be no cause for worry because as long as they have the power to tax, they could always take away from the people whatever they needed to bail them out of trouble. And they're doing just that.

A young man, 21 years of age, working at an average salary—his Social Security contribution would, in the open market, buy him an insurance policy that would guarantee 220 dollars a month at age 65. The government promises 127. He could live it up until he's 31 and then take out a policy that would pay more than Social Security. Now are we so lacking in business sense that we can't put this program on a sound basis, so that people who do require those payments will find they can get them when they're due—that the cupboard isn't bare? Barry Goldwater thinks we can.

No government ever voluntarily reduces itself in size. So, government programs, once launched, never disappear. Actually, a government bureau is the nearest thing to eternal life we'll ever see on this earth. Federal employees—federal employees number two and a half million; and federal, state, and local, one out of six of the nation's work force employed by government. These proliferating bureaus with their thousands of regulations have cost us many of our constitutional safeguards. How many of us realize that today federal agents can invade a man's property without a warrant? They can impose a fine without a formal hearing, let alone a trial by jury? And they can seize and sell his property at auction to enforce the payment of that fine. In Chico County, Arkansas, James Wier over-planted his rice allotment. The government obtained a 17,000 dollar judgment. And a U.S. marshal sold his 960-acre farm at auction. The government said it was necessary as a warning to others to make the system work.

Last February 19th at the University of Minnesota, Norman Thomas, six-time candidate for President on the Socialist Party ticket, said, "If Barry Goldwater became President, he would stop the advance of socialism in the United States." I think that's exactly what he will do. But as a former Democrat, I can tell you Norman Thomas isn't the only man who has drawn this parallel to socialism with the present administration, because back in 1936, Mr. Democrat himself, Al Smith, a great American, came before the American people and charged that the leadership of his Party was taking the Party of Jefferson, Jackson, and Cleveland down the road under the banners of Marx, Lenin, and Stalin. And he walked away from his Party, and he never returned until the day he died—because to this day, the leadership of that Party has been taking that Party, that honorable Party, down the road in the image of the labor Socialist Party of England . . .

Somewhere a perversion has taken place. Our natural, unalienable rights are now considered to be a dispensation of government, and freedom has never been so fragile, so close to slipping from our grasp as it is at this moment. Our Democratic opponents seem unwilling to debate these issues. They want to make you and I believe that this is a contest between two men—that we're to choose just between two personalities. Well what of this man that they would destroy—and in destroying, they would destroy that which he represents, the ideas that you and I hold dear? Is he the brash and shallow and trigger-happy man they say he is? Well I've been privileged to know him . . . long before he ever dreamed of trying for high office, and I can tell you personally I've never known a man in my life I believed so incapable of doing a dishonest or dishonorable thing.

This is a man who, in his own business before he entered politics, instituted a profit-sharing plan before unions had ever thought of it. He put in health and medical insurance for all his employees. He took 50 percent of the profits before taxes and set up a retirement program, a pension plan for all his employees. He sent monthly checks for life to an employee who was ill and couldn't work. He provides nursing care for the children of mothers who work in the stores. When Mexico was ravaged by the floods in the Rio Grande, he climbed in his airplane and flew medicine and supplies down there. An ex-GI told me how he met him. It was the week before Christmas during the Korean War, and he was at the Los Angeles airport trying to get a ride home to Arizona for Christmas. And he said that [there were] a lot of servicemen there and no seats available on the planes. And then a voice came over the loudspeaker and said, "Any men in uniform wanting a ride to Arizona, go to runway such-and-such," and they went down there, and there was a fellow named Barry Goldwater sitting in his plane. Every day in those weeks before Christmas, all day long, he'd load up the plane, fly it to Arizona, fly them to their homes, fly back over to get another load . . .

Those who would trade our freedom for the soup kitchen of the welfare state have told us they have a utopian solution of peace without victory. They call their policy "accommodation." And they say if we'll only avoid any direct confrontation with the enemy, he'll forget his evil ways and learn to love us. All who oppose them are indicted as warmongers. They say we offer simple answers to complex problems. Well, perhaps there is a simple answer—not an easy answer—but simple: if you and I have the courage to tell our elected officials that we want our national policy based on what we know in our hearts is morally right. We cannot buy our security, our freedom from the threat of the bomb by committing an immorality so great as saying to a billion human beings now enslaved behind the Iron Curtain, "Give up your dreams of freedom because to save our own skins, we're willing to make a deal with your slave masters." Alexander Hamilton said, "A nation which can prefer disgrace to danger is prepared for a master, and deserves one." Now let's set the record straight. There's no argument over the choice between peace and war, but there's only one guaranteed way you can have peace—and you can have it in the next second—surrender.

Admittedly, there's a risk in any course we follow other than this, but every lesson of history tells us that the greater risk lies in appeasement, and this is the specter our well-meaning liberal friends refuse to face—that their policy of accommodation is appeasement, and it gives no choice between peace and war, only between fight or surrender. If we continue to accommodate, continue to back and retreat, eventually we have to face the final demand—the ultimatum. And what then—when Nikita Khrushchev has told his people he knows what our answer will be? He has told them that we're retreating under the pressure of the Cold War, and someday when the time comes to deliver the final ultimatum, our surrender will be voluntary, because by that time we will have been weakened from within spiritually, morally, and economically. He believes this because from our side he's heard voices pleading for "peace at any price" or "better Red than dead," or as one commentator put it, he'd rather "live on his knees than die on his feet." And therein lies the road to war, because those voices don't speak for the rest of us.

You and I know and do not believe that life is so dear and peace so sweet as to be purchased at the price of chains and slavery. If nothing in life is worth dying for, when did this begin—just in the face of this enemy? Or should Moses have told the children of Israel to live in slavery under the pharaohs? Should Christ have refused the cross? Should the patriots at Concord Bridge have thrown down their guns and refused to fire the shot heard 'round the world? The martyrs of history were not fools, and our honored dead who gave their lives to stop the advance of the Nazis didn't die in vain. Where, then, is the road to peace? Well it's a simple answer after all. You and I have the courage to say to our enemies, "There is a price we will not pay." There is a point beyond which they must not advance. And this—this is the meaning in the phrase of Barry Goldwater's "peace through strength." Winston Churchill said, "The destiny of man is not measured by material computations. When great forces are on the move in the world, we learn we're spirits—not animals." And he said, "There's something going on in time and space, and beyond time and space, which, whether we like it or not, spells duty."

You and I have a rendezvous with destiny. We'll preserve for our children this, the last best hope of man on earth, or we'll sentence them to take the last step into a thousand years of darkness. We will keep in mind and remember that Barry Goldwater has faith in us. He has faith that you and I have the ability and the dignity and the right to make our own decisions and determine our own destiny. Thank you very much.

DOCUMENT 5: PRESIDENT RICHARD NIXON, "THE SILENT MAJORITY SPEECH" (1969)

Two weeks before this historic address of November 3, 1969, antiwar activists organized the Moratorium to End the War in Vietnam, a nationwide demonstration against President Nixon's handling of the war he "inherited" from Lyndon Johnson. Nixon was compelled to specify the reasons why he would not immediately withdraw the American military, instead outlining his plan of "Vietnamization": the training and build-up of the anti-communist South Vietnamese military, effectively transferring responsibility for the conflict. This strategy for withdrawal, as well as some of the rhetoric in this address, would be echoed in the administrations of Presidents George W. Bush and Barack Obama in their own efforts to end the wars in Afghanistan and Iraq. According to historians Stephen Ambrose and Douglas Brinkley, the plan for Vietnamization:

> proved to be a disastrous choice, one of the worst decisions made by a Cold War President. Some of the direct results were: a prolongation of the war by four years . . . double-digit inflation . . . more bitterness, division, and dissention among the American people; the flouting of the Constitution by the President as he secretly extended the war to Laos and Cambodia, with tragic results for the people of both countries; and the eventual loss of the war.[1]

The speech is also significant because of Nixon's reference to the "silent majority," a pointed solicitation that was designed to mobilize conservative and patriotic citizens to counter the increasingly outspoken critics of the war, whose efforts, Nixon believed, would lead to the "defeat" and "humiliation" of the United States.

Nixon's effort was consistent with his general political strategy to weaken his opponents—including the new left antiwar forces—through fostering what has become known as "backlash" politics.

Less than six months after this speech, Nixon announced an escalation of the war into Cambodia, setting off a new and unprecedented antiwar mobilization that led directly to the killings of four students at Kent State University on May 4, 1970. Four days later, on May 8, a group of construction workers attacked antiwar protesters who had gathered in support of the slain college students. The hardhat thus became a symbol of the silent majority, and Nixon kept various hardhats on display in his office throughout the remainder of his presidency.

Good evening, my fellow Americans. Tonight I want to talk to you on a subject of deep concern to all Americans and to many people in all parts of the world: the war in Vietnam.

I believe that one of the reasons for the deep division about Vietnam is that many Americans have lost confidence in what their government has told them about our policy. The American people cannot and should not be asked to support a policy which involves the overriding issues of war and peace unless they know the truth about that policy. Tonight, therefore, I would like to answer some of the questions that I know are on the minds of many of you listening to me. How and why did America get involved in Vietnam in the first place? How has this administration changed the policy of the previous administration? . . . What choices do we have if we are to end the war? What are the prospects for peace?

Now, let me begin by describing the situation I found when I was inaugurated on January 20: the war had been going on for 4 years; 31,000 Americans had been killed in action; the training program for the South Vietnamese was behind schedule; 540,000 Americans were in Vietnam with no plans to reduce the number . . . the United States had not put forth a comprehensive peace proposal; the war was causing deep division at home and criticism from many of our friends as well as our enemies abroad.

In view of these circumstances there were some who urged that I end the war at once by ordering the immediate withdrawal of all American forces. From a political standpoint this would have been a popular and easy course to follow. After all, we became involved in the war while my predecessor was in office. I could blame the defeat which would be the result of my action on him and come out as the Peacemaker. Some put it to me quite bluntly: This was the only way to avoid allowing Johnson's war to become Nixon's war.

But I had a greater obligation than to think only of the years of my administration and of the next election. I had to think of the effect of my decision on the next generation and on the future of peace and freedom in America and in the world. Let us all understand that the question before us is not whether some Americans are for peace and some Americans are against peace. The question at issue is not whether Johnson's war becomes Nixon's war. The great question is: How can we win America's peace? Well, let us turn now to the fundamental issue. Why and how did the United States become involved in Vietnam in the first place?

Fifteen years ago North Vietnam, with the logistical support of Communist China and the Soviet Union, launched a campaign to impose a Communist government on South Vietnam by instigating and supporting a revolution. In response to the request of the Government of South Vietnam, President Eisenhower sent economic aid and military equipment to assist the people of South Vietnam in their efforts to prevent a Communist takeover. Seven years ago, President Kennedy sent 16,000 military personnel to Vietnam as combat advisers. Four years ago, President Johnson sent American combat forces to South Vietnam.

Now, many believe that President Johnson's decision to send American combat forces to South Vietnam was wrong. And many others—I among them—have been strongly critical of the way the war has been conducted. But the question facing us today is: Now that we are in the war, what is the best way to end it? In January I could only conclude that the precipitate withdrawal of American forces from Vietnam would be a disaster not only for South Vietnam but for the United States and for the cause of peace. For the South Vietnamese, our precipitate withdrawal would inevitably allow the Communists to repeat the massacres which followed their takeover in the North 15 years before.

They then murdered more than 50,000 people and hundreds of thousands more died in slave labor camps. We saw a prelude of what would happen in South Vietnam when the Communists entered the city of Hue last year. During their brief rule there, there was a bloody reign of terror in which 3,000 civilians were clubbed, shot to death, and buried in mass graves.

With the sudden collapse of our support, these atrocities of Hue would become the nightmare of the entire nation—and particularly for the million and a half Catholic refugees who fled to South Vietnam when the Communists took over in the North.

For the United States, this first defeat in our Nation's history would result in a collapse of confidence in American leadership, not only in Asia but throughout the world. Three American presidents have recognized the great stakes involved in Vietnam and understood what had to be done. In 1963, President Kennedy, with his characteristic eloquence and clarity, said, "We want to see a stable government there, carrying on a struggle to maintain its national independence. We believe strongly in that. We are not going to withdraw from that effort. In my opinion, for us to withdraw from that effort would mean a collapse not only of South Vietnam, but Southeast Asia. So we are going to stay there." President Eisenhower and President Johnson expressed the same conclusion during their terms of office.

For the future of peace, precipitate withdrawal would thus be a disaster of immense magnitude. A nation cannot remain great if it betrays its allies and lets down its friends. Our defeat and humiliation in South Vietnam without question would promote recklessness in the councils of those great powers who have not yet abandoned their goals of world conquest. This would spark violence wherever our commitments help maintain the peace—in the Middle East, in Berlin, eventually even in the Western Hemisphere. Ultimately, this would cost more lives. It would not bring peace, it would bring more war.

For these reasons, I rejected the recommendation that I should end the war by immediately withdrawing all of our forces. I chose instead to change American policy on both the negotiating front and battlefront. In order to end a war fought on many fronts, I initiated a pursuit for peace on many fronts. In a television speech on May 14, in a speech before the United Nations, and on a number of other occasions I set forth our peace proposals in great detail. We have offered the complete withdrawal of all outside forces within one year. We have proposed a cease-fire under international supervision. We have offered free elections under international supervision with the Communists participating in the organization and conduct of the elections as an organized political force. And the Saigon Government has pledged to accept the result of the elections.

We have not put forth our proposals on a take-it-or-leave-it basis. We have indicated that we are willing to discuss the proposals that have been put forth by the other side. We have declared that anything is negotiable except the right of the people of South Vietnam to determine their own future . . . Hanoi has refused even to discuss our proposals. They demand our unconditional acceptance of their terms, which are that we withdraw all American forces immediately and unconditionally and that we overthrow the Government of South Vietnam as we leave . . .

Now let me turn, however, to a more encouraging report on another front. At the time we launched our search for peace I recognized we might not succeed in bringing an end to the war through negotiation. I, therefore, put into effect another plan to bring peace—a plan which will bring the war to an end regardless of what happens on the negotiating front. It is in line with a major shift in U.S. foreign policy which I described in my press conference at Guam on July, 25. Let me briefly explain what has been described as the Nixon Doctrine: a policy which not only will help end the war in Vietnam, but which is an essential element of our program to prevent future Vietnams.

We Americans are a do-it-yourself people. We are an impatient people. Instead of teaching someone else to do a job, we like to do it ourselves. And this trait has been carried over into our foreign policy. In Korea and again in Vietnam, the United States furnished most of the money, most of the arms, and most of the men to help the people of those countries defend their freedom against Communist aggression. Before any American troops were committed to Vietnam, a leader of another Asian country expressed this opinion to me when I was traveling in Asia as a private citizen. He said: "When you are trying to assist another nation defend its freedom, U.S. policy should be to help them fight the war but not to fight the war for them."

Well, in accordance with this wise counsel, I laid down in Guam three principles as guidelines for future American policy toward Asia: First, the United States will keep all of its treaty commitments. Second, we shall provide a shield if a nuclear power threatens the freedom of a nation allied with us or of a nation whose survival we consider vital to our security. Third, in cases involving other types of aggression, we shall furnish military and economic assistance when requested in accordance with our treaty commitments. But we shall look to the nation directly threatened to assume the primary responsibility of providing the manpower for its defense.

After I announced this policy, I found that the leaders of the Philippines, Thailand, Vietnam, South Korea, and other nations which might be threatened by Communist aggression, welcomed this new direction in American foreign policy. The defense of freedom is everybody's business, not just America's business. And it is particularly the responsibility of the people whose freedom is threatened. In the previous administration, we Americanized the war in Vietnam. In this administration, we are "Vietnamizing" the search for peace.

The policy of the previous administration not only resulted in our assuming the primary responsibility for fighting the war, but even more significantly did not adequately stress the goal of strengthening the South Vietnamese so that they could defend themselves when we left. The Vietnamization plan was launched following Secretary Laird's visit to Vietnam in March. Under the plan, I ordered first a substantial increase in the training and equipment of South Vietnamese forces . . . Under the new orders, the primary mission of our troops is to enable the South Vietnamese forces to assume the full responsibility for the security of South Vietnam . . .

We have adopted a plan which we have worked out in cooperation with the South Vietnamese for the complete withdrawal of all U.S.

combat ground forces, and their replacement by South Vietnamese forces on an orderly scheduled timetable. This withdrawal will be made from strength and not from weakness. As South Vietnamese forces become stronger, the rate of American withdrawal can become greater. We must retain the flexibility to base each withdrawal decision on the situation as it is at that time rather than on estimates that are no longer valid.

Along with this optimistic estimate, I must—in all candor—leave one note of caution: if the level of enemy activity significantly increases we might have to adjust our timetable accordingly . . .

My fellow Americans, I am sure you can recognize from what I have said that we really only have two choices open to us if we want to end this war. I can order an immediate, precipitate withdrawal of all Americans from Vietnam without regard to the effects of that action. Or we can persist in our search for a just peace through a negotiated settlement if possible, or through continued implementation of our plan for Vietnamization if necessary—a plan in which we will withdraw all of our forces from Vietnam on a schedule in accordance with our program, as the South Vietnamese become strong enough to defend their own freedom. I have chosen this second course. It is not the easy way; it is the right way. It is a plan which will end the war and serve the cause of peace, not just in Vietnam but in the Pacific and in the world.

In speaking of the consequences of a precipitate withdrawal, I mentioned that our allies would lose confidence in America. Far more dangerous, we would lose confidence in ourselves. The immediate reaction would be a sense of relief that our men were coming home. But as we saw the consequences of what we had done, inevitable remorse and divisive recrimination would scar our spirit as a people. We have faced other crisis in our history and have become stronger by rejecting the easy way out and taking the right way in meeting our challenges. Our greatness as a nation has been our capacity to do what had to be done when we knew our course was right.

I recognize that some of my fellow citizens disagree with the plan for peace I have chosen. Honest and patriotic Americans have reached different conclusions as to how peace should be achieved. In San Francisco a few weeks ago, I saw demonstrators carrying signs reading, "Lose in Vietnam, bring the boys home." Well, one of the strengths of our free society is that any American has a right to reach that conclusion and to advocate that point of view. But as President of the United States, I would be untrue to my oath of office if I allowed the policy of this Nation to be dictated by the minority who hold that point of view and who try to impose it on the Nation by mounting demonstrations in the street.

For almost 200 years, the policy of this Nation has been made under our Constitution by those leaders in the Congress and the White House elected by all of the people. If a vocal minority, however fervent its cause, prevails over reason and the will of the majority, this Nation has no future as a free society. And now I would like to address a word, if I may, to the young people of this nation who are particularly concerned, and I understand why they are concerned, about this war. I respect your idealism. I share your concern for peace. I want peace as much as you do. There are powerful personal reasons I want to end this war. This week I will have to sign 83 letters to mothers, fathers, wives, and loved ones of men who have given their lives for America in Vietnam. It is very little satisfaction to me that this is only one-third as many letters as I signed the first week in office. There is nothing I want more than to see the day come when I do not have to write any of those letters. I want to end the war to save the lives of those brave young men in Vietnam. But I want to end it in a way which will increase the chance that their younger brothers and their sons will not have to fight in some future Vietnam someplace in the world. And I want to end the war for another reason. I want to end it so that the energy and dedication of you, our young people, now too often directed into bitter hatred against those responsible for the war, can be turned to the great challenges of peace, a better life for all Americans, a better life for all people on this earth.

I have chosen a plan for peace. I believe it will succeed. If it does succeed, what the critics say now won't matter. If it does not succeed, anything I say then won't matter. I know it may not be fashionable to speak of patriotism or national destiny these days. But I feel it is appropriate to do so on this occasion.

Two hundred years ago this Nation was weak and poor. But even then, America was the hope of millions in the world. Today we have become the strongest and richest nation in the world. And the wheel of destiny has turned so that any hope the world has for the survival of peace and freedom will be determined by whether the American people have the moral stamina and the courage to meet the challenge of free world leadership.

Let historians not record that when America was the most powerful nation in the world we passed on the other side of the road and allowed the last hopes for peace and freedom of millions of people to be suffocated by the forces of totalitarianism. And so tonight, to you, the great silent majority of my fellow Americans, I ask for your support. I pledged in my campaign for the Presidency to end the war in a way that we could win the peace. I have initiated a plan of action which will enable me to keep that pledge.

The more support I can have from the American people, the sooner that pledge can be redeemed. For the more divided we are at home, the less likely the enemy is to negotiate ... Let us be united for peace. Let us also be united against defeat. Because let us understand: North Vietnam cannot defeat or humiliate the United States. Only Americans can do that. Fifty years ago, in this room and at this very desk, President Woodrow Wilson spoke words which caught the imagination of a war-weary world. He said, "This is the war to end war." His dream for peace after World War I was shattered on the hard realities of great power politics and Woodrow Wilson died a broken man.

Tonight I do not tell you that the war in Vietnam is the war to end wars. But I do say this: I have initiated a plan which will end this war in a way that will bring us closer to that great goal to which Woodrow Wilson and every American President in our history has been dedicated—the goal of a just and lasting peace. As President, I hold the responsibility for choosing the best path to that goal and then leading the Nation along it. I pledge to you tonight that I shall meet this responsibility with all of the strength and wisdom I can command in accordance with your hopes, mindful of your concerns, sustained by your prayers.

Thank you and goodnight.

DOCUMENT 6: RONALD REAGAN, "LAW AND ORDER" (1975)

Ronald Reagan delivered an estimated 1,000 radio commentaries during the roughly five-year period separating his tenure as Governor of California, which ended on January 6, 1975, and his 1980 campaign for president. The commentaries addressed a wide range of social, political, and economic issues. Some of the commentaries were quite serious, while others were more lighthearted. This particular commentary is on the topic of law and order, which was a key component of conservative ideology during the late-1960s and early 1970s. Reagan effectively used the law-and-order theme in response to the student uprisings at Berkeley, as well as the Watts Riots of 1965, to win election as governor. Spiro Agnew and Richard Nixon also used similar rhetoric, but in an ironic twist of fate, it was their own corruption and lawlessness that largely discredited the ideology of law and order.

But the resignations of Agnew and Nixon were not the only reason why the rhetoric of law and order had fallen out of favor among conservative politicians. The idea had been critiqued for its disregard for social problems, and for the extent to which it failed to address the grievances of various constituencies, whether on college campuses or in the ghettoes. Here, Reagan defends law and order against persistent claims that it was an inherently racist ideology. As in so many examples of Reagan's biography, there was a blurred distinction between his background in show business and his "real life"; as he notes, he starred in a 1953 film entitled Law and Order.

I once appeared in a movie called *Law and Order*, if it were being made today the title would probably be changed. I'll be right back.

Not too long ago, any discussion of crime and its rapid rate of increase would find the term "law and order" used as a matter of course. Those who feel the courts have been too lenient and that permissiveness has played a part in crime's increase would use the term to describe what should be restored.

I played in a movie some years ago called *Law and Order*. It wasn't a very good movie, as some of you who stay up for the late show have probably discovered. But it was the story of a town marshal who was dedicated to preserving law and order, hence the title. The phrase is perfectly respectable—at least it always has been. We are a nation of laws, proud that we place our faith in law rather than in men. And of course civilization is built upon the ability of humans to live together in an orderly society.

In the last few years however, the phrase has become unfashionable. Those who made it so began looking askance at anyone who used the words. Their arched eyebrows were a reaction to what they had determined was an expression of bigotry. If pressed for an explanation, they would inform you that law and order were code words that really meant a call for racial discrimination. By coincidence, those who made the decision to outlaw this simple phrase are usually against our penal system, against capital punishment, and believe that society, not the criminal, is to blame for crime. Well, I think this inference of bigotry is, in itself, bigoted. Not only does it impugn, without proof, that the character of the person who uses an appropriate phrase to describe what is all too lacking today, but it casts a slur on an entire racial group. Are they not implying that our fellow citizens, who happen to be black, are so given to crime that a call for law and order is automatically a call for a curb on the black community?

The truth is that blacks in America are victims of crime far out of proportion to their numbers. They are roughly 10 percent or 12 percent of our population, but more than half of all the murder victims are black. If law and order is a code word for racism, then explain away the survey done by American University in the nation's capital. It seems that the black residents of the District of Columbia are calling for law and order far more than their white neighbors. 74 percent of them want sterner action against criminals. With whites, it was only 61 percent. 82 percent of blacks, compared to only 62 percent of whites think tougher parole policies would cut down on crime. On the death penalty there was a closer ratio: it was believed to be an effective deterrent by 56 percent of the blacks and 54 percent of the whites. Black citizens are well aware that criminals are color-blind. They practice no discrimination in plying a despicable trade. Law and order isn't a code word to blacks, it's a cry for help. And we'd better join in.

This is Ronald Reagan. Thanks for listening.

DOCUMENT 7: RONALD REAGAN, "THE MODERN LITTLE RED HEN" (1976)

"The Little Red Hen" is an old folktale used to teach children the importance of hard work. The traditional story focuses on the title character, the Red Hen, who goes about planting and harvesting wheat in order to make bread. Despite the repeated requests of the Red Hen, the other barnyard animals refuse to cooperate in the reaping and sowing, and instead only want to eat the bread, the finished product of the Red Hen's labor. Here, in Reagan's retelling, the lazy pig, duck, goose, and cow, are replaced by welfare recipients, union members, and government bureaucrats. The commentary exemplifies Reagan's political style: just below its humorous and lighthearted surface lies an unmistakable backlash appeal.

A modern-day Little Red Hen may not appear to be a quotable authority on economics—but then, some authorities on economics aren't worth quoting. I'll be right back.

About a year ago, I imposed a little poetry on you. It was called "The Incredible Bread Machine," and it made a lot of sense with reference to matters economic. You didn't object too much, so, having gotten away with it once, I'm going to try again. This is a little treatise on basic economics called, "The Modern Little Red Hen."

Once upon a time there was a little red hen who scratched about the barnyard, until she uncovered some grains of wheat. She called her neighbors and said, "If we plant this wheat, we shall have bread to eat. Who will help me plant it?"

"Not I," said the cow; "Not I," said the duck; "Not I," said the pig; "Not I," said the goose.

"Then I will," said the little red hen. And she did. The wheat grew tall and ripened into golden grain. "Who will help me reap my wheat?" asked the little red hen.

"Not I," said the duck; "Out of my classification," said the pig; "I'd lose my seniority," said the cow; "I'd lose my unemployment compensation," said the goose.

"Then I will," said the little red hen. And she did.

At last it came time to bake the bread. "Who will help me bake the bread?" asked the little red hen.

"Oh, that'd be overtime for me," said the cow; "I'd lose my welfare benefits," said the duck; "I'm a dropout and never learned how," said the pig. "Well, if I'm going to be the only helper, that's discrimination," said the goose.

"Then I will," said the little red hen.

She baked five loaves and held them up for her neighbors to see. They all wanted some—and in fact, demanded a share. But the little red hen said, "No." "I can eat the five loaves myself."

"Excess profits!" cried the cow; "Capitalist leech!" screamed the duck; "I demand equal rights!" yelled the goose. And the pig just grunted. And they painted "UNFAIR" picket signs and marched round and round the little red hen, shouting obscenities.

When the government agent came, he said to the little red hen, "You must not be greedy."

"But I earned the bread," said the little red hen.

"Exactly," said the agent. "That's the wonderful free enterprise system. Anyone in the barnyard can earn as much as he wants. But under our modern government regulations, the productive workers must divide their product with the idle."

And they lived happily ever after, including the little red hen, who smiled and clucked, "I am grateful, I am grateful." But her neighbors wondered why she never again baked anymore bread.

I guess a lot of us have been wondering something like that. Incidentally, if you'd like to have a copy of "The Modern Little Red Hen," don't write to me. Write to the station to which you're listening, and they'll send you a copy.

This is Ronald Reagan. Thanks for listening.

DOCUMENT 8: RONALD REAGAN, "RELIGION AND EDUCATION" (1977)

Ronald Reagan was not a particularly religious man. He did not belong to or regularly attend church. Nevertheless, he gave lip service to a number of issues that appealed to the religious right, particularly in the period that preceded the 1980 presidential election. Although the Supreme Court banned school-sponsored prayer during the early 1960s, it was not until the following decade that conservatives mobilized in opposition to what they referred to as "secular humanism" in the public school system. Throughout the 1970s the issue of school prayer, sex education, and the teaching of evolution were part of the larger "culture wars" that gave rise to the religious right as co-constitutive of the American conservative movement, and Reagan was well aware of the role this group could play in the formation of a new conservative coalition. Reagan did not know what it meant to be "born again" in 1976, but by 1980 he had "mastered the code" of appealing to religious conservatives. Reagan made few policy decisions consistent with the issues supported by religious conservatives, and on several occasions he advocated legislation or supported individuals despised by the movement. Here, however, he laments what he characterizes as the "expulsion" of God from public education.

Some time ago, God was expelled on constitutional grounds from our public schools. Did we really do this to preserve separation of church and state? I'll be right back.

Determined to avoid the domination of government by a religious order or a situation where religious belief could be dictated by the government, the framers of our Constitution made sure that our new nation would enjoy a separation of church and state. They intended that individuals be free to worship as each chose. That government could not favor or discriminate against particular religions or denominations, nor could any denomination assume a role in government.

I challenge anyone to prove that a "clear and present danger" to that constitutional protection has ever existed for even one moment in all the years since the Constitution was ratified. And yet, a few years ago, a suit, brought by an avowed atheist, led to a Supreme Court ban on voluntary prayer in our schools. Have we, as a result, let some among us make atheism a religion, and impose it on those of us who believe in our Judeo-Christian traditions?

There is a fundamental difference between the separation of church and state, and denying the spiritual heritage of this country. Inscribed in the Jefferson Memorial in Washington, D.C., are Jefferson's words, "God who gave us life gave us liberty. Can the liberties of a nation be secure when we have removed a conviction that these liberties are the gift of God?" Our coins bear the words, "In God We Trust." We take the oath of office, asking God's help in keeping that oath. And we proclaim that we are a nation, "under God," when we pledge allegiance to the flag.

But we can't mention God's name in a public school—or even sing religious hymns that are non-denominational. Christmas can be celebrated in the school room with pine trees, tinsel and reindeers, but there must be no mention of the man whose birthday is being celebrated. One wonders how a teacher would answer if a student asked why it was called Christmas. We've gone so far that it almost seems a rule, originally designed to guard against violation of the Constitution, has become an aggressive campaign against religion itself. And isn't that the very thing we set out to guard against—domination of religion by the state—in this case, by public school officials?

A case in point: in an elementary school in St. Petersburg, Florida, two teachers came to class wearing lapel buttons which read, "I found it." Such buttons, bumper stickers and even billboards are widespread around the whole country. There have even been spot ads on television with people declaring, "I found it." At any rate, the school principal inquired what the buttons meant, and was shocked to learn the wearers were simply acknowledging they had found God.

Now you'd think this was a personal thing with each of the two teachers, but the principal didn't see it that way. She said, "I feel if the buttons are worn in the school building and a child asks what they mean, it would be bringing religion into the schools." Well, it would seem that not only is religion lacking in the schools, so is common sense. I wonder what a teacher is supposed to say if a kid asks about those four small words on a dime, "In God We Trust." Or could it be, that's why they aren't being taught how to read these days?

This is Ronald Reagan. Thanks for listening.

DOCUMENT 9: RONALD REAGAN, "HYPHENATED NAMES" (1977)

In this commentary from 1977, Reagan addresses the issue of hyphenated surnames, a practice that was on the rise during the 1970s.[2] In a formula that was a regular part of his public speaking, Reagan, through a letter he claimed to have received from a listener, speculates as to how the practice of surname retention, if it continued through generations, would lead to an absurd state of affairs that would cast a burden upon more traditionally minded Americans. The address is vintage Reagan. Through a humorous and nostalgic style that harkens back to an earlier, simpler American age, he also implicitly presents a criticism of the feminist movement by portraying the retention of a woman's maiden name as yet another unnecessary complication of the modern world—and one that would lead to an expansion of the federal government bureaucracy.

What's in a name? That's a well-known clichéd question that could become something of a study if a new idea in marriage catches on. I'll be right back.

In a recent edition of the alternative magazine being published by the *Saturday Evening Club*, a gentleman named Joseph McGrath wrote tellingly of something that could change our society more than switching to the metric system. Mr. McGrath had seen an item in his local paper about an upcoming marriage. The thing that had caught his eye was the announcement that the young couple, in keeping with some of the ideas floating around these days, intended to keep both their surnames. They would, as a married couple, be known as the Schwam-Bukowskis, not Mr. and Mrs. Bukowski. Now, if I'd seen that item, I must confess that I probably would have shrugged it off as a little silly, but certainly that's their right if that's what they wanted to put on their mailbox.

But Mr. McGrath, while conceding that latter point, has a more inquiring mind. He looked into the future, not only at the Schwam-Bukowskis, but at the future of society if such an idea catches on. Envisioning parenthood for the happy couple, Mr. McGrath does some supposing. Suppose a daughter, Janet, is born—Janet Schwam-Bukowski—who grows up and marries a young man who also has a dual name, the idea having caught on. Janet Schwam-Bukowski and Jack Cramwinkle-Roget become the Schwam-Bukowski-Cramwinkle-Rogets. Time passes and they're blessed with a son they promptly name Frank. Reaching the age of 21, Mr. McGrath envisions Frank Schwam-Bukowski-Cramwinkle-Roget falling in love with and marrying a lovely Juanita Hallerin-Schwam—no relation—Morningside-Lucarelli. This nice young couple, being sentimental and nostalgic over earlier times, name their first born after a favorite great-granduncle named John Smith. And there it is on the birth certificate: John Smith Hallerin-Schwam-Morningside-Lucarelli-Schwam-Bukowski-Cramwinkle-Roget.

Without getting into additional generations, Mr. McGrath then took up some of the associated problems started by the young couple, the Schwam-Bukowskis, who set us off on this course. Roll calls at the start of the school day could conceivably take until lunchtime. Of course, he points out there would be rejoicing on the bureaucratic front. The computers would be humming, and the Form 10–40 would have to have a lot of additional lines. Telephone directory printing would be a great growth industry. And how about all those monogrammed items: towels, bed linens, handkerchiefs and even shirts; monogrammed jewelry—tie-clips, cufflinks, earrings, etcetera. Well, we'd probably just have to give up on those. But how about those conventions and business meetings where a sticker bearing your name is stuck to your lapel? It would become an 11 × 14 placard hung around your neck like a bib.

Mr. McGrath carried his vision of the future to other problem areas: the engravers of tombstones for example. He may have created a new parlor game. Try it at your next social gathering. I've thought of one already—probably because of an earlier occupation of mine. Can't you hear a sports announcer now saying excitedly, "John Smith Hallerin-Schwam-Morningside-Lucarelli-Schwam—no relation—Bukowski-Cramwinkle-Roget is fading back to pass . . ." I wonder if we could get Miss Schwam and Mr. Bukowski to reconsider.

This is Ronald Reagan, thanks for listening.

DOCUMENT 10: RONALD REAGAN, "SOCIALIZED MEDICINE" (1977)

In 1961, Ronald Reagan released a well-known LP entitled Ronald Reagan Speaks Out Against Socialized Medicine, *which was funded by the American Medical Association. That project was part of the conservative attempt to prevent the creation of Medicare, the federal program of health coverage for the elderly. Here, Reagan returns to the issue, more than 15 years later, in another broadcast entitled "Socialized Medicine." He connects the issue to some of his favorite topics, including government bureaucracy, taxes, and labor unions.*

We've all heard the admonition, "physician, heal thyself." Maybe it should be changed to read, "physician, defend thyself." I'll be right back.

The campaign goes on to bring healthcare in America out of the free market system and into the protective custody of government. Those who brought us the Postal Service and Amtrak are anxious to provide medical service of the same high caliber. What is hard to understand—well, come to think of it, may not be so hard to understand—is the American Medical Association's reluctance to fight back. After decades of all out war against socialized medicine, is it possible that combat fatigue is beginning to set in?

Heaven knows the energy and determination of those who want to put government in charge of our health has been untiring and persistent. The medical association gave in to war-weariness and endorsed a national health insurance bill that would force all employers to provide health insurance benefits for their employees. Probably the association figured that government would have less chance to interfere in the doctor-patient relationship under such a program. Some place along the line however, the troops rallied, and the association withdrew its support for the bill.

But the defense line, once breached, is hard to restore. The insurance business, which should be opposed to government medicine, is supporting a bill which—just by coincidence, I'm sure—calls for a heavy government subsidy for the buying of private health insurance. Much of the opposition to government medicine has been based on the better quality of medicine we have here in America, where the providing of healthcare is still largely in the free market.

On these broadcasts, I've tried to debunk the claims of the socialized medicine advocates by citing comparisons between medical availability and cost here and in other countries. A typical example is an incident told by Congressman Bob Donald. On a trip to England, he asked an Englishwoman—attractive, except for some facial scars—what she thought of the National Health Service. She approved of it, and said, "We all get our medical care free, you know." That isn't true of course, they're taxed far more heavily than we are, and their health service takes a big bite out of those taxes. Then she said, "It is rather slow. I had to wait eight years for an appointment with a dermatologist about my face." She then had to wait another year before treatment could begin. She repeated though, "But it is free."

There's another argument against socialized medicine which hasn't been used as much as it should, when you think of the sense of fair play that is characteristic of Americans. George Meany of the AFL-CIO is all-out for a national health plan. But how would he react if someone proposed that the skilled workers he represents would have to become government employees to practice their skill? Do any of us have the right to tell the members of any profession or trade they must become government employees in order to pursue their chosen work? Of course we want to insure that no one is denied medical care because of poverty. And we've done better than most countries to provide that care. But wouldn't it violate everything we believe in to adopt a system based on the idea that the patients have a right to the doctor's services without regard for his right to say how, and on what terms those services will be delivered.

This is Ronald Reagan. Thanks for listening.

DOCUMENT 11: RONALD REAGAN, "STUDENT LETTER" (1977)

In this commentary from 1977, Reagan again uses a letter he received that purports to illustrate the virtues of free market capitalism. The results of the student's in-class experiment supported the idea that "socialized" benefits reduce the individual's incentive to work, thereby lowering overall productivity. Reagan was fond of the use of simplistic examples to underscore his pro-business, anti-labor, and anti-tax worldview (see also Document 7). As the 1970s were a time of tremendous corporate "investment" in colleges, universities, and high schools aimed at convincing the nation's youth not only of the benefits of a corporate career but of the virtues of the unfettered free market (see Chapter 4), one cannot help but wonder if the high school student who wrote this letter had been on the receiving end of such a program during his education.

Are you worried that our sons and daughters are being led to believe that socialism offers advantages capitalism can't match? I'll be right back.

Economists—at least the good old fashioned kind—have written countless books and essays trying to explain that a free market economy is superior to the collectivism of Karl Marx. There really shouldn't be much of an argument, with all the examples we have for comparison. Everywhere there is a socialist nation, there is a failure to meet the needs of the people of that nation—except by calling on capitalist neighbors for help. Still, it's the socialist world that is expanding, while ours grows smaller. Well, how would you like to feel a little better about the whole thing?

I received a letter a couple of weeks ago that brightened my whole day. Paul A. Leonard, a sophomore at Mayo High School in Rochester, Minnesota, wrote me a letter saying he had listened to some of these radio broadcasts. Then he wrote, "In view of your support of free enterprise, I thought you might be interested in an experiment that I recently conducted in my history class. Fifteen volunteers were selected with an eye to an approximate balance of athletes, non-athletes, boys and girls. The volunteers were not informed of the purpose of the experiment. The first day, a socialist-like system was set up. The subjects were informed that they had volunteered to do push-ups, in return for which they would be given candy."

Now, push-ups and candy—what do they have to do with socialism? Well, Paul Leonard explained to the 15 volunteers that they would do push-ups, with a limit of 30 on how many anyone would have to do, or could be allowed to do. For every five push-ups, they would each get a piece of candy. And here's where the political science comes in: the total number of push-ups accomplished by the volunteers, would be divided by 15, the number of volunteers, and each would receive a piece of candy for every five push-ups. Those who did 30, and those who couldn't get off the floor once, would share equally in the candy. Four managed to do the maximum, and the overall average was 16.2 push-ups. So, everyone received three pieces of candy. That was half the experiment: the socialist half.

The next day was capitalism's turn. The volunteers found they were going to do push-ups again. Same limit: no more than 30; and same reward: one piece of candy for each five push-ups. Just one difference: they were capitalists this time. No averaging. They would each get one piece of candy for every five push-ups that each one was able to do. In other words, there was an incentive for each one to do his or her very best. The average of 16.2 on the socialist day went up to 21.2, nearly a one-third increase in productivity. And this time, almost half the volunteers, seven, not four, did the maximum of 30.

I gathered from Paul Leonard's letter that he really wasn't too surprised about that. If I could deliver a personal message to Paul, the sophomore at Mayo High, it would be this: Congratulations Paul. You've demonstrated that you understand the difference between the magic of the free market system and the idiocy of Karl Marx. There are some pretty eminent PhDs in economics who can't figure that out.

End of message. This is Ronald Reagan. Thanks for listening.

DOCUMENT 12: RONALD REAGAN, "SANCTIONS AGAINST SOUTH AFRICA" (1978)

In 1978, the year of this commentary, Pieter Willem Botha, head of the Afrikaner National Party apartheid government, became the Prime Minister of South Africa. In contrast to the growing international condemnation of the apartheid regime, the United States had supported the National Party to act as a bulwark against communism on the African continent. Here, in his characteristic style, which makes use of the story of an unnamed black journalist and two anonymous volunteers, Reagan casts the issue of United States investment in South Africa as an act of benevolence and "friendship." Reagan used what he referred to as "constructive engagement" to rationalize his veto of the Comprehensive Anti-Apartheid Act of 1986, a veto that was overridden by Congress.

We have a lot of people in our land who like to take a hand in creating foreign policy. They are diplomats without portfolio. I'll be right back.

It's the right of every American to have opinions, and to express them, and when the occasion warrants, to urge our public officials to take action based on such opinions. We can all criticize our national policies and suggest changes. We can vote against elected officials who refuse to heed our suggestions. But whether as private citizen or public servant, we can't have our own foreign policy and privately establish our own international relations.

The U.S. maintains trade and diplomatic relations with South Africa. South Africans have fought beside Americans in two world wars. It is true however, that most Americans find South Africa's policy of apartheid repugnant, and hope very much that those South Africans who share our repugnance will strive until they succeed in righting what we perceive to be a great wrong. Some Americans think we should end our friendship with South Africa, refuse to allow American businesses to set up branches there and simply ostracize South Africa until it meets our own standards of racial tolerance.

But since we've only recently achieved our present level of racial tolerance, and have a fresh memory of an America where intolerance, bigotry and prejudice were fairly widespread, isn't it possible that we could be more helpful? A friendly America acting with understanding and compassion, based on our own experience could be of more help in resolving apartheid than we could by turning our back.

A black journalist recently returning from a trip to South Africa told me of American industries there who were showing the way in hiring practices and even in providing employee housing. He said that black employees of American firms said that it would be terribly hurtful to South African blacks if the American firms were forced to close up shop.

The other day I came across an item that shows how ridiculous people can be when motivated by prejudice. It seems that the lady in charge of the American Peace Corps is so bitter about South Africa and its policies, that she won't allow any Peace Corps volunteers to serve in that country. It does seem as though she's making a policy determination that is, or should be, beyond her authority. But never mind that.

Recently, two young volunteers serving in Botswana, which borders on South Africa, came down with back ailments. They were not allowed to seek treatment in a nearby South African hospital. Madame Director had them flown to Frankfurt, Germany—that's a 14 hour flight, one way. One of the young men said he flew 14 hours, waited another four-and-a-half hours to spend 20 minutes with a doctor, then flew 14 hours back. And here's the tag-line: Madame Director, who wouldn't allow treatment in the South African Hospital, sent them to Germany, on a plane of South African Airways. Cost? $3,000.

This is Ronald Reagan. Thanks for listening.

DOCUMENT 13: RONALD REAGAN, "GUANTANAMO NAVAL BASE" (1978)

During the late 1970s in the aftermath of the American military defeat in Vietnam, the United States had entered a period of détente with the Soviet Union. During this brief moment of the Cold War, several foreign policy issues appeared to illustrate the decline of American geopolitical power. Among these issues was the Panama Canal, which had been under American control since it opened in 1914, and the Canal Zone had been under American control since 1903. Reagan, who opposed the ratification of the canal treaties that ceded the canal to the Panamanian government, used the issue to argue that a "domino effect" would lead to communist expansion in the region. Here, Reagan attempts to use the canal treaty to suggest that the communists would demand the closure of the entire Guantanamo Naval Base in Cuba, a move that was not under consideration in the United States at the time. Indeed, the Guantanamo base and the Panama Canal were historically intertwined, as both came into existence as part of American expansion related to the Spanish-American War. The conservative movement would successfully use the canal treaty (and other issues of the 1970s) to push for a restoration of militarism as a leading component of American foreign policy.

When the Panama Canal giveaway was ratified by the Senate, some of us suggested that it might be the first of other dominos to fall. I'll be right back.

Since Spanish-American War days and the freeing of Cuba, the United States has maintained a naval base on the island of Cuba at Guantanamo Bay. There is nothing imperialistic about this, nor does it infringe upon Cuban sovereignty the way that some Panamanians thought our canal across Panama did. The Guantanamo base is on Cuban territory, leased by us, the lease to run in perpetuity.

I won't get into the strategic importance of this base, other than to point out that its location off the entrance to the Panama Canal, and the added range it gives us in securing the South Atlantic sea lands. It was key to the Monroe Doctrine—back when we enforced the Monroe Doctrine.

During the long debate over the Panama Canal treaties, many opponents of those treaties, particularly men with great experience in naval strategy, pointed to the obvious close relationship between Castro and Panama's dictator General Torrijos. Predictions were made that the canal, if given up, would only be the first of several dominos, and the next could very well be the Guantanamo Naval Base. This of course was passed off by the State Department as having no real basis in fact, as we were assured that we were buying the gratitude and friendship of the Panamanians with our magnanimous gesture.

Well, the treaties have been ratified. And recently Castro ordered a weeklong celebration of the revolution by which he seized the reins of government in Cuba. We could also add that he has made Cuba a satellite of the Soviet Union. In his speeches, during the celebration, he brought up Guantanamo, using all the phrases that were used all so often by the advocates of the canal treaties: the base was an affront to Cuba's sovereignty, it was colonialism, it was imperialism, and of course, he wasn't going to stand for its continued presence. Right on cue, those new friends we supposedly made in Panama were redefining Panama's foreign policy in a 14-page document. Foreign Minister, Nicolas Gonzalez Revilla, observed that the centerpiece of Panama's foreign policy had been the canal. Now that agreement has been reached on that, they can lay the groundwork for future foreign policy.

Their groundwork covered quite a bit of ground. For example, the Torrijos government is calling for Israel to yield all occupied Arab lands. Closer to home, they want self-determination for Puerto Rico—never mind that Puerto Rico has that already, and that more than 90 percent of its citizens want to stay right where they are: very close to Uncle Sam. Finally, Panama's new foreign policy called for the United States to give up its naval base on Guantanamo Bay. Now, will it be a surprising coincidence if some of our State Department types discover that we don't need that naval base, and that giving it away will win the friendship of Castro?

This is Ronald Reagan, thanks for listening.

Notes

Preface

1. Kathleen Frankovich, "Public Opinion Trends," in *The Election of 1980: Reports and Interpretations*, ed. Marlene Michels Pomper (Chatham, New Jersey: Chatham House Publishers, 1981), 113.

1 Introducing American Conservatism

1. Gil Troy, *Morning in America: How Ronald Reagan Invented the 1980s* (Princeton: Princeton University Press, 2005), 50.
2. Sean Wilentz, *The Age of Reagan: A History, 1974–2008* (New York: HarperCollins, 2008), 127.
3. Lou Cannon, *President Reagan: The Role of a Lifetime* (New York: PublicAffairs, 2000), 119.
4. Anne Edwards, *Early Reagan: The Rise to Power* (New York: William & Morrow, 1987), 144.
5. Gary Wills, *Reagan's America* (New York: Penguin, 2000), 298–307.
6. Wills, *Reagan's America*, 332.
7. Kim Phillips-Fein, *Invisible Hands: The Making of the Conservative Movement from the New Deal to Reagan* (New York: W.W. Norton and Company, 2009), 98.
8. Thomas W. Evans, *The Education of Ronald Reagan: The General Electric Years and the Untold Story of His Conversion to Conservatism* (New York: Columbia University Press, 2006), 4.
9. Evans, *Education of Ronald Reagan*, 38–9.
10. Wills, *Reagan's America*, 337.
11. Frances Fitzgerald, *Way Out There in the Blue: Reagan, Star Wars and the End of the Cold War* (New York: Simon & Schuster, 2000), 57.
12. Matthew Dallek, *The Right Moment: Ronald Reagan's First Victory and the Decisive Turning Point in American Politics* (Oxford: Oxford University Press, 2004), 39.
13. Dallek, *Right Moment*, 68.
14. Edwards, *Early Reagan*, 242.
15. Hunter S. Thompson, *The Proud Highway: Saga of a Desperate Southern Gentleman 1955–1967* (New York: Ballantine Books, 1997), 492.

16 Dallek, *Right Moment*, 197.
17 Mona Charen, "Who's the True Conservative?" *National Review Online*, March 2, 2012, available online at www.nationalreview.com/articles/292419/who-s-true-conservative-mona-charenpg=1.
18 George Nash, *The Conservative Intellectual Movement in America since 1945* (Wilmington, ISI Books, 2006), 198.
19 Theda Skocpol and Vanessa Williamson, *The Tea Party and the Remaking of Republican Conservatism* (New York: Oxford University Press, 2012), 39.
20 Phillips-Fein, *Invisible Hand*, 36.
21 Anthony DiMaggio, *The Rise of the Tea Party: Political Discontent in the Age of Obama* (New York: Monthly Review Press, 2011), 41.
22 Geoffrey Kabaservice, *Rule and Ruin: The Downfall of Moderation and the Destruction of the Republican Party, From Eisenhower to the Tea Party* (New York: Oxford University Press, 2012), 20.
23 Murray N. Rothbard, "Life in the Old Right," in *The Paleoconservatives: New Voices of the Old Right*, ed. Joseph Scotchie (New Brunswick, NJ: Transaction Publishers, 1999), 20.
24 Gary Gerstle, "Race and the Myth of the Liberal Consensus," *The Journal of American History* 82 (1995): 579.
25 John A. Andrew, III, *The Other Side of the Sixties: Young Americans for Freedom and the Rise of Conservative Politics* (New Brunswick: Rutgers University Press, 1997), 35.
26 Phillips-Fein, *Invisible Hand*, 78.
27 Martin Walker, *America Reborn: A Twentieth-Century Narrative in Twenty-six Lives* (New York: Knopf, 2000), 248.
28 Michael W. Miles, *The Odyssey of the American Right* (New York: Oxford University Press, 1980), 285.
29 Barry Goldwater, *The Conscience of a Conservative* (BN Publishing, [1964] 2007), 16.
30 Elizabeth Tandy Shermer, "Origins of the Conservative Ascendancy: Barry Goldwater's Early Senate Career and the De-Legitimization of Organized Labor," *The Journal of American History* 95 (2008): 678.
31 Kabaservice, *Rule and Ruin*, 90.

2 The South, Civil Rights, and the Transformation of the Republican Party

1 Ronald Reagan, "States' Rights Speech," Neshoba County Fair, Mississippi, August 3, 1980. The transcript for Reagan's address has been reprinted online at http://neshobademocrat.com/main.asp?SectionID=2&SubSectionID=297&ArticleID=15600&TM=60417.67.
2 Ann Coulter, "Civil Rights and the Mob: George Wallace, Bull Conner, Orval Faubus and Other Democrats," *Human Events*, June 13, 2011, 16.
3 Todd Tiahrt, "Take a Right Turn: My Conversion from a Democrat to a Conservative Republican," in *Why I am a Reagan Conservative*, ed. Michael K. Deaver (New York: HarperCollins, 2005), 194.

4   Rush Limbaugh, "How Reagan Attracted Independents," radio broadcast transcript, September 28, 2011, available online at www.rushlimbaugh.com/daily/2011/09/28/how_reagan_attracted_independents.
5   Kabaservice, *Rule and Ruin*, 101.
6   Eric Foner, "The Ideology of the Republican Party," in *The Birth of the Grand Old Party: the Republicans' First Generation*, eds. Robert F. Engs and Randall M. Miller (Philadelphia: University of Pennsylvania Press, 2002), 9.
7   Claude Bowers, *The Tragic Era: The Revolution after Lincoln* (Cambridge, Massachusetts: The Riverside Press, 1929); William Dunning, *Reconstruction Political and Economic 1865–1877* (New York: Harper & Brothers, 1907).
8   W.E.B. Du Bois, *Black Reconstruction in America, 1860–1880* (New York: Touchstone, [1935] 1992), 670–709.
9   C. Vann Woodward, *The Strange Career of Jim Crow* (New York: Oxford University Press, 2001), 82–3.
10 Aldon D. Morris, *The Origins of the Civil Rights Movement: Black Communities Organizing for Change* (New York: The Free Press, 1984).
11 Eric Foner, *Reconstruction: America's Unfinished Revolution 1863–1877* (New York: Harper and Row, 1988), 603.
12 George Lewis, *Massive Resistance: The White Response to the Civil Rights Movement* (Oxford: Hodder Arnold, 2006), 15.
13 Earl Black and Merle Black, *The Rise of the Southern Republicans* (Cambridge, Massachusetts: Belknap, 2002), 40.
14 V.O. Key, *Southern Politics in State and Nation* (Knoxville: The University of Tennessee Press, [1949] 1977), 16.
15 Miles, *Odyssey of the Right*, 18.
16 Phillips-Fein, *Invisible Hand*, 9; Eric Rauchway, *The Great Depression and New Deal: A Very Short History* (Oxford: Oxford University Press, 2008), 67.
17 Pat Dunham, *Electoral Behavior in the United States* (Englewood Cliffs, New Jersey: Prentice Hall, 1991), 79.
18 Meg Jacobs, "The Conservative Struggle and the Energy Crisis," in *Rightward Bound: Making America Conservative in the 1970s*, eds. Bruce J. Schulman and Julian E. Zelizer (Cambridge, Massachusetts: Harvard University Press, 2008), 202.
19 Phillips-Fein, *Invisible Hand*, 56.
20 The full report can be found on the Truman Presidential Library website, available online at www.trumanlibrary.org/civilrights/srights1.htm.
21 Mary Dudziak, *Cold War, Civil Rights: Race and the Image of American Democracy* (Princeton, New Jersey: Princeton University Press, 2000).
22 George Lewis, "White South, Red Nation: Massive Resistance and the Cold War," in *Massive Resistance: Southern Opposition to the Second Reconstruction*, ed. Clive Webb (Oxford: Oxford University Press, 2005), 119.
23 Thomas Borstelmann, *Apartheid's Reluctant Uncle: The United States and Southern Africa in the Early Cold War* (New York: Oxford University Press, 1993), 4.
24 Ronald Story and Bruce Laurie, *The Rise of Conservatism in America, 1945–2000: A Brief History with Documents* (New York: Bedford/St. Martin's, 2008), 39.
25 Numan Bartley, *The Rise of Massive Resistance: Race and Politics in the South during the 1950s* (Baton Rouge: Louisiana State University Press, 1997), 33.
26 Morris, *Origins of the Civil Rights Movement*.

27 Jason Sokol, *There Goes My Everything: White Southerners in the Age of Civil Rights* (New York: Knopf, 2006), 4.
28 Stokely Carmichael and Charles V. Hamilton, *Black Power: The Politics of Liberation in America* (New York: Vintage Books, 1967), 89.
29 Joseph Crespino, *In Search of Another Country: Mississippi and the Conservative Counter-Revolution* (Princeton, New Jersey: Princeton University Press, 2007), 102–3.
30 Black and Black, *Rise of Southern Republicans*, 4, 205.
31 Kabaservice, *Rule and Ruin*, 118.
32 Harold H. Martin, "George Wallace, the Angry Man's Candidate," *Saturday Evening Post*, June 15, 1968, 23.
33 Dan T. Carter, *The Politics of Rage: George Wallace, the Origins of the New Conservatism, and the Transformation of American Politics* (Baton Rouge, LA: Louisiana State University Press, 2000), 474.
34 Lewis, "White South, Red Nation," 122.
35 Sokol, *There Goes My Everything*, 86.
36 Story and Laurie, *The Rise of Conservatism*, 53.
37 Andrew, *Other Side of the Sixties*, 181.
38 Goldwater, *Conscience of a Conservative*, 23.
39 Goldwater, *Conscience of a Conservative*, 31.
40 The previous quotation from Goldwater's speech on the senate floor also appears in Rick Perlstein, *Before the Storm: Barry Goldwater and the Unmaking of the American Consensus* (New York: Nation Books, 2001), 364.
41 Kabaservice, *Rule and Ruin*, 102–3.
42 Kabaservice, *Rule and Ruin*, 113.
43 William F. Buckley Jr., *Let Us Talk of Many Things: The Collected Speeches* (New York: Basic Books, 2008b), 77–8.

3 The Social Backlash: Riots, Religion, and Realignment

1 Kabaservice, *Rule and Ruin*, 121, 123.
2 Thomas Borstelmann, *The 1970s: A New Global History from Civil Rights to Economic Inequality* (Princeton, New Jersey: Princeton University Press, 2012), 114.
3 Dallek, *Right Moment*, 84–5.
4 Samuel Walker, *Presidents and Civil Liberties from Wilson to Obama: A Story of Poor Custodians* (New York: Cambridge University Press, 2012), 384.
5 Dallek, *Right Moment*, 137.
6 Donna Murch, "The Many Meanings of Watts: Black Power, *Wattstax*, and the Carceral State," *OAH Magazine of History* 26 (2012): 37.
7 Dallek, *Right Moment*, 145.
8 Phillips-Fein, *Invisible Hand*, 143.
9 Dallek, *Right Moment*, 188.
10 Charles Holden and Zach Messitte, "Spirogate: *The Washington Post* and the Rise and Fall of Spiro Agnew," *Maryland Historical Magazine* 102 (2007): 177.
11 Justin P. Coffey, "Spiro T. Agnew and Middle Ground Politics," *Maryland Historical Magazine* 98 (2003): 443.

12 The quotations in this paragraph are from the University of Baltimore, Langsdale Library Special Collections, "Baltimore '68: Riots and Rebirth," at http://archives.ubalt.edu/bsr/index.html.
13 David J. Garrow, *The FBI and Martin Luther King, Jr.* (New York: Penguin Books, 1981), 185.
14 Daniel Walker, *Rights in Conflict/The Walker Report* (New York: Bantam Books, 1968).
15 Dean J. Kotlowski, *Nixon's Civil Rights: Politics, Principle, and Policy* (Cambridge, Massachusetts, 2001).
16 Chris Bonastia, "Hedging His Bets: Why Nixon Killed HUD's Desegregation Efforts," *Social Science History* 28 (2004): 42.
17 James Boyd, "Nixon's Southern Strategy: 'It's All in the Charts,'" *New York Times*, May 17, 1970. Available online at http://www.nytimes.com/packages/html/books/phillips-southern.pdf.
18 Suleiman Osman, "The Decade of the Neighborhood," in *Rightward Bound: Making America Conservative in the 1970s*, eds. Bruce J. Schulman and Julian E. Zelizer, (Cambridge, Massachusetts: Harvard University Press, 2008), 118.
19 Thomas Sugrue and John D. Skrentny, "The White Ethnic Strategy," in *Rightward Bound: Making America Conservative in the 1970s*, eds. Bruce J. Schulman and Julian E. Zelizer, (Cambridge, Massachusetts: Harvard University Press, 2008), 175.
20 James Boyd, "Nixon's Southern Strategy 'It's All in the Charts,'" *New York Times*, May 17, 1970. Available online at www.nytimes.com/packages/html/books/phillips-southern.pdf.
21 Michael Drosnin, "After 'Bloody Friday' New York Wonders If Wall Street Is Becoming a Battleground," *Wall Street Journal*, May 11, 1970. Available online at http://chnm.gmu.edu/hardhats/homepage.html.
22 Homer Bigart, "War Foes Here Attacked by Construction Workers," *New York Times*, May 9, 1970. Available online at http://chnm.gmu.edu/hardhats/homepage.html.
23 Bigart, "War Foes."
24 Marc Linder, *Wars of Attrition: Vietnam, the Business Roundtable, and the Decline of Construction Unions* (Iowa City: Fanpihua Press, 2000), 279–80.
25 Francis X. Clines, "For the Flag and for Country, They March," *New York Times*, May 21, 1970. Available online at http://chnm.gmu.edu/hardhats/homepage.html.
26 Drosnin, "After 'Bloody Friday.'"
27 Kabaservice, *Rule and Ruin*, 305.
28 James C. Cobb, "From Muskogee to Luckenbach: Country Music and the Southernization of America," *The Journal of Popular Culture* 16 (1982): 86.
29 James N. Gregory, "Southernizing the American Working Class: Post-War Episodes of Class Transformation," *Labor History* 39 (1998): 151.
30 n.a., "Readers' views," *Louisville Courier-Journal*, September 4, 1975a, A16.
31 n.a., "Readers' views," *Louisville Courier-Journal*, September 3, 1975b, A24.
32 n.a., "Those arrested in clashes . . . ," *Louisville Courier-Journal*, September 7, 1975, A4.
33 n.a., "Thousands peacefully protest . . . ," *Louisville Courier-Journal*, September 28, 1975, A1.

34 Matthew D. Lassiter, *The Silent Majority: Suburban Politics in the Sunbelt South* (Princeton: Princeton University Press, 2006), 154.
35 n.a., "Harlan union man finds role ...," *Louisville Courier-Journal*, September 6, 1975, A7.
36 n.a., "Activity back to normal ...," *Louisville Courier-Journal*, September 6, 1975, B1.
37 Jon Hillson, *The Battle of Boston* (New York: Pathfinder Press, 1977), 164.
38 Paul Boyer, "The Evangelical Resurgence in 1970s American Protestantism," in *Rightward Bound: Making America Conservative in the 1970s*, eds. Bruce J. Schulman and Julian E. Zelizer (Cambridge, Massachusetts: Harvard University Press, 2008), 29.
39 Dan T. Carter, *The Politics of Rage: George Wallace, the Origins of the New Conservatism, and the Transformation of American Politics* (Baton Rouge, Louisiana: Louisiana State University Press, 2000), 451–5.
40 Carl Bernstein and Bob Woodward, *All the President's Men* (New York: Simon and Schuster, 1974), 26.
41 Conrad Black, *Richard M. Nixon: A Life in Full* (New York: PublicAffairs, 2007), 630.
42 Jonathan Aitken, "The Great Chuck Colson," *The American Spectator*, July/August 2012, 67.
43 William Martin, *With God on Our Side: The Rise of the Christian Right in America* (New York: Broadway, 2005), 98–9.
44 Frank Lambert, *Religion in American Politics: A Short History* (Princeton: Princeton University Press, 2008), 17.
45 Lambert, *Religion in American Politics*, 107.
46 Martin, *With God on Our Side*, 11.
47 Martin, *With God on Our Side*, 70.
48 Martin, *With God on Our Side*, 40–1.
49 Daniel Williams, *God's Own Party: The Making of the Christian Right* (Oxford: Oxford University Press, 2010), 179.
50 Boyer, "The Evangelical Resurgence," 41.
51 Jackson Putnam, "Governor Reagan: A Reappraisal," *California History* 83 (2006): 27.
52 Martin, *With God on Our Side*, 193.
53 Williams, *God's Own Party*, 121.
54 Graham Noble, "The Rise and Fall of the Equal Rights Amendment," *History Review* 72 (2012): 32.
55 Noble, "Rise and Fall," 33.
56 Marjorie Spruill, "Gender and America's Right Turn," in *Rightward Bound: Making America Conservative in the 1970s*, eds. Bruce J. Schulman and Julian E. Zelizer (Cambridge, Massachusetts: Harvard University Press, 2008), 79.
57 Williams, *God's Own Party*, 149.
58 Matthew D. Lassiter, "Inventing Family Values," in *Rightward Bound: Making America Conservative in the 1970s*, eds. Bruce J. Schulman and Julian E. Zelizer (Cambridge, Massachusetts: Harvard University Press, 2008), 27.
59 Michael W. Flamm, *Law and Order: Street Crime, Civil Unrest, and the Crisis of Liberalism in the 1960s* (New York: Columbia University Press, 2005), 67.

4 Crises, Carter, and the Triumph of Ronald Reagan

60 Tracey E. K'Meyer, *Civil Rights in the Gateway to the South: Louisville, Kentucky, 1945–1980* (Lexington: The University Press of Kentucky, 2009), 259.

1 Wilentz, *The Age of Reagan*, 65.
2 Frye Gaillard, *Prophet from Plains: Jimmy Carter and His Legacy* (Athens, Georgia: The University of Georgia Press, 2007), 3.
3 Martin, *With God on Our Side*, 154.
4 Borstelmann, *The 1970s*, 57.
5 Gerald Epstein, "Domestic Stagflation and Monetary Policy: The Federal Reserve and the Hidden Election," in *The Hidden Election: Politics and Economics in the 1980 Presidential Campaign*, eds. Thomas Ferguson and Joel Rodgers (New York: Pantheon Books, 1981), 144.
6 Quoted in Phillips-Fein, *Invisible Hand*, 158.
7 Bethany E. Moreton, "Make Payroll, Not War," in *Rightward Bound: Making America Conservative in the 1970s*, eds. Bruce J. Schulman and Julian E. Zelizer (Cambridge, Massachusetts: Harvard University Press, 2008), 67.
8 Moreton, "Make Payroll, Not War," 68, 62.
9 Martin, *With God on Our Side*, 140–1.
10 Phillips-Fein, *Invisible Hand*, 194–5.
11 Phillips-Fein, *Invisible Hand*, 182.
12 Daniel A. Smith, "Howard Jarvis, Populist Entrepreneur: Reevaluating the Causes of Proposition 13," *Social Science History* 23 (1999): 202.
13 All quotations in this paragraph are taken from the KPBS video, "Proposition 13".
14 Smith, "Howard Jarvis," 178.
15 Smith, "Howard Jarvis," 203.
16 Walter Dean Burnham, "The 1980 Earthquake: Realignment, Reaction, or What?" in *The Hidden Election: Politics and Economics in the 1980 Presidential Campaign*, eds. Thomas Ferguson and Joel Rodgers (New York: Pantheon Books, 1981), 110.
17 Howard Zinn, *A People's History of the United States* (New York: HarperPerennial, 1995), 460.
18 Jeremi Suri, "Détente and Its Discontents," in *Rightward Bound: Making America Conservative in the 1970s*, eds. Bruce J. Schulman & Julian E. Zelizer (Cambridge, Massachusetts: Harvard University Press, 2008), 234, 236–7.
19 William F. Buckley Jr., *The Reagan I Knew* (New York: Basic Books, 2008), 99.
20 Wilentz, *The Age of Reagan*, 67.
21 Derek N. Buckaloo, "Carter's Nicaragua and Other Democratic Quagmires," in *Rightward Bound: Making America Conservative in the 1970s*, eds. Bruce J. Schulman and Julian E. Zelizer (Cambridge, Massachusetts: Harvard University Press, 2008), 255.
22 Wilentz, *The Age of Reagan*, 103.
23 Tim Weiner, *Legacy of Ashes: The History of the CIA* (New York: Penguin, 2007), 428.
24 Weiner, *Legacy of Ashes*, 429.
25 Weiner, *Legacy of Ashes*, 424–5.
26 Wilentz, *The Age of Reagan*, 109.

27 Andrew E. Busch, *Reagan's Victory: The Presidential Election of 1980 and the Rise of the Right* (Lawrence: Kansas: University Press of Kansas, 2005), 137.
28 Thomas Ferguson and Joel Rogers, "The Reagan Victory: Corporate Coalitions in the 1980 Campaign," in *The Hidden Election: Politics and Economics in the 1980 Presidential Campaign*, eds. Thomas Ferguson and Joel Rodgers (New York: Pantheon Books, 1981), 38.
29 Ronald Reagan, *An American Life* (New York: Simon & Schuster, 1990), 217.
30 Gerald Pomper, "The Nominating Contests," in *The Election of 1980: Reports and Interpretations*, ed. Marlene Michels Pomper (Chatham, New Jersey: Chatham House Publishers, 1981), 15.
31 Wilentz, *The Age of Reagan*, 123.
32 Cannon, *The Role of a Lifetime*, 114.
33 Pomper, "The Nominating Contests," 82–3.
34 Robert Whitaker, *The New Right Papers* (New York: St. Martin's Press, 1982), ix.
35 The demographic breakdown of election results can be found, among other places, in Gerald Pomper, "The Presidential Election," in *The Election of 1980: Reports and Interpretations*, ed. Marlene Michels Pomper (Chatham, New Jersey: Chatham House Publishers, 1981), 65–96.
36 Charles E. Jacob, "The Congressional Elections," in *The Election of 1980: Reports and Interpretations*, ed. Marlene Michels Pomper (Chatham, New Jersey: Chatham House Publishers, 1981), 122.
37 Jacob, "The Congressional Elections," 122.
38 Hastings Wyman, "The Southern Strategy since Carter," *National Review*, June 9, 1978, 701.

5 The Image and Reality of Ronald Reagan and American Conservatism

1 Robert Lynd and Helen Lynd, *Middletown: A Study in Modern American Culture* (New York: Harcourt Brace & Company, 1929), 421.
2 C. Wright Mills, *White Collar: The American Middle Classes* (New York: Oxford University Press, 1951), 233, 327.
3 Jonathan Schoenwald, *A Time for Choosing: The Rise of Modern American Conservatism* (New York: Oxford University Press, 2001), 125.
4 Jacobs, "The Conservative Struggle," 198.
5 Bruce Schulman and Julian Zelizer, introduction to *Rightward Bound: Making America Conservative in the 1970s* (Cambridge, Massachusetts: Harvard University Press, 2008), 2.
6 Burnham, "The 1980 Earthquake," 98.
7 Wilson Carey McWilliams, "The Meaning of the Election," in *The Election of 1980: Reports and Interpretations*, ed. Marlene Michels Pomper (Chatham, New Jersey: Chatham House Publishers, 1981), 170.
8 Gil Troy, *The Reagan Revolution: A Very Short Introduction* (New York: Oxford University Press, 2009), 52.
9 David Harvey, *A Brief History of Neoliberalism* (Oxford: Oxford University Press, 2007), 1.
10 Busch, *Reagan's Victory*, 188.

11 Troy, *The Reagan Revolution*, 1–19.
12 Irving Goffman, *The Presentation of Self in Everyday Life* (Edinburgh: University of Edinburgh Social Sciences Research Center Monograph Series, 1956), 10.
13 Troy, *The Reagan Revolution*, 98.
14 Cannon, *The Role of a Lifetime*, 32.
15 Cannon, *The Role of a Lifetime*, 120.
16 Cannon, *The Role of a Lifetime*, 17.
17 Edwards, *Early Reagan*, 137, 145.
18 Edwards, *Early Reagan*, 167.
19 Michael Rogin, *Ronald Reagan, the Movie and Other Episodes in Political Demonology* (Berkeley: University of California Press, 1987), 11.
20 Edwards, *Early Reagan*, 272–3.
21 Dallek, *Right Moment*, 163.
22 Dallek, *Right Moment*, 233.
23 Wills, *Reagan's America*, 392–3.
24 Jane Mayer and Doyle McManus, *Landslide: The Unmaking of the President 1984–1988* (Boston: Houghton Mifflin Company, 1988), 92–3.
25 Fitzgerald, *Way Out There*, 22–3.
26 Rogin, *Reagan, the Movie*, 4.
27 Edwards, *Early Reagan*, 53–4.
28 Reagan, *An American Life*, 150.
29 Stephen Vaughn, "Ronald Reagan and the Struggle for Black Dignity in Cinema, 1937–1953," *Journal of African American History* 87 (2002): 83.
30 Vaughn, "Reagan and Black Dignity," 84.
31 Nancy Reagan gave remarks at the Goldwater Institute in 1995, and excerpts of her speech can be found online at www.youtube.com/watch?v=ec_Nunb6izo.
32 M.E. Bradford, "George Wallace and the American Conservatives: The Nexus," *National Review*, April 25, 1975, 442.
33 Jeremy D. Mayer, "Reagan and Race: Prophet of Colorblindness, Baiter of the Backlash," in *Deconstructing Reagan: Conservative Mythology and America's Fortieth President*, ed. Kyle Longley et al. (Armonk, NY: M.E. Sharpe, 2007), 77.
34 Burnham, "The 1980 Earthquake," 105.
35 Reagan, *An American Life*, 401.
36 Martin, *With God on Our Side*, 48.
37 Jeffrey L. Brudney and Gary W. Copeland, "Evangelicals as a Political Force: Reagan and the 1980 Religious Vote," *Social Science Quarterly* 65 (1984): 1073.
38 Martin, *With God on Our Side*, 208.
39 Martin, *With God on Our Side*, 209.
40 Phillips-Fein, *Invisible Hand*, 232.
41 Aaron Haberman, "Into the Wilderness: Ronald Reagan, Bob Jones University, and the Political Education of the Christian Right," *Historian* 67 (2005): 240.
42 David John Marley, "Ronald Reagan and the Splintering of the Christian Right," *Journal of Church and State* 48 (2006): 853.
43 Ferguson and Rogers, "The Reagan Victory," 3–4.
44 Haberman, "Into the Wilderness," 244.
45 Haberman, "Into the Wilderness," 245, 246.
46 Williams, *God's Own Party*, 195–6.

47 Marley, "Ronald Reagan," 866, 867.
48 Paul Frymer, *Uneasy Alliances: Race and Party Competition in America* (New York: Oxford University Press, 1999), 8.
49 Buckley, *Let Us Talk of Many Things*, 381–2.
50 Michael Schaller, "Reagan and the Cold War," in *Deconstructing Reagan: Conservative Mythology and America's Fortieth President*, ed. Kyle Longley et al. (Armonk, NY: M.E. Sharpe, 2007), 33.
51 Suri, "Détente and Its Discontents," 243.
52 Schaller, "Reagan and the Cold War," 30–1.
53 Krauthammer, Charles. "Essay: The Reagan Doctrine," *Time*, April 1, 1985. Available online at http://www.time.com/time/magazine/article/0,9171,964873,00.html. For a discussion of the Reagan Doctrine, see Chester Pach, "The Reagan Doctrine: Principle, Pragmatism, and Policy," *Presidential Studies Quarterly* 36 (2006): 75–88.
54 James Graham Wilson, "How Grand Was Reagan's Strategy?" *Diplomacy and Statecraft* 18 (2007): 773.
55 Schaller "Reagan and the Cold War," 33.
56 This and the previous quotation are from Robert Samuel, "Conservative Intellectuals and the Reagan–Gorbachev Summits," *Cold War History* 12 (2012): 141.
57 Mayer and McManus, *Landslide*, 91.
58 Mayer and McManus, *Landslide*, 98.
59 Mayer and McManus, *Landslide*, 316.
60 Joseph A. McCartin, *Collision Course: Ronald Reagan, the Air Traffic Controllers, and the Strike that Changed America* (New York: Oxford University Press, 2011).
61 McCartin, *Collision Course*, 300.
62 John W. Sloan, "The Economic Costs of Reagan Mythology," in *Deconstructing Reagan: Conservative Mythology and America's Fortieth President*, ed. Kyle Longley et al. (Armonk, NY: M.E. Sharpe, 2007), 47.
63 Thomas Frank, *What's the Matter with Kansas? How Conservatives Won the Heart of America* (New York: Holt, 2004), 148.
64 Phillips-Fein, *Invisible Hand*, 114.
65 Troy, *The Reagan Revolution*, xiv.
66 Wilentz, *The Age of Reagan*, 335.
67 Harvey, *Neoliberalism*, 23.
68 Robert Scheer, *The Great American Stickup: How Reagan Republicans and Clinton Democrats Enriched Wall Street While Mugging Main Street* (New York: Nation Books, 2010), 100.
69 Gregory Albo, "Neoliberalism from Reagan to Clinton," *Monthly Review*, April 2001, 86.

Documents

1 Stephen E. Ambrose and Douglas G. Brinkley, *Rise to Globalism: American Foreign Policy since 1938* (New York: Penguin, 1997), 228.
2 Claudia Goldin and Maria Shim, "Making a Name: Women's Surnames at Marriage and Beyond," *Journal of Economic Perspectives* 18 (2004).

Bibliography

Agnew, Spiro. *Frankly Speaking: A Collection of Extraordinary Speeches.* Washington D.C.: Public Affairs Press, 1980.
Aitken, Jonathan. "The Great Chuck Colson," *The American Spectator*, July/August 2012, 66–7.
Albo, Gregory. "Neoliberalism from Reagan to Clinton," *Monthly Review*, April 2001, 81–9.
Ambrose, Stephen E. and Douglas G. Brinkley. *Rise to Globalism: American Foreign Policy since 1938.* New York: Penguin, 1997.
Andrew, John A., III. *The Other Side of the Sixties: Young Americans for Freedom and the Rise of Conservative Politics.* New Brunswick, New Jersey: Rutgers University Press, 1997.
Bartley, Numan V. *The Rise of Massive Resistance: Race and Politics in the South during the 1950s.* Baton Rouge: Louisiana State University Press, 1997.
Bernstein, Carl and Bob Woodward. *All the President's Men.* New York: Simon and Schuster, 1974.
Bigart, Homer. "War Foes Here Attacked by Construction Workers," *New York Times*, May 9, 1970.
Black, Conrad. *Richard M. Nixon: A Life in Full.* New York: PublicAffairs, 2007.
Black, Earl and Merle Black. *The Rise of the Southern Republicans.* Cambridge, Massachusetts: Belknap, 2002.
Bonastia, Chris. "Hedging His Bets: Why Nixon Killed HUD's Desegregation Efforts," *Social Science History* 28 (2004): 19–52.
Borstelmann, Thomas. *Apartheid's Reluctant Uncle: The United States and Southern Africa in the Early Cold War.* New York: Oxford University Press, 1993.
———. *The 1970s: A New Global History from Civil Rights to Economic Inequality.* Princeton: Princeton University Press, 2012.
Bowers, Claude G. *The Tragic Era: The Revolution after Lincoln.* Cambridge, Massachusetts: The Riverside Press, 1929.
Boyd, James. "Nixon's Southern Strategy 'It's All in the Charts'," *New York Times*, May 17, 1970. Available online at www.nytimes.com/packages/html/books/phillips-southern.pdf.

Boyer, Paul. "The Evangelical Resurgence in 1970s American Protestantism." In *Rightward Bound: Making America Conservative in the 1970s*, edited by Bruce J. Schulman and Julian E. Zelizer. Cambridge, Massachusetts: Harvard University Press, 2008, 29–51.

Bradford, M.E. "George Wallace and the American Conservatives: The Nexus," *National Review*, April 25, 1975.

Brudney, Jeffrey L. and Gary W. Copeland. "Evangelicals as a Political Force: Reagan and the 1980 Religious Vote," *Social Science Quarterly* 65 (1984): 1072–9.

Buckaloo, Derek N. "Carter's Nicaragua and Other Democratic Quagmires." In *Rightward Bound: Making America Conservative in the 1970s*, edited by Bruce J. Schulman and Julian E. Zelizer. Cambridge, Massachusetts: Harvard University Press, 2008, 246–64.

Buckley, William F., Jr. *The Reagan I Knew*. New York: Basic Books, 2008a.

———. *Let Us Talk of Many Things: The Collected Speeches*. New York: Basic Books, 2008b.

Burnham, Walter Dean. "The 1980 Earthquake: Realignment, Reaction, or What?" In *The Hidden Election: Politics and Economics in the 1980 Presidential Campaign*, edited by Thomas Ferguson and Joel Rodgers. New York: Pantheon Books, 1981, 98–140.

Busch, Andrew E. *Reagan's Victory: The Presidential Election of 1980 and the Rise of the Right*. Lawrence, Kansas: University Press of Kansas, 2005.

Cannon, Lou. *President Reagan: The Role of a Lifetime*. New York: PublicAffairs, 2000.

Carmichael, Stokely and Charles V. Hamilton. *Black Power: The Politics of Liberation in America*. New York: Vintage Books, 1967.

Carter, Dan T. *The Politics of Rage: George Wallace, the Origins of the New Conservatism, and the Transformation of American Politics*. Baton Rouge, Louisiana: Louisiana State University Press, 2000.

Charen, Mona. "Who's the True Conservative?" *National Review Online*, March 2, 2012. Available online at www.nationalreview.com/articles/292419/who-s-true-conservative-mona-charenpg=1.

Clines, Francis X. "For the Flag and for Country, They March," New York Times, May 21, 1970.

Cobb, James C. "From Muskogee to Luckenbach: Country Music and the Southernization of America," *The Journal of Popular Culture* 16 (1982): 81–91.

Coffey, Justin P. "Spiro T. Agnew and Middle Ground Politics," *Maryland Historical Magazine* 98 (2003): 440–55.

Coulter, Ann. "Civil Rights and the Mob: George Wallace, Bull Conner, Orval Faubus and Other Democrats," *Human Events*, June 13, 2011, 16.

Crespino, Joseph. *In Search of Another Country: Mississippi and the Conservative Counter-Revolution*. Princeton: Princeton University Press, 2007.

Critchlow, Donald T. and Cynthia L. Stachecki. "The Equal Rights Amendment Reconsidered: Politics, Policy and Social Mobilization in a Democracy," *Journal of Policy History* 20 (2008): 157–76.

Dallek, Matthew. *The Right Moment: Ronald Reagan's First Victory and the Decisive Turning Point in American Politics*. Oxford: Oxford University Press, 2004.

DiMaggio, Anthony. *The Rise of the Tea Party: Political Discontent in the Age of Obama*. New York: Monthly Review Press, 2011.

Drosnin, Michael. "After 'Bloody Friday' New York Wonders If Wall Street Is Becoming a Battleground," *Wall Street Journal*, May 11, 1970.

Du Bois, W.E.B. *Black Reconstruction in America, 1860–1880*. New York: Touchstone, 1992.

Dudziak, Mary. *Cold War, Civil Rights: Race and the Image of American Democracy*. Princeton: Princeton University Press, 2000.

Dunham, Pat. *Electoral Behavior in the United States*. Englewood Cliffs, New Jersey: Prentice Hall, 1991.

Dunning, William A. *Reconstruction Political and Economic 1865–1877*. New York: Harper & Brothers, 1907.

Edwards, Anne. *Early Reagan: The Rise to Power*. New York: William & Morrow, 1987.

Epstein, Gerald. "Domestic Stagflation and Monetary Policy: The Federal Reserve and the Hidden Election." In *The Hidden Election: Politics and Economics in the 1980 Presidential Campaign*, edited by Thomas Ferguson and Joel Rodgers. New York: Pantheon Books, 1981, 141–95.

Evans, Thomas W. *The Education of Ronald Reagan: The General Electric Years and the Untold Story of His Conversion to Conservatism*. New York: Columbia University Press, 2006.

Ferguson, Thomas and Joel Rogers. "The Reagan Victory: Corporate Coalitions in the 1980 Campaign." In *The Hidden Election: Politics and Economics in the 1980 Presidential Campaign*, edited by Thomas Ferguson and Joel Rodgers. New York: Pantheon Books, 1981, 3–63.

Fitzgerald, Frances. *Way Out There in the Blue: Reagan, Star Wars and the End of the Cold War*. New York: Simon & Schuster, 2000.

Flamm, Michael W. *Law and Order: Street Crime, Civil Unrest, and the Crisis of Liberalism in the 1960s*. New York: Columbia University Press, 2005.

Foner, Eric. "The Ideology of the Republican Party." In *The Birth of the Grand Old Party: the Republicans' First Generation*, edited by Robert F. Engs and Randall M. Miller. Philadelphia: University of Pennsylvania Press, 2002, 8–29.

———. *Reconstruction: America's Unfinished Revolution 1863–1877*. New York: Harper and Row, 1988.

Formisano, Ronald P. "The 'Party Period' Revisited," *The Journal of American History* 86 (1999): 93–120.

Frank, Thomas. *What's the Matter with Kansas? How Conservatives Won the Heart of America*. New York: Holt, 2004.

Frankovich, Kathleen. "Public Opinion Trends." In *The Election of 1980: Reports and Interpretations*, edited by Marlene Michels Pomper. Chatham, New Jersey: Chatham House Publishers, 1981, 97–118.

Frymer, Paul. *Uneasy Alliances: Race and Party Competition in America*. New York: Oxford University Press, 1999.

Gaillard, Frye. *Prophet from Plains: Jimmy Carter and His Legacy*. Athens, Georgia: The University of Georgia Press, 2007.

Garrow, David J. *The FBI and Martin Luther King, Jr*. New York: Penguin Books, 1981.

Gerstle, Gary. "Race and the Myth of the Liberal Consensus," *The Journal of American History* 82 (1995): 579–86.

Goffman, Irving. *The Presentation of Self in Everyday Life*. Edinburgh: University of Edinburgh Social Sciences Research Center Monograph Series, 1956.

Goldin, Claudia and Maria Shim. "Making a Name: Women's Surnames at Marriage and Beyond," *Journal of Economic Perspectives* 18 (2004): 143–60.

Goldwater, Barry M. *The Conscience of a Conservative*. BN Publishing, [1964] 2007.

Gregory, James N. "Southernizing the American Working Class: Post-War Episodes of Class Transformation," *Labor History* 39 (1998): 135–54.

Haberman, Aaron. "Into the Wilderness: Ronald Reagan, Bob Jones University, and the Political Education of the Christian Right," *Historian* 67 (2005): 234–53.

Harvey, David. *A Brief History of Neoliberalism*. Oxford: Oxford University Press, 2007.

Hillson, Jon. *The Battle of Boston*. New York: Pathfinder Press, 1977.

Holden, Charles J. and Zach Messitte. "Spirogate: *The Washington Post* and the Rise and Fall of Spiro Agnew," *Maryland Historical Magazine* 102 (2007): 176–93.

Jacob, Charles E. "The Congressional Elections." In *The Election of 1980: Reports and Interpretations*, edited by Marlene Michels Pomper. Chatham, New Jersey: Chatham House Publishers, 1981, 119–41.

Jacobs, Meg. "The Conservative Struggle and the Energy Crisis." In *Rightward Bound: Making America Conservative in the 1970s*, edited by Bruce J. Schulman and Julian E. Zelizer. Cambridge, Massachusetts: Harvard University Press, 2008, 193–209.

K'Meyer, Tracey E. *Civil Rights in the Gateway to the South: Louisville, Kentucky, 1945–1980*. Lexington, Kentucky: The University Press of Kentucky, 2009.

Kabaservice, Geoffrey. *Rule and Ruin: The Downfall of Moderation and the Destruction of the Republican Party, From Eisenhower to the Tea Party*. New York: Oxford University Press, 2012.

Key, V.O., Jr. *Southern Politics in State and Nation*. Knoxville, Tennessee: The University of Tennessee Press, [1949] 1977.

Kotlowski, Dean J. *Nixon's Civil Rights: Politics, Principle, and Policy*. Cambridge, Massachusetts: Harvard University Press, 2001.

Krauthammer, Charles. "Essay: The Reagan Doctrine," *Time*, April 1, 1985. Available online at www.time.com/time/magazine/article/0,9171,964873,00.html.

Lambert, Frank. *Religion in American Politics: A Short History*. Princeton: Princeton University Press, 2008.

Lassiter, Matthew D. *The Silent Majority: Suburban Politics in the Sunbelt South*. Princeton: Princeton University Press, 2006.

———. "Inventing Family Values." In *Rightward Bound: Making America Conservative in the 1970s*, edited by Bruce J. Schulman and Julian E. Zelizer. Cambridge, Massachusetts: Harvard University Press, 2008, 171–92.

Lewis, George. *Massive Resistance: The White Response to the Civil Rights Movement*. Oxford: Hodder Arnold, 2006.

———. "White South, Red Nation: Massive Resistance and the Cold War." In *Massive Resistance: Southern Opposition to the Second Reconstruction*, edited by Clive Webb. Oxford: Oxford University Press, 2005, 117–35.

Limbaugh, Rush. "How Reagan Attracted Independents," September 28, 2011. Available online at www.rushlimbaugh.com/daily/2011/09/28/how_reagan_attracted_independents.

Linder, Marc. *Wars of Attrition: Vietnam, the Business Roundtable, and the Decline of Construction Unions*. Iowa City: Fanpihua Press, 2000.

Lowndes, Joseph E. *From the New Deal to the New Right: Race and the Southern Origins of Modern Conservatism*. New Haven, Connecticut: Yale University Press, 2008.

Lynd, Robert and Helen Lynd. *Middletown: A Study in Modern American Culture*. New York: Harcourt Brace & Company, 1929.

Marley, David John. "Ronald Reagan and the Splintering of the Christian Right," *Journal of Church and State* 48 (2006): 851–68.

Martin, Harold H. "George Wallace, the Angry Man's Candidate," *Saturday Evening Post*, June 15, 1968, 23–5.

Martin, William. *With God on Our Side: The Rise of the Christian Right in America*. New York: Broadway, 2005.

———. "How Ronald Reagan Wowed Evangelicals," *Christianity Today*, August 2004, 48–9.

Mayer, Jane and Doyle McManus. *Landslide: The Unmaking of the President 1984–1988*. Boston: Houghton Mifflin Company, 1988.

Mayer, Jeremy D. "Reagan and Race: Prophet of Colorblindness, Baiter of the Backlash." In *Deconstructing Reagan: Conservative Mythology and America's Fortieth President*, edited by Kyle Longley et al. Armonk, New York: M.E. Sharpe, 2007, 70–89.

McCartin, Joseph A. *Collision Course: Ronald Reagan, the Air Traffic Controllers, and the Strike that Changed America*. New York: Oxford University Press, 2012.

McWilliams, Wilson Carey. "The Meaning of the Election." In *The Election of 1980: Reports and Interpretations*, edited by Marlene Michels Pomper. Chatham, New Jersey: Chatham House Publishers, 1981, 170–88.

Miles, Michael W. *The Odyssey of the American Right*. New York: Oxford University Press, 1980.

Mills, C. Wright. *White Collar: The American Middle Classes*. New York: Oxford University Press, 1951.

Morris, Aldon D. *The Origins of the Civil Rights Movement: Black Communities Organizing for Change*. New York: The Free Press, 1984.

Moreton, Bethany E. "Make Payroll, Not War." In *Rightward Bound: Making America Conservative in the 1970s*, edited by Bruce J. Schulman and Julian E. Zelizer. Cambridge, Massachusetts: Harvard University Press, 2008, 52–70.

Murch, Donna. "The Many Meanings of Watts: Black Power, *Wattstax*, and the Carceral State," *OAH Magazine of History* 26 (2012): 37–40.

Nash, George. *The Conservative Intellectual Movement in America since 1945*. Wilmington, Delaware: ISI Books, 2006.

Noble, Graham. "The Rise and Fall of the Equal Rights Amendment," *History Review* 72 (March 2012): 30–3.

Osman, Suleiman. "The Decade of the Neighborhood". In *Rightward Bound: Making America Conservative in the 1970s*, edited by Bruce J. Schulman and Julian E. Zelizer. Cambridge, Massachusetts: Harvard University Press, 2008, 106–27.

Pach, Chester. "The Reagan Doctrine: Principle, Pragmatism, and Policy," *Presidential Studies Quarterly* 36 (2006): 75–88.

Perlstein, Rick. *Before the Storm: Barry Goldwater and the Unmaking of the American Consensus*. New York: Nation Books, 2001.

Phillips-Fein, Kim. *Invisible Hands: The Making of the Conservative Movement from the New Deal to Reagan*. New York: W.W. Norton and Company, 2009.

Pomper, Gerald. "The Nominating Contests." In *The Election of 1980: Reports and Interpretations*, edited by Marlene Michels Pomper. Chatham, New Jersey: Chatham House Publishers, 1981, 1–37.

Putnam, Jackson. "Governor Reagan: A Reappraisal," *California History* 83 (2006): 24–45.

Rauchway, Eric. *The Great Depression and New Deal: A Very Short History*. Oxford: Oxford University Press, 2008.

Reagan, Ronald. *An American Life*. New York: Simon & Schuster, 1990.

Rogin, Michael. *Ronald Reagan, the Movie and Other Episodes in Political Demonology*. Berkeley: University of California Press, 1987.

Rothbard, Murray N. "Life in the Old Right." In *The Paleoconservatives: New Voices of the Old Right*, edited by Joseph Scotchie. New Brunswick, New Jersey: Transaction Publishers, 1999, 19–30.

Samuel, Robert. "Conservative Intellectuals and the Reagan–Gorbachev Summits," *Cold War History* 12 (2012): 135–57.

Schaller, Michael. "Reagan and the Cold War." In *Deconstructing Reagan: Conservative Mythology and America's Fortieth President*, edited by Kyle Longley et al. Armonk, New York: M.E. Sharpe, 2007, 3–40.

Schoenwald, Jonathan. *A Time for Choosing: The Rise of Modern American Conservatism*. New York: Oxford University Press, 2001.

Scheer, Robert. *The Great American Stickup: How Reagan Republicans and Clinton Democrats Enriched Wall Street While Mugging Main Street*. New York: Nation Books, 2010.

Shermer, Elizabeth Tandy. "Origins of the Conservative Ascendancy: Barry Goldwater's Early Senate Career and the De-Legitimization of Organized Labor," *The Journal of American History* 95 (2008): 678–709.

Skocpol, Theda and Vanessa Williamson. *The Tea Party and the Remaking of Republican Conservatism*. New York: Oxford University Press, 2012.

Sloan, John W. "The Economic Costs of Reagan Mythology." In *Deconstructing Reagan: Conservative Mythology and America's Fortieth President*, edited by Kyle Longley et al. Armonk, New York: M.E. Sharpe, 2007, 41–69.

Smith, Daniel A. "Howard Jarvis, Populist Entrepreneur: Reevaluating the Causes of Proposition 13," *Social Science History* 23 (1999): 173–210.

Sokol, Jason. *There Goes My Everything: White Southerners in the Age of Civil Rights.* New York: Knopf, 2006.

Spruill, Marjorie J. "Gender and America's Right Turn." In *Rightward Bound: Making America Conservative in the 1970s*, edited by Bruce J. Schulman and Julian E. Zelizer. Cambridge, Massachusetts: Harvard University Press, 2008, 71–89.

Story, Ronald and Bruce Laurie. *The Rise of Conservatism in America, 1945–2000: A Brief History with Documents.* New York: Bedford/St. Martin's, 2008.

Sugrue, Thomas J. and John D. Skrentny. "The White Ethnic Strategy." In *Rightward Bound: Making America Conservative in the 1970s*, edited by Bruce J. Schulman and Julian E. Zelizer. Cambridge, Massachusetts: Harvard University Press, 2008, 171–92.

Suri, Jeremi. "Détente and Its Discontents." In *Rightward Bound: Making America Conservative in the 1970s*, edited by Bruce J. Schulman and Julian E. Zelizer. Cambridge, Massachusetts: Harvard University Press, 2008, 227–45.

Thompson, Hunter S. *The Proud Highway: Saga of a Desperate Southern Gentleman 1955–1967.* Edited by Douglas Brinkley. New York: Ballantine Books, 1997.

Tiahrt, Todd. "Take a Right Turn: My Conversion from a Democrat to a Conservative Republican." In *Why I am a Reagan Conservative*, edited by Michael K. Deaver. New York: HarperCollins, 2005, 189–94.

Troy, Gil. *The Reagan Revolution: A Very Short Introduction.* New York: Oxford University Press, 2009.

———. *Morning in America: How Ronald Reagan Invented the 1980s.* Princeton: Princeton University Press, 2005.

Vaughn, Stephen. "Ronald Reagan and the Struggle for Black Dignity in Cinema, 1937–1953," Journal of African American History 87 (2002): 83–95.

Walker, Daniel. *Rights in Conflict/The Walker Report.* New York: Bantam Books, 1968.

Walker, Martin. *America Reborn: A Twentieth-Century Narrative in Twenty-six Lives.* New York: Knopf, 2000.

Walker, Samuel. *Presidents and Civil Liberties from Wilson to Obama: A Story of Poor Custodians.* New York: Cambridge University Press, 2012.

Weiner, Tim. *Legacy of Ashes: The History of the CIA.* New York: Penguin, 2007.

Whitaker, Robert (ed.). *The New Right Papers.* New York: St. Martin's Press, 1982.

Wilentz, Sean. *The Age of Reagan: A History, 1974–2008.* New York: HarperCollins, 2008.

Williams, Daniel. *God's Own Party: The Making of the Christian Right.* Oxford: Oxford University Press, 2010.

Wills, Gary. *Reagan's America.* New York: Penguin, 2000.

Wilson, James Graham. "How Grand Was Reagan's Strategy?" *Diplomacy and Statecraft* 18 (2007): 773–803.

Witcover, Jules. *White Knight: The Rise of Spiro Agnew.* New York: Random House, 1972.

Woodward, C. Vann. *The Strange Career of Jim Crow*. New York: Oxford University Press, 2001.
Wyman, Hastings. "The Southern Strategy since Carter," *National Review*, June 9, 1978.
Zelizer, Julian. "Conservatives, Carter, and the Politics of National Security." In *Rightward Bound: Making America Conservative in the 1970s*, edited by Bruce J. Schulman and Julian E. Zelizer. Cambridge, Massachusetts: Harvard University Press, 2008, 265–87.
Zinn, Howard. *A People's History of the United States*. New York: HarperPerennial, 1995.

Videos

KPBS, *Proposition 13*, Envision San Diego Project. Available online at www.kpbs.org/news/envision/prop13/.

Online Archival Sources

University of Baltimore, Langsdale Library Special Collections, "Baltimore '68: Riots and Rebirth". Available online at http://archives.ubalt.edu/bsr/index.html.

Louisville Courier-Journal articles, no author

"Readers' views," *Louisville Courier-Journal*, September 4, 1975a, A16.
"Readers' views," *Louisville Courier-Journal*, September 3, 1975b, A24.
"Those arrested in clashes . . .," *Louisville Courier-Journal*, September 7, 1975, A4.
"Thousands peacefully protest . . .," *Louisville Courier-Journal*, September 28, 1975, A1.
"Absenteeism high . . .," *Louisville Courier-Journal*, September 5, 1975, A1.
"Harlan union man finds role . . .," *Louisville Courier-Journal*, September 6, 1975, A7.
"Activity back to normal . . .," *Louisville Courier-Journal*, September 6, 1975, B1.

INDEX

A Choice, Not an Echo 8, 81; *see also* Schlafly, Phyllis
abolitionism 31
Agnew, Spiro 62–5, 74, 81, 85, 185
Almond, Lindsay 45
Alzheimer's disease 10
American Civil War 30, 32–3
American Federation of Labor–Congress of Industrial Organizations (AFL–CIO) 163, 193
American Jewish Congress 129
Anderson, John 106, 108, 126
anticommunism 5, 7, 12, 14–16, 25, 47, 76, 79, 99, 104, 160, 163, 170
antiwar movement 14, 68–71
apartheid 40, 126, 195–6
Atwater, Lee 27

Baker v. Carr 42
Berlin Wall 118
Bob Jones University 19, 127–9
Bork, Robert 50
Boulware, Lemuel 5–6, 92, 95, 140
Bowie State College 62–3
Bozell, Brent Jr. 24
Brennan, Peter J. 70
Bright, Bill 80
Brown, John 31
Brown, Pat 9, 57–8, 65, 120
Brown v. Board of Education 42, 49, 71
Bryant, Anita 83–4
Buckley, William F. Jr. 23–4, 48, 53, 54, 87, 100, 131, 134, 152

Business Roundtable 94–5
Bush, George H. W. 108–9, 121
Bush, George W. 178
busing 71–3

Calhoun, John C. 31–2
California Proposition 8 (Briggs Amendment) 126
California Proposition 13 (tax revolt of 1978) 96–8
Calvary Chapel Church 79
Campus Crusade for Christ 80
Carter, Jimmy 1, 2, 10, 89, 99–105, 116, 126, 128; 1980 presidential election 106–12
Cato Institute 94
Central Intelligence Agency (CIA) 24, 74, 102–4, 135–6, 151
Chaney, James 28, 45
Charen, Mona 12
China 14, 65, 99, 149, 180
Choice 61
Christian Coalition 130
Christianity *see* religious right
Civil Rights Act of 1964 20, 28–9, 42, 50, 67, 124–5
civil rights movement 7, 14, 23, 28, 42–51, 152
Civilian Conservation Corps (CCC) 174
classical liberalism 13
Clinton, Bill 140–3
Cold War 4, 14, 16, 40, 42, 47, 100, 115–16, 131–3, 137, 154–5, 160, 165–7, 177, 179, 196

color blind ideology 45–7
Colson, Charles "Chuck" 74–5, 127
Commodity Futures Modernization Act of 2000 141
Commodity Futures Trading Commission 143
communism *see* Soviet Union
Comprehensive Anti-Apartheid Act of 1986 *see* apartheid
Congress of Racial Equality (CORE) 42, 57, 63
Conlan, John 80
Conscience of a Conservative 25, 49
Coors, Joseph 94, 135
Coulter, Ann 28

Davis, Nancy *see* Reagan, Nancy
Deficit Reduction Act of 1984 139
Democratic Party 21–2, 30, 32, 34–40, 42–3, 48, 104, 106–7, 140–1, 159, 165, 176
détente 99–100, 132–3, 196
Dixiecrat Party 40–1, 158, 163, 165, 168
Dixon, Illinois 2, 27
Dobson, James 84
Douglass, Frederick 31
Dylan, Bob 16

economic conservatism *see* libertarianism
Economic Recovery Act of 1981 95, 137–9
Eisenhower, Dwight D. 22, 38–9, 47–8, 152, 180
Environmental Protection Agency (EPA) 65, 91
Equal Rights Amendment (ERA) 16, 65, 81–2
evangelicalism *see* religious right

Falwell, Jerry 77–8, 83, 130
Family Research Council 84
family values ideology 83–5
Farmer, James 63
Faubus, Orval 45
Federal Bureau of Investigation (FBI) 5, 165
Federal Deposit Insurance Corporation (FDIC) 38
feminism 14, 81, 190

Feulner, Edward 94
Financial Services Modernization Act of 1999 141
Focus on the Family 84
Ford, Gerald 81, 87–8, 100, 108–9, 111, 120, 125
Forman, James 42, 77
free speech movement 14, 57–8, 115; *see also* University of California, Berkeley
Freedom Council 130

Gann, Paul 97
Garrison, William Lloyd 31
Geithner, Timothy 143
General Electric Company (GE) 5–7, 28, 92, 118, 170
General Electric Theatre 5
Gingrich, Newt 12, 124
Goldman Sachs 143
Goldwater, Barry 1, 8, 23–6, 28–9, 43–4, 49–53, 54, 56, 60–1, 81, 85, 87, 95, 100–1, 109, 114, 124–6, 152, 160, 170, 173, 175, 178
Goodman, Andrew 28, 45
Gorbachev, Mikhail 132, 134
Graham, Billy 77
Great Depression 3, 13, 36, 42, 54, 89, 92, 174
Great Migrations 58
Great Society 67, 172
Greenspan, Alan 142
Guantanamo Naval Base 196

hardhat riots 68–70, 179
Hargis, Billy James 76
Hayek, Friedrich 13
Heritage Foundation 93–4
Hinckley, John Jr. 122
Hoover, Herbert 36–7, 54
House Un-American Activities Committee 5, 167

Internal Revenue Service (IRS) 128–9
Iran-contra affair 57, 135–7
Iranian Revolution 89, 102–3

Jarvis, Howard 96
John Birch Society 7, 15, 77, 170

Johnson, Lyndon B. 8, 60, 64, 67, 178, 180

Kemp, Jack 95
Kemp-Roth tax cut *see* Economic Recovery Act of 1981
Kennedy, Edward "Ted" 81, 106, 108
Kennedy, John F. 64, 180–1
Kennedy, Robert "Bobby" 165
Kent State University 68–9, 179
Kerner Commission Report 60
Keynes, John Maynard 38
King, Martin Luther Jr. 42, 62, 77
Ku Klux Klan (KKK) 45, 123–4

Laffer, Arthur 95
laissez faire capitalism 13, 20, 24, 36; *see also* libertarianism
law and order ideology 58–64, 74, 85, 185
libertarianism 12–13, 56, 137–43, 170, 194
Limbaugh, Rush 29
Lincoln, Abraham 29, 32
Lindsay, John 68
Little Rock, Arkansas 48
Lott, Trent 27, 40

McCarthy, Joseph 15, 24, 77, 157, 163
McGovern, George 81
McIntire, Carl 76
Manhattan Institute for Policy Research 94
Meese, Edwin III 57–8
Mills, C. Wright 113, 147, 152; "Letter to the New Left" (transcript) 147–52
Mises, Ludwig von 13
Mississippi Freedom Democratic Party (MFDP) 43–4
modern (moderate) Republicans *see* Republican Party
Moral Majority 78, 130
Murphy, George 9

Nader, Ralph 92
National Advisory Commission on Civil Disorders *see* Kerner Commission Report
National Association for the Advancement of Colored People (NAACP) 39, 42
National Association of Evangelicals 133

National Federation of Republican Women (NFRW) 81
National Journalism Center 94
National Organization for Women (NOW) 81
National Review 12, 23, 48, 125, 134
National Woman's Party 81
neoliberalism 141–3
Neshoba, Mississippi 27–8
New Deal 4, 6, 14, 20–2, 38, 48, 92, 111, 114–15, 131, 137, 171
New Deal coalition 36–9, 41, 48, 67, 106, 114, 140
new left 21, 152, 169, 179; *see also* Mills, C. Wright
new right 21, 152
Nixon, Richard 55, 62, 64–71, 74–5, 79, 81, 85, 87, 89, 92, 114, 124, 127, 178–9, 185; "Silent Majority Speech" 179–85 (transcript)
North American Free Trade Agreement (NAFTA) 140
North Atlantic Treaty Organization (NATO) 20, 147–8
North, Oliver 135
nullification 32

Obama, Barack 16, 98, 143, 178
Occupational Safety and Health Administration (OSHA) 65, 91
O'Connor, Sandra Day 129–30
old right 20–1
Organization of Petroleum Exporting Countries (OPEC) 90–1, 103

Panama Canal 88, 100, 196–8
Parents Television Council 24
Paul, Alice 81
Phillips, Kevin 66–7, 125, 154
Plessy v. Ferguson 34
Powell, Lewis 92
Professional Air Traffic Controllers Organization (PATCO) Strike 138
Prohibition 76–7

Rand, Ayn 17
Reagan Democrats 100
Reagan Doctrine 133, 137

Reagan, Jack 21, 123
Reagan, Nancy 4, 124
Reagan, Neil 5
Reagan, Ronald 1, 2, 7–8, 27–8, 30, 45, 54, 56, 58, 60–2, 80, 83, 85, 95, 98, 100, 114–17, 152; 1976 presidential election 87–9, 120; 1980 presidential election 103, 106–12; "A Time for Choosing" 8, 28, 58, 170–78 (transcript); anticommunism of 131–7; biography 3–10; economic conservatism (libertarianism) of 137–43; as Governor of California 9, 58, 80, 126; presentation of reality 117–23; radio commentaries 186–98 (transcripts); social conservatism of 123–31
Red Scare 14
Rehnquist, William 50
religious right 17, 55, 74–85, 123, 126–31, 188–9
Religious Roundtable 128, 130
Republican Party 8, 19–26, 28–30, 32–7, 42–3, 48, 51, 62, 74, 87–9, 112, 114–15, 123–4, 131, 139, 154, 160, 168; modern (moderate) Republicans 19–22, 26; stalwart Republicans 20–2
Reynolds v. Simms 42
Ripon, Wisconsin 32
Robertson, Pat 78, 83, 130
Rockefeller, Nelson 26, 51–2, 61, 81
Roe v. Wade 79–80
Romney, Mitt 12
Ronald Reagan Radio Commentary 10
Roosevelt, Franklin D. 4, 38, 54
Rubin, Robert 142
Rusher, William 48
Russian Revolution 14

Sandinista National Liberation Front 101; see also Iran-contra affair
Santorum, Rick 12
Save Our Children 84
Schlafly, Phyllis 8, 81–4
Schwerner, Michael 28, 45
Scopes, John 76
Screen Actors Guild (SAG) 5, 9, 118, 124
Securities and Exchange Commission (SEC) 38

silent majority 55, 64–73; see also Richard Nixon
Smith, Al 35, 52, 176
Smith v. Allwright 39, 42
social conservatism 12, 16–17, 47, 123–31, 170; see also religious right
Social Security 67, 175
socialism see communism
solid South 34–5
South Africa see apartheid
Southern Christian Leadership Conference (SCLC) 42
southern strategy 66
Soviet Union 7, 10, 16, 40, 47, 131–4, 149, 164–5, 180; invasion of Afghanistan 89, 102–4
Spanish–American War 34, 196–8
States' Rights Democratic Party see Dixiecrat Party
states' rights ideology 27–8, 41, 49
Stonewall riots 83
Stop Taking Our Privileges (STOP ERA) 82
Strategic Arms Limitation Treaty (SALT) 104
Student Nonviolent Coordinating Committee (SNCC) 42–3, 57
Students for a Democratic Society (SDS) 154; "The Port Huron Statement" (transcript) 154–70
Students in Free Enterprise (SIFE) 93
Summers, Lawrence 142
supply-side economics 95, 98
Swann v. Charlotte/Mecklenburg 72

Taft family 20, 38, 87
Tampico, Illinois 2
Tax Equity and Fiscal Responsibility Act of 1982 139
taxation 19, 94–7, 127–30, 194; see also libertarianism
tea party movement 18, 98, 140
Tennessee Valley Authority (TVA) 38
Thatcher, Margaret 18, 142
Therapeutic Abortion Act of 1967 80, 126
Thompson, Hunter S. 9
Thurmond, Strom 40–1, 44, 81
Tiahrt, Todd 29, 51

Torrijos, Omar 100, 197
Towson State College 63
traditionalism *see* social conservatism
Truman, Harry 39–40, 47
Turner, Nat 31

United Electrical Workers (UE) 6
United Nations (UN) 20
United Organizations of Taxpayers (UOT) 97; *see also* Jarvis, Howard
United States Constitution 49–50, 59
University of California, Berkeley 57, 59, 85, 185

Vesey, Denmark 31
Vietnam War 9, 55–6, 64, 67, 85, 87–9, 91, 99, 171, 178–85
Viewpoint with Ronald Reagan 10
Voting Rights Act of 1965 42, 67, 125

Walker, David 31
Wallace, George 42, 45–6, 81, 125–6
Wanniski, Jude 95

Warner Brothers 4
Watergate affair 1, 74, 85, 87, 99
Watts Riots 59–60, 115, 185
Welfare Reform Bill of 1996 142–3
Weyrich, Paul 94, 130
Whig Party 32, 54
White Citizens Councils 45
WHO Radio 3
Williams v. Mississippi 34
Wilson, Woodrow 185
Wood, Sam 9
Works Progress Administration (WPA) 38
World Court 20
World War Two 4, 11, 20, 24, 99, 110, 113, 161, 163
Wyman, Jane 4

Yeltsin, Boris 132
Yorty, Sam 120
Young Americans for Freedom (YAF) 25, 100, 152; "Sharon Statement" (transcript) 153–4

www.routledge.com/history

You may be interested in the other titles in this series ...

Critical Moments in American History

Series Editor: **William Thomas Allison,**
Georgia Southern University

The Battle of the Greasy Grass/Little Bighorn:
Custer's Last Stand in Memory, History, and Popular Culture
By Debra Buchholtz
ISBN 13: 978-0-415-89559-0 (pbk)

The Assassination of John F. Kennedy:
Political Trauma and American Memory
By Alice L. George
ISBN 13: 978-0-415-89557-6 (pbk)

Freedom to Serve:
Truman, Civil Rights, and Executive Order 9981
By Jon E. Taylor
ISBN 13: 978-0-415-89448-7 (pbk)

The Battles of Kings Mountain and Cowpens:
The American Revolution in the Southern Backcountry
By Melissa Walker
ISBN 13: 978-0-415-89561-3 (pbk)

The Nativist Movement in America:
Religious Conflict in the 19th Century
By Katie Oxx
ISBN 13: 978-0-415-80748-7 (pbk)

The Cuban Missile Crisis:
The Threshold of Nuclear War
By Alice L. George
ISBN 13: 978-0-415-89972-7 (pbk)

The 1980 Presidential Election:
Ronald Reagan and the Shaping of the American
Conservative Movement
By Jeffrey D. Howison
ISBN 13: 978-0-415-52193-2 (pbk)

For additional resources visit the series website at:
www.routledge.com/cw/criticalmoments

Available from all good bookshops

www.routledge.com/history

Democracy as a Way of Life in America
A History

Richard Schneirov
and **Gaston A. Fernandez**

The United States is a nation whose identity is defined by the idea of democracy. Yet democracy in the U.S. is often taken for granted, narrowly understood, and rarely critically examined. In *Democracy as a Way of Life in America*, Schneirov and Fernandez show that, much more than a static legacy from the past, democracy is a living process that informs all aspects of American life.

The authors trace the story of American democracy from the revolution to the present, showing how democracy has changed over time, and the challenges it has faced. They examine themes including individualism, foreign policy, the economy, and the environment, and reveal how democracy has been deeply involved in these throughout the country's history.

Democracy as a Way of Life in America demonstrates that democracy is not simply a set of institutions or practices such as the right to vote or competing political parties, but a complex, multi-dimensional phenomenon, whose animating spirit can be found in every part of American culture and society. This vital and engaging narrative should be read by students of history, political science, and anyone who wants to understand the nature of American democracy.

978-0-415-83612-8 (pbk)
978-0-415-83611-1 (hbk)
September 2013

For more information and to order a copy visit
www.routledge.com/9780415836128

Available from all good bookshops

www.routledge.com/history

Presidential Documents
Words that Shaped a Nation from Washington to Obama, 2nd Edition

Edited by
Thomas J. McInerney
and **Fred L. Israel**

"State papers are instruments of power, and Presidential Documents illustrates the diverse ways American presidents have striven to mold the nation's destiny. This collection, well-selected and ably annotated, is a fine introduction to the perennial mysteries of the American presidency."
– Arthur Schlesinger, Jr

In this lively, authoritative collection, Thomas J. McInerney presents famous and lesser-known speeches, letters, and other important documents from every U.S. president from George Washington to Barack Obama.

Whether printed in full or excerpted, these history-making documents are an invaluable resource as well as a fascinating browse. Including familiar documents such as the Emancipation Proclamation, to personal correspondence such as a letter from George H.W. Bush to his children, this collection brings together the famous statements that came to represent each administration with intimate glimpses into the thought processes of various presidential leaders.

Now in its second edition, *Presidential Documents* has been re-designed to increase its usefulness in the classroom. Part openers introduce each era of the American presidency with a concise political and historical overview, highlighting the challenges each leader faced, and placing the documents in context. Whether used as a complement to an American history survey text or as a collection of primary documents for courses on the American Presidency, *Presidential Documents* provides an engrossing look at the work of the leaders of the United States, in all their complexity.

978-0-415-89575-0 (pbk)
978-0-415-89574-3 (hbk)
September 2012

For more information and to order a copy visit
www.routledge.com/9780415895750

Available from all good bookshops

www.routledge.com/history

If you liked this book, you may also be interested in our series of biographies ...

Routledge Historical Americans

Series Editor: **Paul Finkelman**, Albany Law School

Frederick Douglass
By L. Diane Barnes
ISBN 13: 978-0-415-89112-7 (pbk)

Woody Guthrie
By Ronald D. Cohen
ISBN 13: 978-0-415-89569-9 (pbk)

Thurgood Marshall
By Charles L. Zelden
ISBN 13: 978-0-415-50643-4 (pbk)

Harry S. Truman
By Nicole L. Anslover
ISBN 13: 978-0-415-89567-5 (pbk)

John Winthrop
By Michael Parker
ISBN 13: 978-0-415-81812-4

John F. Kennedy
By Jason K. Duncan
ISBN 13: 978-0-415-89563-7 (pbk)

Bill Clinton
By David H. Bennett
ISBN 13: 978-0-415-89468-5 (pbk)

Routledge Historical Americans is a series of short, vibrant biographies that illuminate the lives of Americans who have had an impact on the world. Each book includes a short overview of the person's life and puts that person into historical context through essential primary documents, written both by the subjects and about them. A series website supports the books, containing extra images and documents, links to further research, and where possible, multi-media sources on the subjects. Perfect for including in any course on American History, the books in the Routledge Historical Americans series show the impact everyday people can have on the course of history.

For additional resources visit the series website at:
www.routledge.com/cw/historicalamericans

Available from all good bookshops

Taylor & Francis
eBooks
FOR LIBRARIES

ORDER YOUR FREE 30 DAY INSTITUTIONAL TRIAL TODAY!

Over 23,000 eBook titles in the Humanities, Social Sciences, STM and Law from some of the world's leading imprints.

Choose from a range of subject packages or create your own!

Benefits for **you**
- ▶ Free MARC records
- ▶ COUNTER-compliant usage statistics
- ▶ Flexible purchase and pricing options

Benefits for your **user**
- ▶ Off-site, anytime access via Athens or referring URL
- ▶ Print or copy pages or chapters
- ▶ Full content search
- ▶ Bookmark, highlight and annotate text
- ▶ Access to thousands of pages of quality research at the click of a button

For more information, pricing enquiries or to order a free trial, contact your local online sales team.

UK and Rest of World: **online.sales@tandf.co.uk**
US, Canada and Latin America:
e-reference@taylorandfrancis.com

www.ebooksubscriptions.com

A flexible and dynamic resource for teaching, learning and research.

CPSIA information can be obtained
at www.ICGtesting.com
Printed in the USA
LVHW03s0100121018
593322LV00006B/90/P